praise for *Loving Life on the Margins*

Feeling hopeless? Isolated? Overwhelmed? Loving Life on the Margins *is the antidote. Sit with these stories, these lives of active contemplation, practiced faith, and engaged, examined nonviolence and be restored. Thank you, Suzanne and Brayton, for crafting an honest, inviting, inspiring portrait of a centered life at the margins.*

—Frida Berrigan,
columnist for *Waging Nonviolence*
author of *It Runs in the Family: On Being Raised by Radicals and Growing into Rebellious Motherhood*

The Agape story is truly a real life story that follows the command of Jesus: take the gospel to all the world. Suzanne and Brayton will show you, the reader, just how the gospel is lived in this day and time.

—William Neal Moore
Pentecostal minister, international speaker against the death penalty, and former Death Row inmate in Jackson, Georgia, for seventeen years

In these challenging times, we need people who give us hope in the struggle for peace, justice, and equality. This is where the Agape Community comes in. I highly recommend the book, Loving Life on the Margins.

—Roy Bourgeois
laicized Roman Catholic priest expelled from the Maryknoll order because of his advocacy for ordination of women and founder of the human rights School of the Americas Watch, SOA Watch

This stunning new volume recounts more than four decades of faith-filled companionship, radical nonviolence, environmental sustainability, simplicity of lifestyle, solidarity with the poor, artistic beauty, and prayerful community. Against great odds, Agape and its co-founders have kept hope alive for so many.

—Thomas Massaro, SJ
professor of moral theology,Fordham, University
author of books on peacemaking, including the recent publication,
Living Justice: Catholic Social Teaching in Action

This is a story of spiritual adventure. From prison journals and composting toilets to confronting cardinals about war to chasing woodchucks from the garden, Loving Life on the Margins *is full of life and hope, part of a witness the authors call, "the vast network of God's womb love."*

—Eric Martin
co-editor of *The Berrigan Letters*
activist, teacher, and candidate for the doctor of philosophy degree at
Fordham University

In today's world, we desperately need beautiful models of those who break away from the dominant paradigm and choose to embrace lives of prophetic witness. Loving Life on the Margins *gives us the nitty gritty story of how two people of faith moved from a middle-class upbringing toward a lifestyle dedicated to ecological restoration, social justice, and nonviolent resistance, thereby challenging all of us to move beyond our comfort zones and find our own vocations.*

—Brenna and Eric Cussen Anglada
homesteaders, resisters. and authors
among founders of Saint Isidore Catholic Worker Farm and
Agronomic University in southwest Wisconsin

A beautiful memoir of a marriage, a symbol of unity of Christ and the church, a shining example of what Peter Maurin, one of the founders of the Catholic Worker movement, intended as an agronomic university. Brilliant, far reaching, rooted . . . a treasure.

—Daniel Marshall
historian of the Catholic Worker movement

Brayton and Suzanne's memoir shows us how for over forty years they loved and cared for each other and cultivated mutual understanding among cultures and religious traditions. Their way of peacebuilding and concern for immigrants and refugee families are exemplary and something that we at the Islamic Center have supported and participated in.

—Mohammad Saleem Bajwa, MD
director, Islamic Society of Western Massachusetts

I am very thankful to Suzanne and Brayton for the wonderful experience of their lives. For more than forty years, a testimony that they leave for future generations, they have proclaimed the Gospel of Jesus in their lives.

—Hazel Dardano
medical worker for the poor in her home country, El Salvador, during
the 1970s until she was forced to flee and,
now a US citizen, protestor for immigrant lives and advocate for
immigrants in need of housing

LOVING LIFE ON THE MARGINS

Loving Life

on the

Margins

the story of the Agape community

Suzanne Belote Shanley

and

Brayton Shanley

Haley's
Athol, Massachusetts

Haley's
488 South Main Street
Athol, MA 01331
haley.antique@verizon.net

Library of Congress Cataloging-in-Publication Data
Names: Shanley, Suzanne Belote, author. | Shanley, Brayton, author.
Title: Loving life on the margins : the story of the Agapáe Community /
   Suzanne Belote Shanley, Brayton Shanley.
Description: Athol, MA : Haleys, 2019.
Identifiers: LCCN 2019008946 | ISBN 9781948380034
Subjects: LCSH: Agapáe Community. | Christian communities--Catholic Church. |
   Basic Christian communities--Massachusetts--Hardwick. | Shanley, Suzanne
Belote. | Shanley, Brayton.
Classification: LCC BX2347.72.U6 S53 2019 | DDC 267/.1827443--dc23
LC record available at https://lccn.loc.gov/2019008946

hardcover ISBN: 9781948380065
watermarked pdf for e-reading ISBN: 9781948380072

For our mothers
Ellen McDonald Shanley and Olga Ralicki Belote
who loved us into Agape

Peace I leave you; my peace I give to you.
I do not give to you as the world gives.
Do not let your hearts be troubled, and do not let them be afraid."

—John14:27
NRSV • New Revised Standard Version
Oxford University Press, 1989

Contents

Photos and Illustrations

Agape: Creating New Beginnings

a foreword by David O'Brien

Loving Life on the Margins: the Story of the Agape Community, like the remarkable life work of Brayton and Suzanne Shanley, is an American Catholic story. America in imagination, and sometimes in fact, has always been about new beginnings, about self-making personal lives and creating fresh and free communities. The Shanleys call their creation Agape, an intentional community. It is among the latest in a long line of creatively constructed American communities, some religious like Amish farms; some ethnic like a Polish neighborhood; some provisional like wagon trains; some enduring, like those whose white-steepled churches dot our country's landscapes. As one learns about Agape, one easily pictures smiles on the faces of earlier American resisters who lived in the Shanleys' central Massachusetts neighborhood:

- dreamer Bronson Alcott of Fruitlands
- peacemaker Adin Ballou of Hopedale
- abolitionist Abbey Kelley Foster and her husband, Stephen, on Liberty Farm in Worcester

Many Americans, alive to the promise of liberty and justice for all, have made acts of self-giving love, agape, through resistance, disobedience, and community creation. Agape's history is another compelling story of resisting violence and injustice and trying to create what Peter Maurin called "a new society within the shell of the old."

The Shanleys wisely call their memoir *Loving Life on the Margins* about loving the complicated, messy life around them, in the right now, right here, in the heart of the USA as it is and still may someday become. Their dream combines Quaker Edward Hicks's portrait of "The Peaceable Kingdom" and Martin Luther King's "beloved community." Such a world becomes imaginable as a little gift in the lives of people in communities like Agape and the peace and justice movements they serve. So, yes, Agape's story is a very American story.

And it is also a Catholic story. The Shanleys, like so many Catholics of their 1960s generation, started their life together with Catholicism but now seem a little unsure of where they fit in the larger Catholic community. They have tried, in Brayton's phrase, to find "a new way of being Catholic." To be sure, some Catholics may not be sure the Shanleys and their friends still belong. Perhaps they sometimes reach the boundaries of the Church. Nevertheless, the Shanleys, with their close friends and many of their multiple "allies" in the Agape story, are sure of one thing: they have been called. They have tried the best they could to live out in daily life the Gospel message of Jesus.

Drawing upon the sacramentally rich subcultural Catholic world of mass, confession, and moral certainty, they encountered war, racism, and economic and social unfairness. Neither America nor the church turned out to be quite "what they were supposed to be," to use a sixties term. Students of the Shanleys' generation usually focus on liberation stories, often trivializing the pain of the period. Only a few catch the way so many young men and women discovered that their new-found freedom, the ability to be intentional, came with a partner, a share of responsibility for the evils of violence and racism and inequality exploding around them. Certainties of all sorts gave way to searches.

More than a few Catholics joined movements to confront problems of American society for which they, like the Shanleys, felt personally responsible. Feeling cut off from traditional Catholic moral righteousness, such Catholics asked themselves the simple question posed a century earlier by the storyteller Charles Sheldon for a similarly adrift generation of young Protestants: What would Jesus do?

If there is a central theme of the Agape story told by the Shanleys, it is surely this: a loving couple and their many friends have tried for four decades to live an answer to that question in daily life. They may be, in the Shanleys' telling, "maladjusted," and they surely are "creative," but they are also intentionally Catholic. With many priests, nuns, and lay people, they have been exploring, on behalf of all of us, new ways of being Catholic, ways of faith, hope, and agape love.

So, Brayton and Suzanne Shanley, with seriousness, humility, and an occasional touch of humor, tell a very old American and a somewhat new Catholic story. They love each other, the world, and the human family as they find it, and they have spent their life together trying to share responsibility for the history all of us are living together. They think their life choices took them to the margins, or to what Pope Francis calls "the periphery." That sounds right, as they describe protests, arrests, going back to the land, and building a house of straw.

When Pope Francis addressed the United States Congress, he chose Abraham Lincoln and Martin Luther King as exemplary Americans. As representative American Catholics, the Pope chose two who lived on the margins, Agape icons Dorothy Day and Thomas Merton. Lincoln, who presided over war and brutal violence, and King, the courageous apostle of nonviolence, help us rethink our America country: should we be the empire-seeking world dominator that Agape worries about, or should we have a different center?

Few Christian Americans lived further from what we think of as the center of public life than the pacifist, near anarchist Dorothy Day and the Trappist monk Merton, who followed a radical discipline of prayer, poverty, and silence. Yet the Pope said we might learn from Merton and Day what Catholic Christianity has to offer America and the world. Perhaps Merton, Day, and nonviolent resisters like the Shanleys live at history's center.

And perhaps it is the rest of us, from Popes to presidents to members of Congress to people like us in middle-class suburbs, rural townships, and urban neighborhoods who live at the margins. There, barely holding onto our integrity and our faith, in our families, workplaces, and civic squares, we deal with our complicated, paradoxical history. We at the secular margins look to intentional peacemakers like King, Day, and Merton, and to interfaith communities like Agape to see what the beloved community we desire and hope for might look like.

David O'Brien is professor emeritus of history, College of the Holy Cross, Worcester, Massachusetts.

*Suzanne Belote Shanley and Brayton Shanley stroll up
the springtime path from Agape's Brigid House, constructed of straw bales.*

Entering Life on the Margins

an introduction by Suzanne Belote Shanley and Brayton Shanley

When we decided to write the story of our small intentional community, we felt that what has happened at Agape over thirty-six years may prove meaningful to our readers. Agape has been identified over the years as a nonviolent lay Christian community, although we have always sensed the inadequacy of attempting to define a fluid, evolving, and multidimensional living entity. After years of studying and praying over Jesus' teachings on enemy love, we named our community Agape. We learned that agape expresses the greatest love as it exceeds Eros, or desire, and philia, or friendship, and refers to new, transformative, unconditional agape love as outlined in Jesus's Sermon on the Mount. (Matthew 5-7)

Martin Luther King's concept of agape love drew us in as he reminded Christians that, when Jesus commands us to "love our enemies," Jesus is speaking of agape, a love that is creative, understanding goodwill for all people.

As we resonated with the power of Christ's words and those of King, we found ourselves following King's example in merging Gandhi's evocative notion of soul force or satyagraha with the impulse of agape love.

Much as we had done over the years in *Servant Song*, the community journal, we set out to convey the intensity, joy, and bonding that have flourished during our Agape sojourn with so many motivated and committed friends. That which is precious and real about Agape reflects the lives of those who believed in and supported the vision for the long haul.

Not liking the term "memoir" as too self-referential, we began to see ourselves as co-authors of a spiritual journal, the testimony of one small endeavor in the lineage of nonviolent intentional communities.

Prior to Agape's co-founding, we had been involved as a couple in several other community experiments. The unfolding of our individual and married lives took place over four decades within the sweep of the cultural, spiritual, and historic eras we lived through. We began to see nonviolence, peacemaking, resistance, and interfaith practice as the engines of change, pointing the way to what could happen if Christians followed their lineage, the teachings of Jesus.

In 1974, the year we met, we had been radicalized by the never-ending horror of war, the specter of nuclear winter and nuclear annihilation. After Vietnam, the near meltdown of Three Mile Island, the overthrow of governments in Latin America, and the build-up of American military bases across the globe formed our decision as a couple to withdraw from and not cooperate with the madness of the war machine. Evolving Catholic social teaching, the influence of Oscar Romero and Latin American resistance communities, inspired and emboldened our quest.

As our opposition to the sway of empire grew, we were beginning to base our lives on the social gospel and teachings of Jesus, rooted in our study of nonviolence and its early preachers and practitioners, Gandhi, King, Dorothy Day, and so many others. The fire was lit.

We enriched our perspective with scripture study through Asian religions that embraced Gandhi whose practice of ahimsa, Sanskrit for non-injury, included vegetarianism and a constructive program for nonviolent living.

We experienced in prayer, meditation, and scripture study that Jesus speaks to us in the deepest recesses of our hearts, creating in them a profound transformation. In addition, we experienced a call to do this while pursuing, as lay people, a life in community.

Our emerging desire to transcribe the Agape story involved telling about the lives we lived with those who make the story. Over these years, a blend of voices and backgrounds—interns, volunteers, benefactors, and friends—established the community rhythm and practice. The word legacy comes to mind, a collective memory, a holding of years in trust. Our role as scribes, keepers of the flame of resistance, involved the duty to remember and record what we realize will not be replicated, at least not in the form it was founded.

Agape's early core consisted of a group of friends from various walks of life who coalesced around a passion for world peace and making nonviolent teachings relevant. The resistance-shaped spirit of the sixties and seventies fostered ferment and solid energy for experimentation. Co-founding Ailanthus, we planted early antiwar seeds in Boston in 1979 with an interfaith group of friends. We all gravitated to the name, Ailanthus, a resilient shrub also known as the Tree of Life, that defied uprooting and could be found growing through cracks in inner-city cement.

In a very clear sense, friendship became the catalyst for like-minded people drawn to each other with excitement and purpose to live outside of dominant cultural mayhem. Together we conceived of leaving jobs, pooling finances, and plunging into voluntary displacement to live counter-culturally.

We forged bonds across the faith spectrum with members of Cambridge Friends Meeting, the Buddhist Peace Pagoda, Pax

Christi, Catholic Worker communities, and Catholic parishes throughout New England. After formative years in Boston and Brockton, we relocated to the woods of Hardwick, Massachusetts, in the Quabbin Reservoir watershed.

Moving into the deep woods required reshaping our identity as individuals and as a married couple. We were academically inclined, primarily city dwellers who went from the city of Brockton to Hardwick, a farm town of two thousand. After the main building was in place, unfinished but habitable, we began growing our own food and creating a school of nonviolence. With like-minded others, we constructed every building from the ground up.

We married into our tribe when most of us were in our twenties and thirties. Our family of nonconformists originated in the Boston area. On the opening day of Agape's residence in Hardwick, in 1989, we experienced a love feast as someone called it, a family reunion, a blessing of the clan.

Bishop Timothy Harrington of the Diocese of Worcester joined a diverse collection of friends including Father Richard McSorley, Society of Jesus, Georgetown University; Sister Jane Morrissey, Sisters of Saint Joseph, Springfield, Massachusetts; and Tom Cornell, Catholic Worker, New York. Opening day included comrades from the Buddhist Peace Pagoda and the Bruderhof as well as other regional and national resistance communities. We celebrated our lives as participants in the Beloved Community advanced by King.

The day we opened Agape's residence, several hundred of us heard Kaddish, the Jewish mourner's prayer of praise to God, chanted by our old Ailanthus friend, Jim Levinson, outside of Saint Francis House. That first Agape building housed our family and all who might come to live with us.

We were stirred to the depths by the plaintive remembrance of our Judeo-Christian heritage. Taking our cues from diverse faith traditions, we embraced interfaith practice. Going forward, we saw our lives and the lives of those who lived and worked with us becoming what Rabbi Abraham Heschel speaks of in his book, *I Asked for Wonder*, "a work of art."

In *Loving Life on the Margins: the Story of the Agape Community,* we attempt to do what Jesus asked: "Interpret the present time" (Luke 12:56) through the lens of the past. We hope that you, the reader of this book, will find in the Agape story something worthy of interpretation as a commentary on the lineage and future of small faith communities like ours.

Over the years, we have been drawn to the image of God as the Divine Feminine, that God's heart and ungraspable power is Mother as well as Father. We have come to believe that the womb-love of God gives birth to voices joined in prayer and song, souls born into longing and pain, struggling to be reflections of what is possible in our short time on this imperiled, glorious planet.

Three Deadly Crises That Saved My Life

Brayton

I was in the Bronx in the late 1980s giving a presentation to a Catholic parish conference on nonviolence. A woman asked a challenging question: "How does a guy like you from Pelham, a wealthy suburb of New York City, end up with simple living and nonviolence?"

I remember being stumped by the question. I grew up in a town of white Anglo-Saxon Protestant privilege, although my Irish Catholic father took home a middle-class salary. Born into Roman Catholic faith but functioning as agnostics, my parents were classic periodic church attenders. God was never important enough to discuss around the dinner table.

As an adult, I follow the nonviolent Jesus, and the social climb is decidedly downward on the American Dream ladder. But it is a good question: "How *did* this happen to me?" Part of my confusion around the question reflects my conviction

In 1952, Brayton's family included, from left front, Brayton;
Bruce, the Collie dog; Tricia Shanley, Brayton's sister; back,
Brayton's mother, Ellen McDonald Shanley, and his father, Tom Shanley.

that I didn't think my lifestyle, though considered radical by mainstream standards, was that extreme. I knew others living much more demanding lives of social activism and voluntary poverty. Nevertheless, let's take the question seriously. How did this happen?

Real moments of childhood crisis started me in the direction of a contrarian life. I grew up during the 1950s economic boom of suburbs made possible by the World War II generation. Although not at all an eccentric, I felt drawn to Bohemians, the Beat generation, and gifted intellectual types. So-called

As he plays with war toys at four,
Brayton wears a World War II
German army helmet liberated by his
father during the war.

Brayton's father, Tom, right, trains on maneuvers in 1943 at Camp Edwards, Cape Cod, Massachusetts, to prepare to go overseas.

success stories of elder males among family and friends who had made it financially didn't hold my attention.

Almost Deadly Fall

On a sunny February morning just before my fourteenth birthday, my life took a major involuntary turn. I thought I knew what I wanted when I was thirteen. Along with every other budding teenager, I craved social acceptance. I longed for the attention of athletic stardom, playing noticeably well at football, baseball, and basketball. My football-playing friend, Bill Solimene, reminded me that football was "the glory sport," and all other athletics were window dressing. Even academic achievement paled in significance to the pure aphrodisiac of scoring touchdowns along with the adoring attention and status that came with it.

My dream all ended when I fell twenty feet out of a tree while climbing onto a roof. With a bunch of my guy friends at my buddy Jimmy Philson's house, we were playing ring-a-lievio, a hide-and-seek game replete with fake rifles to "kill" each other. After my descent, I learned that I had fractured my third cervical vertebra. Even worse, the second, third, and fourth vertebrae were knocked out of alignment. My spinal cord was miraculously unharmed. I escaped a quadriplegic fate.

When I was discharged from my doctor's care six months later, my orthopedist, Dr. William Oetting, informed me that all contact sports for me were out. His advice: "Don't let anyone grab your head." Except for baseball, my promising athletic career ended before it began. How could this happen?

At the tender age of fourteen, I was given no choice but to reinvent myself, yet, I was too young and uninvented to begin with. My mother, realizing this drastic turn, asked her friend, Polly Paine, "What will Brayton do now that he can't play football?"

"He will begin to think," Polly predicted.

When all I felt was the pain of the loss, I asked myself, "What is left?" I felt strangely crippled, and it would be a good while before I would have any "thinking" to point to. I apparently needed to ride out my teenage years, biding my time wondering over my fragile teenage self with football stardom off the table forever.

By my late teens, a new person, buried deep inside, began slowly, imperceptibly, to emerge, a person freer to become something more than an athlete. At first, this freedom was imposed on me, but it eventually bore miraculous fruit, though only after ten years lost in wild, hedonistic pursuits so typical of the age.

The next drastic turn in the road came four years later when my mother, who had just turned fifty, died unexpectedly in the space of three horrifying weeks of complications of pneumonia after a serious flu. At the woefully immature age of eighteen, I was left helpless, stunned, and abandoned. As in most families I knew, Mother was the rock who formed my moral sense of self as I faced that scary adolescent world in front of me. It was her compassionate embrace of the disturbed or those who had a bad hand dealt to them that informed how I began to look at people, especially those most troubled among us. Even as a thrill-seeking, parents-be-damned teenage boy on the outside, I was always her disciple on the inside.

As the American Civil Rights Movement brought twentieth century African-American struggles for human dignity onto our TV screens, Mother made it clear that we should stand with them and care that they suffered such a tormented fate. How strange, then, that she hired a black woman to do her ironing, which Mom hated to do.

An African-American maid was certainly an evolutionary remainder of a house slave. But, my mother's love and respect for Vivian was one of the most memorable family relationships of my childhood. Without any lecturing, Mother taught our white-privileged family to treat the Vivians of this world as family.

I adored Vivian. Every time she came to iron, I gladly left all my neighborhood friends in order to spend the afternoon gabbing with Vivian on every conceivable topic. What an unusual friendship choice for a ten-year-old boy.

It was like breaking my neck again when mother died when I wasn't ready to do without her nor to negotiate my life decisions in her absence. It afforded me no choice but to gird myself and start growing up fast. The reality was that I would decide things on my own and be off to college in Boston a few months later.

My father was still in the picture, but he was never really present in my adolescent dilemmas. Within six months of my mother's death, Dad confided to me in a painfully lonely moment, "Men were not meant to be alone." He eventually remarried and lived a quiet life, dealing as best he could as a functional alcoholic but steady breadwinner. My sister Trish, four years older, soon joined me living in Boston where I landed in college without any money in my pocket. After being my chief sibling antagonist throughout my childhood, Trish became my trusted guide and surrogate mother.

After years of my parents living beyond their means, my father was more or less broke and pressured by debt. As a result, I lasted only a semester at Emerson College. I ran out of tuition money by second semester of my freshman year, and Shawmut Bank rejected my loan request. My father, strapped with some debt, was unable to afford my tuition costs. Out of luck, out of school, and out of money on the streets

Brayton, right, takes a break during a 1973 visit in Tucson, Arizona, with his former college roommate Pat Brown.

in Boston, I was eighteen and looking for work. These shocking realities became essential preparation for the next great dramatic moment in my young life that defined my values to this moment.

Uncle Sam's Long, Deadly Arm

When I was forced to quit school in February, 1966, Emerson College sent my name into the selective service board as "no longer matriculating at the college." Within weeks, I received my first draft notice at my father's home in New York. I was to appear for a draft physical at the notorious Whitehall Street Draft Board, made famous by Arlo Guthrie's sixties antiwar anthem, "Alice's Restaurant."

I wrote the draft board to say that I no longer resided in New York: Would they please advise? From the moment I dropped that letter in the mail, it was official: I was running from the draft. The prospect of being drafted sent me and many in my generation into sheer existential panic. My utter terror of being dragged into the army served to clarify something about me and many of the peers I grew up with. Reared among wealth and privilege, most of my friends had no particular love, fascination, nor career interest in anything military. As a teenager, I grew to disdain the army as macho and too déclassé for the educated and moneyed class I identified with.

Paradoxically, I grew up captivated by my father's proud stories of liberating Europe with General George S. Patton's Third Army, including fighting in the Battle of the Bulge, a campaign where Americans took their greatest casualties of the entire war. My dad, a duty-bound, true patriot who loved being associated with the victorious Patton, never talked about his combat experience. I often wondered why.

By the time I was eighteen, I realized just how different I was from my father and many in his generation who possessed a deep and abiding trust in their government and military. Many of their children, who came of age in the 1960s, grew suspicious of American foreign policy and American wars. By 1966, we began to view the Vietnam War as a lie advanced because of the domino theory, the unproven concept that Asian countries collapsed like a row of falling dominoes at the hands of Communists. The domino theory extends the lie perpetuated by Lyndon Johnson and his old World-War-II generation. Add to that deluded course the fact that, by the mid-1960s, the war in Vietnam—morally questionable for starters—looked like a catastrophic, losing proposition.

The sixties antiwar movement was fueled not only by morally refined and prepared conscientious objectors but also by legions of young white men raised in privilege, who enjoyed many options and advantages more attractive than joining the army. We white men of means were terrified at the prospect of being sucked into a cruel, doomed war that could get us killed or worse. No panic was more terrifying to an inexperienced and sheltered eighteen-year-old like me than ending up in Vietnam.

I continued to run from the draft throughout the summer, moving from Boston to New York and back to Boston, hoping to postpone the physical until January of 1967 when I was safely back in college, making me exempt from the lethal clutches of the army. After three or four letters and missed physical appointments, the selective service informed me that I was scheduled to appear in Boston for my physical in October. If I failed to appear, the letter warned, "You will be draft delinquent." Did that mean "under arrest"? I didn't know.

My decision process was faulty and morally limited because, concerned my father would discover what his draft-dodger son was up to, I was deciding my moves alone. My father and I never talked about the draft or whether it was my duty to defend my country in Vietnam. I assumed that Dad was pro-war when necessary. He was a patriot, a person who would unhesitatingly support his country's decision to wage war. What I knew was Dad was not pleased with the long-haired hippie look of his only son.

I had been accepted at St. Anselm College in New Hampshire, but my entrance was three months off. I had only a month to mull over my next move.

I decided to play my disability card rather than risk a further run, get caught, and have no options left. "Once you are drafted" my already-drafted friends reminded me, "you are theirs." With fear and trembling, I showed up at the South Boston Draft Board for my physical. Hand shaking, I clutched a letter from Dr. Oetting, the orthopedist who treated my neck fracture and vertebrae displacements. I bet the entire ranch that I would be saved by his letter alone and the up or down vote by the attending doctor, clearly a risky wager.

I checked in and began the two-hour physical. I expected to eliminate the whole nerve-wracking physical exam by submitting my letter first and getting out of the draft, as we said affectionately in those days. But no, I was required to take the complete physical. My anxiety was total as I passed each test with perfect combat readiness. I would wager that not one young man present that day was more militarily fit than I.

Free at Last

Then I heard the voice of salvation: "All those who have letters that refer to medical problems, please see the doctor in Room 17." With insides churning, I handed the doctor my letter. After reading the short, three-paragraph letter, the doctor looked up at me and asked in some disbelief: "Is this true?"

As if I had achieved some great super human feat, I proudly proclaimed, "Yessir."

With a slight shaking of his head, he stamped my file "1Y, medical deferment." I was exempt from the draft. How ironic that a deadly fall from a tree saved my life.

The tough-guy draft board routine alienated me permanently from what appeared to be absolute obedience to a regimented world that brainwashed and intimidated young men.

Something was very rotten in my nineteen-year-old paradise. I was face-to-face with the reality that our war in Vietnam was not only a war of bad judgment but also a clear sign of a war-dependent, First-World foreign policy bent on world domination. To live questioning authority and embracing the alternative political narratives of the remaining sixties became the trajectory of my college years.

In a few months, I began my studies at St. Anselm. Two years later, my father died of kidney failure, his death signaling my final boyhood rite of passage. An unsteady adult, I was beginning to think, as my mother's friend Polly had predicted. Unready to be on my own without the benefit of parental love and care, I became what my friends referred to as an orphan. The death of my parents before their time left me feeling like the line from a blues song by Dave Van Ronk: "Motherless children have a hard time when their mother is dead."

I found myself at St. Anselm College, a conservative Benedictine liberal arts college in Manchester, New Hampshire. I ended up there because my Uncle Joe was a legendary philosophy chair at the college, and I knew that I could gain a speedy acceptance. In his twenties, Joe McDonald befriended pacifists Dorothy Day and Peter Maurin of the Catholic Worker and began a Catholic Worker farm with others in the late 1930s. While my sister was enrolled there in the early sixties, my uncle invited Dorothy Day to St. Anselm every year. Yet the political scene there was conservative against the backdrop of the radical and raucous sixties. Within a decade. I joined others similarly converted to a vision of simple-living nonviolence and making my way back to my Catholic roots.

In 1970, Brayton graduated from St. Anselm College, Manchester, New Hampshire, with a degree in urban studies.

"How does a guy like you from Pelham, a wealthy suburb of New York City, end up with simple living and nonviolence?" If that woman in the Bronx who asked me the question had had the time to listen to my recounting of my childhood, it would have been as good an answer as I could have mustered.

Early Years

Suzanne

The desire to attend Catholic school came to me quite forcefully as a young child living in Cheektowaga, New York, where our family attended weekly mass at St. Bernard's, which also had a parish school.

The periodic carpentry jobs held by my father, Harold, bore the stamp of suffering and failure both for him personally as well as for us as a family. Everything was a struggle financially. As children, we were aware of debt, unpaid bills, and worry about being evicted from our rental apartments.

Polish and Poor

My mother, Olga Ralicki, the daughter of Russian-Polish father, Stanislaus, and mother, Pelagia, eked out a hardscrabble existence with Polish immigrant families in the section of Buffalo called Black Rock. Named after a Russian princess, my mother, whose father and brothers ran a saloon, was not able, at least initially, to shield her own children from similar, though less severe, deprivation such as she had endured during the Depression.

Suzanne's uncle and aunt, Edward and Bella Ralicki, support Suzanne on her 1951 First Communion day in Buffalo.

I realized gradually that many a kid did not share a bed with her sister in an arrangement that lasted for my sister Beverly and me in a tiny room in a pillbox of a house until I was eighteen. My brothers also shared a separate, small room.

Embarrassment and anger accompanied my wearing hand-me-downs from relatives. I fought with Beverly, five years younger than I, over clothes, which we hung in a shared tiny closet. Down the center of our shared bed, we drew an imaginary line which the other was not to cross even in her sleep.

The only time in my entire life that my mother hit me

was when I grabbed and pushed Beverly, who had worn one of my new outfits, the color and style of which (cranberry dress with knee-length miniskirt and white bodice) made me look skinnier than I was.

Beverly looked adorable in the outfit, but I wasn't thinking then about how much she suffered as a child with severe scoliosis and other health issues, nearly dying at age two. I just wanted my dress—on me, not Beverly.

My early life consisted of catastrophic near-death circumstances in my sister's toddler years, my own almost fatal peritonitis, and my mother's kidney cancer, diagnosed as potentially fatal. Defying all odds, both my mother and my sister experienced seemingly miraculous recoveries.

Bev lay in a coma, unresponsive at age two after a nearly lethal dose of an experimental drug. Defying the advice of the experts that she would not improve, my parents brought her home. My mother hovered over Beverly, lifting her fingers, talking to her constantly even though she was for the most part unresponsive. My parents encouraged the rest of us to do the same. Beverly seldom met our gaze or seemed to hear us talking. She lay there, helpless and beautiful.

My very Polish-looking uncle Eddie Ralicki—square chin, sloping Slavic nose, heavy set, a bit swarthy in complexion—took me for a novena to seven Catholic churches, both of us praying over and kissing relics to encourage saints to intercede for my sister's recovery. Eventually, over a period of months, Beverly did slowly awaken, but she had to learn to walk and talk all over again. My mother enlisted the aid of us three siblings in the task.

Polishness marked our lives, including our shopping at the Broadway Street meat market where people spoke Polish and we kids took in the aroma of sauerkraut and kielbasa filling the air. The family legend was that my grandfather, from Bialystok, supposedly jumped overboard at Ellis Island and never sought nor was ever granted citizenship. Even though my father ridiculed and

Suzanne's mother, Olga, and father, Harold, from left,
supervise her brother Harry, on tricycle, and Suzanne at the
Perry Street Projects in Buffalo in 1947.

joked derisively about the "Polacks" on my mother's side, I loved to hear her speak in Polish.

Shopping at the Polish meat market where some of my relatives worked provided an excuse for my father to get drunk in a nearby bar early in the day as he downed one shot and a beer after another. One or two of us kids sat with cokes and a cherry on a stick. I hated the smell of beer and booze and being left alone, fidgeting and restless at a table in a dismal, nearly empty bar. Despite his low self-esteem, my father's French last name, Belote, gave him a sense of superiority over my mother, resulting in his mockery of things Polish, including my relatives who lent him money to pay the bills.

My mother possessed a thirst for knowledge and new experiences, resulting in her completing nursing school and becoming a registered nurse. We kids were all very proud of her. Our enthusiasm only increased my father's sense of inferiority.

I loved to see her in her uniform and starched nurse's hat with the single line of thin black velvet in the front. My mom seemed so happy going to her job in the preemie ward of a local hospital, and our financial circumstances began to improve slightly because of her.

Shaped by Catholicism

We went to church weekly as a family, and eventually, after my father's baptism and entry into the Catholic Church, he became a church usher. When he came to our row, pushing a basket with a long pole-extension handle down the aisle, I was both proud and humiliated.

As a child, I wrestled with the thought that "I should be proud of him," yet I experienced the opposite. I was mortified when he fell into the bathtub in a drunken stupor after my mother locked their bedroom door to keep him out. Groaning, he often walked up and down the hallway leading to our rooms.

At Sunday mass, I learned about St. Bernard's Elementary School and saw students sitting with the Felician nuns, whose full habits with starchy white neck covers intrigued me. I decided I wanted to go to school there. The pageantry of high mass and the strange sense of comfort I received from it led to my begging my mother to transfer me on scholarship from my public elementary school to St. Bernard's.

I was drawn to Catholic ritual, experiencing early on in life, probably from the suggestion of the nuns, that if I stared hard enough at the statues in church, they would speak to me. I wanted to hear the voices of Mary, Joseph, and other saints whose lips I was convinced were moving. The fact that saints knew my thoughts and cared for me became early consolations, a welcome escape from my dreary circumstances.

But mysticism didn't make up for the stark reality of us four kids sitting with my mother at the kitchen table with the smell of pork chops, steak, or ham, potatoes boiling, meal prep done, plates out, waiting for my father and our family meal. Every time we heard a car, we ran to the window, but no father. We ate in silence, and after we went to our rooms, my mother slammed the cupboard doors over and over to cover her crying.

My longing for a father was met in a superficial way at St. Bernard's by Father Kiefer, the quintessential parish priest. Father Keifer was handsome, elderly, white-haired, soft-spoken, and kind. He visited our elementary school and the nuns weekly, entering our fourth grade classroom, expecting and receiving our high-pitched greeting. We all stood and chortled in unison, "Good morning, Father Keifer. . . . No, Father. Yes, Father. Thank you, Father." He was a distant, apparently holy, male figure I was taught to revere.

I had visions of convent life, of quiet dark rooms where nuns prayed in silence and calm. For a short time, I thought I had a vocation, the calling we prayed for every day in school. In a vague way I did feel a call to flee, to escape. A convent seemed like a restful place compared to my life.

But I was more strongly drawn to Jimmy Larkin, my thirteen-year-old classmate with curly dark brown hair and tantalizing eyes. We shared a clandestine kiss on the lips behind closed doors while playing a spin-the-bottle game at Suzie Ostrowski's house on her thirteenth birthday.

Routinely not wanting to wake my sister in the bed next to me and keeping flashlights and novels under my pillow at night, I found refuge and delight in books and study. I came to understand at an early age, that education was my ticket out of Cheektowaga— the boredom and stifling sameness.

Years of Rebellion

Eventually, as a teen, I attended another Felician school, Bishop Colton High School, also on a scholarship, where the Felician nuns imparted discipline, study habits, and a sense of the sacred. The discipline was rigid, the lack of creativity relieved by the guidance of a lay teacher, Mrs. Mischka, who took me to my first Shakespearean play at age fifteen.

My rebellion against the authoritarian structure of the school peaked when one of my best friends quit after being harassed by the nuns and publicly humiliated for her "subversive" reading of

Suzanne, senior class president and student council member, discusses programs with other students in 1961 at Bishop Colton High School.

Mein Kampf and other offenses of "attitude." In an early taste of defiance and disobedience, I began to express my righteous anger and gained a reputation as something of a non-conformist, a presage of things to come.

As the senior class president, I gave a talk at graduation in the school gym, exhilarated by the freedom at hand, and decided on a secular college in Buffalo, after having turned down a scholarship to an all-women's Catholic college.

After graduation from State University of New York at Buffalo, I began teaching high school English in West Seneca, New York, for two years while simultaneously attending grad school for a master's in English. Sometimes, I traveled with a friend to Boston and fell in love with the city, moving there before completing my master's degree.

In Boston, I felt the loss of familiar moral certitudes while testing my newfound freedom, frequenting bars, restless, adrift, and catapulting into a period of dread. I returned to Buffalo to complete my master's degree on the topic of existential absurdity in the novels of John Updike. Absurdity appealed to me more than faith. What was God doing for me anyway? Maybe life was absurd.

Finding a Partner for Life

By the time I met Brayton Shanley and the destiny that was to be my next stage began to unfold, I was struggling intensely with the ever-present figure of my drunken father, his rejection and harassment. A series of boyfriends, proposals, and a strong conviction never to marry came and went. It was during a breakup period with my most recent boyfriend that I met Brayton.

When I met Brayton, I knew that he was unlike anyone I had previously encountered. He was a vegetarian and yoga practitioner into faith and eastern religions. Our first conversation was about Franco Zeffirelli's movie, *Romeo and Juliet.*

For the first time in a long time, while with Brayton, I felt real happiness. Our lives were filled with conversations about religion and study of faith traditions.

We lived together in Cambridge near Harvard Square, jogging, watching sailboats on the Charles River, and attending Quaker Friends Meeting in Longfellow Center, both of us alienated from our Catholic roots. With Brayton, I felt a unique thrill of urgency, expectation, and ease of relating. We took our eastern religion practices quite seriously—mantras, yoga, reading Ram Das, meditation.

I began rejecting deeply ingrained notions of patriotism, unquestioning obedience to authority, and the false sense of security that came from surrendering to the powers that be. I was breaking open a churning post-Vietnam, pre-return-to-God consciousness. Our love for each other reinforced our mutual desire for a spiritual return to the not-quite-dead roots of our Christianity. Much like the hemorrhaging woman, I was touched by Jesus, and I felt the power of connection. I found that afflictions and fear, regret and recrimination fast become moments of healing.

For the first time, I read books that portrayed Jesus as an outlaw, a renegade, an outsider who preached solidarity with the oppressed, the poor, and the victimized. Our eclectic tastes led us to Alan Watts, Elizabeth Schussler Fiorenza, Rosemary Radford Reuther, and Krishnamurti. We began groups for study and discussion. In various settings with others similarly searching, we examined the social gospel and base communities, which led to questioning the power structure of church and country.

I continued to pursue my lifelong goal of a PhD in English, eventually taking a job teaching freshman English at Simmons College. Nevertheless, I wanted something outside of my own personal gratification of academic and intellectual advancement. I was on the brink of something transformative.

My feelings were not unlike what the poet Mary Oliver observes as an epiphany as she "emerged from the woods in the early morning" into "the mild, pouring-down sunlight" to experience "a sudden impact, *a seizure of happiness.*" At that moment, Oliver writes:

> Time seemed to vanish. Urgency vanished. Any important difference between me and all other things vanished. I knew that I belonged to the world and felt comfortably my own containment in the totality.

I, too, was beginning to feel that I belonged to the world.

Entering Communities of Nonviolence

Suzanne

By 1979, a year after we met Philip Berrigan and Elizabeth McAlister, Brayton and I were affiliating with Boston area peacemakers including Quakers. We were increasingly drawn to protests against nuclear war and proliferation of nuclear weapons and power. Boston was a hub of radicalism, and the excitement was contagious.

The bold raid in Catonsville, Maryland—where Phil Berrigan and eight others, including his Jesuit brother, Daniel, destroyed draft files with homemade napalm—electrified the country and the world. I took note, as a silent sister non protester, thinking: "A *Catholic priest*?" Philip and Daniel Berrigan, co-conspirators, brothers and both priests, appeared on the cover of *Time* magazine, the title reading simply, "The Berrigans."

In the infantry during World War II, Phil Berrigan attained the rank of second lieutenant. A former priest of the Josephite order, he had secretly married Elizabeth McAlister, a nun, artist, and antiwar activist. Their marriage came at the peak of resistance to and at the height of the Vietnam War. Phil faced stiff jail time for his arrests, thus creating a stir in Catholic circles and emboldening activists in successive waves of arrests.

The photos of the Catonsville group, Dan and Phil in black priest garb, faces etched in anguish, became icons of resistance opening a new chapter in what would become known as the Catholic Left.

In the meantime, Vietnamese people died by the thousands along with American troops. Amidst draft protests, the shock and horror of it all ignited college campuses nationally. For me, the high-profile priest resisters gave impetus to a new and dramatic rendition of my faith as it did for millions of other Catholics.

Like most Catholics, knowing little about anything remotely related to taking one's faith to a public forum, I didn't associate Catholicism with bold, mesmerizing drama. My conscience was barely awakened but, in the space of a few years, the Berrigans and Catonsville so captivated me that I chose to include *The Diary of a Priest Revolutionary* by Philip Berrigan, in a Literature of Dissent course I created at Arlington, Massachusetts, High School.

Fellow teachers, themselves young radicals, inspired me to lift my voice in protest and wear my George McGovern button in the classroom. I committed to the 1972 presidential peace candidate who stood, as the Berrigans did, for truth and conviction unparalleled in my emerging activist soul.

Rowe Camp: Meeting Philip Berrigan and Elizabeth McAlister

By the time we met Liz and Phil in 1978, Brayton and I had launched not only our relationship but a desire for a more radical life together. My activist yearnings were blossoming, whereas Brayton had been a long-time peacemaker. Brayton heard that Liz and Phil were to speak at Rowe Camp and Conference Center in western Massachusetts on the topic of community and resistance. Since we were actively exploring both, we leapt at the chance to learn firsthand from them about community life on the edge.

We arrived late at Rowe as did Liz and Phil. The center director, Doug Wilson, himself a resister who spent time in jail during the Vietnam War, put the four of us together in a small room for a quick dinner before the conference began.

Phil and Liz were candid and open. Our rapport was established, at least in my mind, almost immediately. That weekend was the beginning of my conversion to radical nonviolence and of seeing Jesus in a staggeringly new light. The experience was riveting, even though Liz and Phil were remarkably humble, even reserved in their presentation.

In all of my years as a Catholic, I had never heard of a Jesus spoken of in the way that Liz McAlister and Philip Berrigan spoke of him: Jesus acted in the world. Faith was a risk. Faith was action. Jesus's teachings related to life in community and ongoing resistance. Jesus, the prisoner, resister of empire, molder of enemy love, took on a new scale of importance.

We were impressed by Liz and Phil standing as a married couple in community in opposition to the American war machine. Brayton and I were headed in the same direction. Phil and Liz's non dramatic, stick-to-the-point presentation of Gospel imperatives to resist war and emphasis on lives lived together contrasted with chilling, horrifying scenarios for nuclear war and qualified as anything but academic. They urged the small group gathered that night to resist nuclear Armageddon and fast-approaching planetary devastation by withdrawing support from a government playing nuclear roulette.

The solution? Follow Jesus. Live simply. Non-cooperate with the war-making state. Put your body on the line in acts of civil disobedience. Do all within the context of community.

Both Liz and Phil stressed that following Christ and the Gospel led inevitably to risk, especially jail witness. I learned about jail witness, when resisters modeled nonviolent behavior in jail during their sentences, and about Gandhian tactics, when unarmed and disarmed resisters confronted armed forces to encourage change. I heard the antiwar messages of Leo Tolstoy and Dorothy Day. By the end of the weekend, I was on board. I joked with Brayton that I was ready to sign up and move to Jonah House.

Overcoming Fear

How does one resist? The Berrigan-McAlister prescription: Acts 4:44-46: "All who believed were together and had all things in common; they would sell their property and possessions and divide them among all according to each one's needs." The theory was that a life shared with others made resistance and jail witness possible.

All of it meant a pretty deep plunge for me.

I had only recently climbed out of poverty into academia. Now, two charismatic, Christ-centered resisters tugged at my lagging faith, saying: Listen up. This is a radical call. You can do it. This is the essence of Jesus, your God. This is the Truth. Jesus tells us to reject the great lie, Satanic deception, the governments who wreak death and havoc on the planet. Jesus breaks the law. He suffers consequences. Do you?

Notwithstanding my childhood worry about money, the Berrigans and others I was meeting and reading introduced me to the concept of voluntary poverty as an antidote to the evils of American capitalism. The message: Divest for the sake of and in solidarity with those who have nothing.

Sharing income with members dipping into a common pot provided the foundational principle for operation of Jonah House which had income coming from painting houses often belonging to the wealthy in Baltimore and environs. Liz, Phil, and the cohort at Jonah House brought to life early Christian communities depicted in Acts 4:32: " . . . believers were of one heart and one mind. None of them ever claimed anything as his/her own . . . " Modeling one's life after first-century Christians constituted a huge but appealing leap for me. It made sense: no one was needy, if "all who owned property or houses, sold them and donated the proceeds" to the larger goal of the common good, solidarity with the poor. (Acts 4:34-36)

Mesmerized by the power of convictions so emphatically stated, I realized that Jonah House's Yes! was also a resounding No! No! We will *not* support the murderous rampage in Vietnam, Cambodia, and the rest of Southeast Asia nor will we prop up dictators in Latin America with our money. Such moral stands of unflinching

Suzanne, left, and the poet Denise Levertov at a 1979 Clamshell Alliance protest against the Seabrook, New Hampshire,Nuclear Power Plant. Activists claimed success in blocking construction of one of two reactors.

conscience and conviction from Jonah House, Catholic Worker communities, and others like them crystallized the desire in both Brayton and me to pursue life in community and solidarity with the network of faith-based resistance communities.

Brayton and I had become increasingly more involved in campaigns against nuclear power at the Seabrook Nuclear Power Plant in New Hampshire, a burning issue during the 1970s. While I taught at Simmons, several students, Simmons faculty members, and I founded an antinuclear group at the college, a first of its kind. We called ourselves Simmons for Survival.

Simmons College Teach-In: Meeting the Resistance Family

The lowest paid teacher in the college, I taught freshman English at Simmons where, out of a humble base of a small band of students and faculty and with Brayton's help, we began preparations for an antiwar teach-in at Simmons College. Filled with out-sized optimism, we organizers secured the auditorium at Simmons for the event. Many faculty members of the liberal or radical persuasion signed on.

We had begun corresponding with Liz and Phil, so the teach-in a few months after meeting them provided an opportunity for inviting Phil to be the keynote speaker. Excitedly, we also invited Tony Mullaney, one of a group of resisters known as The Milwaukee Fourteen, who participated in a dramatic draft-card burning with homemade napalm in a Catonsville-like action in Wisconsin. Tony had taught at St. Anselm College, where Brayton's uncle Joseph McDonald chaired the philosophy department.

The Simmons teach-in offered a microcosm of the momentum-gathering national debate over nuclear weapons. Constructs like Mutually Assured Destruction, MAD, offered a rationale for governments to foster nuclear weapons and to escalate the international arms race. Doomsday scenarios of total annihilation through nuclear war became part of the political landscape.

As an English teacher and sometime poet, I learned that Denise Levertov, arguably one of the best American poets of the twentieth century, lived in Somerville, Massachusetts. An admirer of her poetry, I assumed that Denise with her reputation as a protest poet of some note would know the Berrigans. After finding her address, I rushed off an invitation asking her to speak at the Simmons teach-in. Almost immediately, Denise responded with a firm yes. In a matter of weeks, I met the poet who had accompanied Wendell Berry to Gethsemane in 1967 for a visit with Thomas Merton.

So much happened so quickly in my life that I thought things unfolded just like the Book of Acts "signs and wonders" and God pointing us in a direction.

Soul-making days multiplied until the moment finally arrived several days before the teach-in when we picked up Phil from Logan Airport in Boston. We were on the threshold of a new realm of meaning affirmed by the stirring within us. Phil strode off the plane full of purpose and passion with his serious expression and magnetic blue eyes.

Described at the time of his death in various news outlets as a moral giant and the conscience of our generation, Phil represented someone I had respected and admired from a distance. During the teach-in, he would stay at my home and speak at my college. Compassionate and intense, Phil possessed a natural gregariousness, an inquiring ease of manner, his focus unfalteringly on the other.

The Simmons College Teach-In

The night of the teach-in, the Simmons auditorium was packed to overflowing with more than five hundred people. Charlie King, folksinger and activist, opened the night with a rousing peace ballad. From my position at the podium as the facilitator of the teach-in, I spotted a diminutive and exotic-looking man in an orange robe in the back of the auditorium. He appeared to be a Japanese monk. He carried a hoop-shaped drum and held a slightly crooked drumstick. Later that evening, I learned that, indeed, he was a monk dedicated to peace and nuclear disarmament. His name was Gyoway Kato. He had recently arrived in the United States from Japan and would eventually found the New England Peace Pagoda.

Though Phil was not an electrifying speaker with the smooth, riveting style of Howard Zinn, he was a prophet. His destiny, as

Participants in a 1979 Simmons College teach-in include, from left, Philip Berrigan, Tony Mullaney, State Representative Doris Bunte of Roxbury, Denise Levertov, and Mark Solomon of the Simmons history department.

defined by Rabbi Abraham Heschel in his book, *The Prophets, Part II*, was to be "an assaulter of the mind" whose words, once you heard them, "begin to burn where conscience ends." The power of Phil's "burning words" lay in the enormity of his sacrifice, five years in prison thus far.

Suzanne and Phil Berrigan confer at the 1979 Simmons College teach-in.

Planting Seeds of Resistance in Boston

Suzanne

That night, those of us who knew each other only briefly and those of us who met each other for the first time planted seeds of a resistance community in Boston modeled after Jonah House and eventually called Ailanthus: A Nonviolent Witness for Peace.

photo copyright by Robert Thiefels

Suzanne takes a stand at the June 12, 1982, rally for nuclear disarmament in New York City with Brayton, right.

The reception room after the teach-in was so packed that the poet Denise Levertov and I couldn't find a place to sit. She grabbed my arm conspiratorially, pulled me toward her, and said: "Let's sit on the floor." A close relationship with Denise began from that floor moment. I counted it as another among converging signs—literary, moral, and spiritual.

Simmons College became an incubator for

A group from Ailanthus, including Brayton, second row, left, and Suzanne, next to him with bandanna, attended the June 12, 1982 rally for nuclear disarmament in New York City.

the meeting of antiwar activists like Paul Hood, who was to become a co-founder of Ailanthus. When we first met Paul, he lived frugally, refused war taxes, and eschewed a car as he rode his bike around Boston.

Ailanthus: A Nonviolent Witness for Peace

With its call for resistance and civil disobedience, Ailanthus wasn't for everyone. We had followed a mix of faith journeys— Buddhist, Catholic, and Quaker. None of us yet counted as seasoned resisters, but all of us were drawn to public witness during the escalation of the nuclear war/doomsday scenarios of the 1980s.

Paul and Dinah Starr, both Quakers, and a few others eventually to include Kato, the future leader (or shonin in

Japanese) of the New England Peace Pagoda in Leverett, Massachusetts, and Sister Clare Carter comprised the backbone of Ailanthus. Both Kato, Shonin, who grew up in Japan, and Sister Clare, who grew up in Boston, were separately ordained by the Japanese antinuclear Buddhist monastic order, Nipponzan Myhoji, which builds peace pagodas around the world. Kato lived with us in Belmont, Massachusetts, for a short time as he daily walked the twenty or so miles for thirty days from Boston to Walden Pond and back. He prayed and drummed for peace, one of the first United States occasions of hundreds of his similar walks all over the world with other antinuclear and peace activists.

Some members of Ailanthus, named for the resilient shrub that grows defiantly sprouting up through concrete, lived at Haley House in Boston, founded in the 1970s as a Catholic Worker community. Haley House consisted of a soup kitchen and two residences where, thanks to property owners Kathe and John McKenna, we held many of our Ailanthus meetings.

While I still taught at Simmons, Ailanthus maintained an ongoing symbolic presence at Charles Stark Draper Laboratory in Cambridge. Draper built guidance systems for first-strike nuclear weapons. We witnessed at Draper in a weekly vigil, greeting employees with fliers asking them to consider the impact of their

Ailanthus vigils in 1979 at Charles Stark Draper Laboratory in Cambridge to oppose weapons, especially first-strike guidance systems, and war.

A late 1970s vigil at Draper Labs focuses on the drumming of
Buddhist monk, Gyoway Kato, center, and Sister Clare Carter,
second from right, of the Nippponzan Myohoji antinuclear monastic order.
The group chants the opening words of the Lotus Sutra,
"Na Mu Myoho Renge Kyo," a call to the eternal Buddha.

complicity in manufacturing the death-dealing technology of
nuclear warfare.

Every Monday for some ten years, anywhere from five to thirty
or more of us from the extended peace community in Boston and
beyond kept a silent vigil at Draper Labs. We held hand-painted
signs: "Blessed are the Peacemakers" and "Nuclear Weapons
are Unsafe for Children and Other Living Creatures." We were
a motley crew. Paul, Ailanthus wisdom figure and World War II
veteran, once described us to a reporter as "small potatoes."

Our community bonding and weekly prayer together with
study of scripture and writings of great peacemakers became the
basis for our witness at Draper and for our preparations for acts of
civil disobedience.

We spent hours processing our concerns in our fliers to Draper
employees as well as in our conversations with them. We also
considered the risk of discipleship and doing jail time. A priority
in our discussions involved confronting violence in our own
hearts with caution about how our arrest preparations could lead
to anger and violence of spirit from those in whose midst we were
supposedly bearing witness.

Arrest, Trial, and Cutting Loose

After one of several arrests, I arrived for my bench trial not expecting to be sent directly to jail. I naively assumed that I could delay or request jail time during the Simmons College spring break. What ignorance! Instead, I received a fourteen-day sentence, and jailers led me out of the courtroom in handcuffs. Only my Quaker friend Paul Hood stood nearby as a support person.

After my fourteen days in jail, Brayton came to pick me up from the Massachusetts Correctional Institution at Framingham, the main women's prison in Massachusetts. The intensity of my jail time, journaling, meeting women in prison, and visits from community friends convinced me that I wanted to practice community and resistance full-time. I felt I could not return to Simmons after the semester ended.

Our original scheme imagined that Brayton would quit his job first and I would support us on my small salary at Simmons. My prayer and experience with the women in prison changed that. Once I left the jail compound and got into our car, I confided my decision to Brayton. "I have to leave Simmons. I just can't continue, even if part time. We'll have to find some other means of support."

A baffled look on his face, Brayton pulled out an official-looking envelope, my letter of termination from the chair of the Simmons College Department of English. "Thank you for your service," the chair wrote, "and I wish you success in your peacemaking endeavors." My college teaching career and PhD plans were over.

We had taken another irreversible step. During that time, we drove back and forth to the Pentagon, deepening our bonds with Phil, Liz, and others at Jonah House. We met more peacemakers who have become life-long friends. When we attended our first Atlantic Life Community meeting of loosely knit communities of resistance, we met others equally drawn to living out Jesus's mandate by following the Hebrew prophets: "But I say to you, offer no resistance to one who is evil. When someone strikes you on your right cheek, turn the other one as well." (Matthew 5: 38-48).

Finding our second family—sisters and brothers whose voices and commitments called us in a direction of risk taking—filled me with a sense of destiny unlike anything I had ever experienced. I felt reborn, full of energy.

Phil as Mentor

During the early years of our friendship with Phil, he was in and out of jail. Brayton and I continued a regular correspondence with him. Phil's letters, which I cherish, include memorable phrases. In one letter, Phil seemed almost to accept the role of prophet as described by his friend Rabbi Abraham Heschel: "Someone, whether God or God's prophet, must tear the veil from a thunderous national silence. . . around . . . the BOMB and war-making." Those twin realities, I heard Phil say repeatedly, comprise "the taproot of violence which kills us all in every conceivable way."

Wanting to "remedy this curse of killing," Phil's solution equaled "an unequivocal stand against killing in war, killing on death row, killing in the womb, killing the elderly, killing in the home or on the street, killing by economics or dictatorship." His inspiration and ironclad conviction provided the foundation of my own discipleship.

Long before the identification of the ecological movement, Phil addressed ecocide and homicide. He linked bombs dropped by the American empire with the irreversible effects of climate change that put future life on the planet at risk. In his cherished, distinctive handwritten letters, Phil issued—succinctly and bluntly, with the forcefulness of John the Baptist—a call to the community for nonviolent faith and *action*:

> I'm writing to Christians—say your prayers, do your homework and take every opportunity to expose nonviolently, the respectable murderers. John *sez* it all—lying always accompanies murder. And both are Satanism.

To me, Phil was a great unraveler systematically undoing my prior conceptions about Jesus, government, just war, complacency, and complicity. In personal conversation and public declaration, Phil encouraged us to "name the beast," the demon of violence within and without.

In the Berrigan exegesis, Jesus stood as more than a symbol of suffering to be avoided at all costs; rather, Jesus becomes the paradigm of nonviolence whose question "Who do you say I am?" must become the central question in Christian life. When we argued in Ailanthus whether or not to use Jesus's name in fliers, possibly risking offense to friends of other faiths, Phil said unequivocally, "You've got to have something that claims you. Scripture and Jesus put a claim on Christians."

As always, Philip Berrigan provided inspiration as our lives gathered momentum around resistance. In a letter Phil wrote from prison, I received my commission:

> I heard a good quote recently, reminiscent of the Roman Empire on the skids with the barbarians at the gate. Some Christians read the signs of the times and built nonviolent communities which later on, preserved the scripture, classics, and art during the Dark Ages.

The difference from the Roman Empire analogy, Phil further commented, is that

> the barbarians are our own people—the politicians, generals, CEOs, and bankers. But the formulas for redress are the same: build nonviolent communities of civil resistance.

And so we did.

Quakers Walk Their Talk

Brayton

A woman I worked with at the Learning Guild in the 1970s shared excitedly about attending the Quaker meeting in Cambridge. I had always associated Quakers with a small Christian sect of pacifists known for living out their religious convictions and paying the price. As a young boy in the early 1950s, my earliest introduction to Quakers was seeing *Friendly*

Persuasion a movie set in Indiana during the Civil War. The lead actor, Anthony Perkins, convincingly portrays Quaker antiwar convictions, my first glimpse of a pacifist stand.

Suzanne and I decided to attend the Quaker meeting, where we found committed and active pacifists who regularly practiced contemplative silence. Sitting in stillness with like-minded members of the Society of Friends reminded me of sitting with yogis and Buddhists as I had done in my twenties. So it felt right to sit with Quakers, peacemakers with contemplative prayer at the center. Suzanne agreed, loving the ambiance and pared-down simplicity.

Christian Nonviolence and the Payment of Taxes

By that time in our lives, we were seriously discerning our future direction as a couple in professional jobs and in making comfortable salaries. After Quaker meeting for worship one Sunday, we spotted a workshop flier entitled "Quakers and War Taxes" led by Alan Eccleston, a weighty Friend and respected war tax refuser. We decided to attend.

Alan delivered his presentation in the measured, sensible way so typical of Quakers. He read from *Christian Faith and Practice*, issued by the Quaker yearly meeting:

> A socially reformed life, which rejects all that is inseparably linked with injury to others will necessarily involve self-sacrifice. We will now reflect on the sacrifices of faith as they pertain to the way we earn money and how our tax money is spent.

Running headlong into the simple Quaker logic, Alan's workshop clearly stated Quaker ethical nonviolence:

> We Quakers cannot by our faith injure or kill anyone or even threaten to do so. But if I cannot do the act of violence, it also follows that I cannot pay for someone else to injure or kill in my name and with my tax dollars.

The statistic that more than fifty percent of every American tax dollar pays for past, present, and future wars staggered us. But the Quaker way manages such hard realities with a truth simple to understand, radical to live, but always compassionately stated. The notion of consequences as a result of religious conviction was a brand new idea for me. Imagine refusing to pay taxes for war based on religious principle?

It was the late 1970s, a time of increased pace of the nuclear arms race between the US and Soviet Union. The acronym MAD described our two countries' breach of sanity in piling up nuclear weapons to avoid Mutually Assured Destruction. Suzanne and I began to ask ourselves risky questions like: Did we really want to pay for the production of weapons that might end life on earth?

As we weighed the question, Quakers in Cambridge offered instructional, action-based workshops laying out strategies for tax resistance and, more importantly, for building a community of faith that would support those who refused to pay war taxes.

Inevitably, we would run into memorable tax refusers Wally and Juanita Nelson, leaders of the New England War Tax Resistance movement. Juanita often shared her frustration about the relative invisibility of the movement. Wally had a great story about the IRS turning up at his door to discuss his tax debt. He greeted the agent warmly, offered him a cup of tea, and they sat down to discuss the matter at hand—the fact that Wally Nelson owed the IRS some back taxes.

Wally promptly stated his case. "Ya know you come into my house and ask me to give you money so that the military can go out and kill people with it, and you don't even apologize. You don't even say, 'Well, sorry I have to come in here and disrupt your day.' You don't even say, 'Look I am sorry I have to do this, but it is my job, and you did break the law.' You think you are making some kind of normal request. Well, I think you're crazy."

Wally's approach was transparent and simple. He often uttered his well-known refrain "you don't gotta do things." Just because people do something in obedience to the law, "*you* don't gotta." Wally had a strong aversion to making moral decisions too complicated. "Oh you don't have to read all these books, discuss it 'til you're blue in the face and wonder about it endlessly. Keep things simple; paying taxes that go for hurting and killing people is crazy. I am not gonna do it."

Juanita often said to me the same thing from a different angle. "Just

Juanita Nelson speaks about tax resistance

because everyone's doing it and it's the rage, does not make it right. I think this is especially true when using the things of this world. Just because someone invents some gadget that has become wildly popular, oh just everyone is using it except you. There's all this pressure to conform."

Most people we meet are satisfied to talk about how bad war is. But we do not want to just *talk* about how bad war is. We need to refuse to pay war taxes. That refusal will cause a complete change in the way we live . . . for the better.

Our initial tax refusal evolved in two steps. First, while we had a full-time taxable income, we paid our taxes under written protest, sending a letter to the Internal Revenue Service with our tax filings. The following year, I withheld all federal taxes through my employer, the Learning Guild, by opting to be paid gross salary without any taxes withheld. For a time, the Internal Revenue Service was quiet on my nonpayment of war taxes, but that changed dramatically after a few years.

Taxes and Death

I never imagined I would *not* pay my taxes, given my parents' oft-quoted, well-worn, World-War-II-generation cliché: "The two things you cannot avoid are death and taxes." With my reading of Adin Ballou and nineteenth-century American Christian anarchists, I ran into the counterpoint to the maxim: "Taxes cause death." Like nothing else I could have imagined, to question war and preparation for war paid for by my taxes altered my assumptions about how I spend money.

A cherished fantasy we harbor as Americans reared in the middle class is that life should get better, easier, and certainly more lucrative as we work our way into our thirties and forties. The progress model, a classic bourgeois falsehood we are all schooled in, suggests that life gets easier with hard work. The assumption of progress and privilege clashes with tax refusal, which brings us closer to the disadvantaged whose lives rarely get easier.

And what if I choose *not* to make a taxable income? Life gets more challenging, more rigorous, more ascetic, and less monetarily lucrative. Can progress actually mean moving downward?

In the late 1970s, Suzanne and I each refused to pay two thousand dollars we legally owed in federal taxes to the IRS. Our refusal was reported directly to the IRS, which responded immediately by putting a lien on the rehabbed and formerly abandoned house we owned in Brockton. This meant that upon sale of our house, the feds would take their cut of four thousand dollars plus penalties—maybe somewhere in the neighborhood of six thousand dollars and counting.

Additional penalties accrued for not filing tax returns. We felt the grip of the IRS as we continued to compound a yearly fine, increasing what the government identified as our debt as our income lessened. We wondered if our tax resistance would ruin us financially and permanently.

Parallel to that dilemma, the wisdom of nonviolent beliefs provides deeper insight into the conflict. Could we engage in a respectful dialogue with the adversary and meet with the IRS agents assigned to each of our cases? In such a meeting, Suzanne and I hoped that the agents could inform us of just how much trouble we were in and give us a clue as to what they thought of our refusal to pay.

Owing back taxes means that the Feds can control your home and assets, levy hefty penalties, seize cars, and garnish wages. It began to occur to us that a life of such tax resistance might not be sustainable from year to year.

Face to Face with the Tax Agent

Although I felt morally right in my stand, I was plenty nervous entering the all-powerful IRS office of the agent assigned to my case. Once we greeted each other and sat down, he was friendly enough, seemed to know my case, how much I owed, and the penalties involved. He informed me of how long what he called my default had been on IRS books and what the future held for me financially as far as the IRS was concerned.

While engaged in our cordial and substantive conversation, his tone changed dramatically after I explained the moral and ethical grounds of our refusal. He offered quite spontaneously, "I respect your position on war and the payment of taxes, and many agents I know respect positions of conscience. But payment of federal taxes in full is the law, and you have broken the law by refusing to pay."

Sounding much like a collection agency, he went on to clarify, "Agents like me are hired to collect back taxes. It appears what you owe is un-collectable given your strong religious convictions. Like most agents I am more interested in collecting from fat cats who are cheating on their taxes."

Then, with stunning brevity, he concluded, "I am going to "file" your case. We call it a '53,' which means your debt will stay on the books with no additional fines now or into the future. The case will reopen only if you start earning a taxable income."

From the outset of our conversation, I felt the enormity of the power leverage of the IRS. At the same time, I felt relief in not having to fork over the tax money and continue the excruciating pressure of increasing fines. A small victory.

I was impressed with how an ordinary and likable tax agent could respect a law-breaking tax refuser, and how I could respect him, as our dialogue unfolded.

The bottom-line reality, however, is that our tax debt would take several years to resolve.

The IRS Comes Calling

Suzanne

At this seminal decision-making time in our lives, we sought out advice from people among the leaders of the small and unheralded tax resistance movement in the US, all of them looking for creative ways to resist supporting war and empire within our considerably reduced lifestyle. We moved in incremental steps in the direction of tax resistance. Once while teaching at Simmons, I went to the bursar's office to request that I be allowed to receive gross salary without taxes deducted. The clear-cut answer: No.

Simultaneous with our tax resistance, we began our community experiment with the McCarthy family. Agape had just published a pamphlet written by Charlie McCarthy called *Christian Nonviolence: the Great Failure, the Only Hope* with an untutored though admirable cover sketch of the face of Jesus drawn by the eldest McCarthy daughter, Kristin, then sixteen.

In our Brockton kitchen, part of a crude and hollowed-out shell of the house, I prepared a mailing of our pamphlets as a community promotion for our programs on nonviolence. As I stuffed envelopes with the Jesus-face covers, I had my first visit from a male IRS agent. Alone with our adopted daughter, Teresa, about thirteen months old, I realized that the IRS was calling.

The agent politely and matter-of-factly informed me that the City of Brockton had received our tax resistance statements and that, after a year of IRS scrutiny, the time for an investigation had arrived. I asked the agent to have a seat and proceeded to share with him information about our path to noncooperation with war taxes. He listened patiently without interruption as we sipped our tea, the face of Jesus staring up at us from the table on multiple book covers.

The IRS agent hesitated briefly, then said, "This is all very interesting. I see the rationale. I even respect it, but you are going to have to deal with the IRS anyway. Now that you own a home, they'll be after it."

The man didn't disagree with what I said about the military budget and the risk of an accidental nuclear war or of destroying the planet. "Who wants to pay for that?" I asked him rhetorically.

He shrugged. "Yeah, I know."

Teresa, who had been skidding around in her little scooter, was getting impatient with the adult blah, blah, blah. My IRS friend left saying: "I have to fill out a report." With a definite sense of chagrin, he apologized, saying that I would lose money or the house or might be called into the IRS office in Brockton or all three.

A short time later, a letter from the IRS arrived, summoning me to appear at the IRS office in downtown Brockton to discuss my taxes. I knew they might put a lien on the house or impose a fine, in effect, taking what we owed from the money we put into the mortgage.

When I arrived at the courthouse, I was escorted into a small room where an affable woman reviewed my years of non-payment, the amount I owed, and the fines that had accrued. Some part of me felt insecure and unsettled. In my mind, I could hear the doubter in me saying, "Oh, no. What have you done?"

To my surprise, the woman who was the head of the branch office sympathetically told me that she respected my actions and wished that she didn't have to recover the money but added, "There has to be a penalty." That penalty, a year later, meant a lien on the house and the collection of back taxes from it.

Eventually, we lived on nontaxable donations from friends, a reliable option without the ongoing worry of squeezing past the ridiculously low level of taxable income.

In the nineties, we joined with Randy Kehler and Betsy Corner and Wally and Juanita Nelson in their two-year protest over seizure of land-trust property by the IRS because of Randy and Betsy's tax refusal. Their house was sold to a low bidder who moved in while hundreds of us protested the immoral IRS seizure and sale of the property.

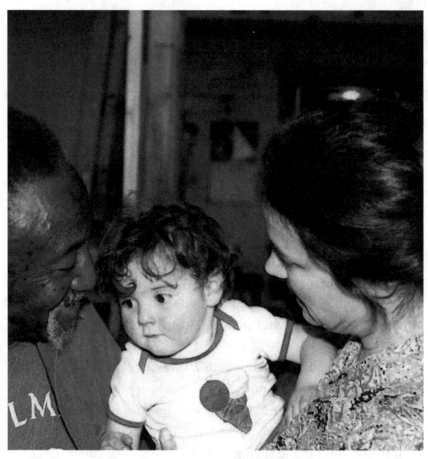

Wally Nelson, left, who founded Pioneer Valley Tax Resisters with his wife, Juanita, admires Teresa Shanley and chats with Suzanne at Agape in 1988.

Randy was arrested and went to jail for more than a month. People from all over the country supported the witness. The action furthered our bond of friendship with the tax resistance community and with Wally and Juanita, who became regulars at Agape gatherings. At Agape, they often spoke about their life at Woolman Hill without heat, electricity, or running water on a little plot of land they called the Bean Patch where we frequently visited.

Wally and Juanita were not Christian, but unfailing in their selflessness, they embodied Jesus to the core as they often sent us a widow's mite from occasional, unsolicited donations they received. Our friendship endured and flourished.

Joanne and Jail

Suzanne

One of the most dramatic and defining experiences of my life involves going to jail several times for acts of civil disobedience while resisting research and design of nuclear weapons at Draper Laboratory in Cambridge, Massachusetts.

My first incarceration in 1980 altered my life forever. During that time of imprisonment, I met Joanne (not her real name) and three of her children. The experiences changed my life.

Jail alone, even for a short two weeks, would have changed my life. Not only did I see life in prison firsthand, but I also met a fellow inmate, a woman of lively intelligence who became my close friend. As if by some mysterious grace, I also met and fell in love with her children. Because Joanne remained incarcerated after I left prison, I became involved in care of her children. I had my first experience of mothering while Joanne completed her sentence. My complex and sometimes painful bonding with Joanne's children continues and grows.

Through meeting Joanne and her children, I saw the inherent racial biases of the prison system, the cruelty and degradation of prisons, and especially the negative effect on incarcerated mothers and their children. I became an advocate for the abolition of prisons and taught courses on nonviolence in the Massachusetts Correctional Institute, Framingham, for women where I served my sentence. I also became a staunch opponent of the death penalty.

I came to treasure and love Joanne's children with a devotion and passion I had not previously known. They responded to my affection with genuine care and love that confirmed my desire to have children.

Brayton and I took the children to our resistance meetings and to the playground. We taught them how to ride bikes and spent holidays and almost every weekend with them for a year.

Our bonding with the children eventually gave Brayton and me emotional reinforcement that led to our decision to marry and have a family. Joanne's children attended our wedding on September 27, 1980.

Today, we consider Joanne's grown children as close relatives. We share a deep and profound connection. It would be impossible to tell the history of Agape without mentioning them, their painful story, and the way it has played out in their lives.

Involved in each others' lives, we see and talk with each other frequently. They live successful adult lives with meaningful jobs, a testimony to their determination and resilience. Early Ailanthus and Agape community networking provided support from hundreds of people who assisted Joanne and her family in countless ways, from setting up apartments and low-rent housing to child care, financial aid, counseling, and friendship.

My rich, indelible relationship with Joanne led to a similar association with Joanne's children that provided me perspective on their struggle of living as biracial children in a racist society and its effects on them. We grew together and learned to love unconditionally with a joy and comfort that sustain me.

I first laid eyes on Joanne in 1980 when, in my thirties, a judge sentenced me to fourteen days in the Framingham prison for civil disobedience at Draper.

Handcuffed after a brief trial and escorted to a police squad car, I felt nervous yet strangely ready as the two male officers chauffeured me to jail. To prepare, I had gone through role-playing exercises simulating arrest, and I had the confidence of that drill. Both officers remained silent and unresponsive when I tried to make conversation about the evils of nukes. Resigned and increasingly apprehensive, I sat back in the police car, .

Shortly after my arrival and initial processing at MCI, Framingham, where I successfully refused the usual vaginal drug search, a guard escorted me into the women's day room complete with institutional linoleum floors and plastic chairs. Some women sat around in their slips, most smoked, and others stared blankly at a battered television on a plastic table in the middle of the room.

I spotted a thin, energetic woman with a commanding, dominating presence who stood out from the rest.

From her perch, one foot on a chair and one foot on the ground, the woman whom I would soon know as Joanne studied me while rapidly puffing on her cigarette. She got up from her chair, stood with hands on hips, pointed to my floral print, hippie skirt (I was dressed for my teaching job at Simmons), took the cigarette out of her mouth, and said, with no little sarcasm for the amusement of the other women, "Now what have we here? A cute little lady in her fancy flower outfit. And what brings you to this fuckin' hole?"

I was embarrassed, taken aback. Her comment was harsh but oddly nonthreatening. I liked her right away. She was rail thin, had a long, prominent nose, deep-set brown eyes, and an alert awareness—a look of intelligence, curiosity, and toughness. She drew me in. I noticed that it was hard for her to sit still.

I stammered a bit and, not wanting to make a fool of myself, tried to get my bearings. So I asserted rather loudly and probably with a little "brag and blow," as the Irish say, "Protesting against nuclear weapons." Several of the women looked at me in disbelief. A few laughed, but not derisively.

The inquiring woman asked more questions, and she seemed genuinely interested in my rap. Yet another cigarette dangling from her mouth, she was expressive, opinionated.

The slip woman grabbed my arm and steered me towards her cell for count, when guards take the roster of prisoners. "Everybody needs a bodyguard in this rat hole. I'll be yours. Don't say nothin' to anyone that you don't have to." She told me her name was Joanne.

1980 Prison Journal Entries

Joanne says that she is thirty, though she looks older with her hardened face, sunken cheeks. She tells me she's a drug addict, in for heroin and gun possession. Her serious, almost scowling demeanor

47

softens with an occasional joke about a guard or an inmate. Then, the hard, cynical look returns, the swagger, the assertive, airtight observations.

Joanne has sad eyes. She tells me that she is married and that her husband, Mark, who is African-American and whom she hasn't seen for over two years, is also in jail in Massachusetts. She is white. They have three children.

She has done time before, knows the ropes, so she lays out her understanding of the system—a blueprint of what I can and cannot do in what she calls a "plantation for the poor." "Watch out," she warned, "for rape by other inmates or guards." Now I was afraid. I hadn't considered *this*.

She refers to the guards as "screws" and "cock-a-roaches" (her inflection emphatically on the first syllable). She's doing a mandatory year for gun possession, with time added for dealing, solicitation, and on.

She is *always* eager to talk, a fabulous relater. We have lots of time on our hands not being out in the population but confined to the medical unit, which for me was my protection. As a white professional woman, I received the kind of solicitude that is not offered to the other women. It was a realization of class, race, and privilege.

Joanne's three kids were on her mind constantly. "My kids are with my sister-in-law, Christine, who really isn't my sister-in-law. She has the same last name, so I call her that so DSS won't get the kids."

Christine has three kids of her own plus Joanne's three and apparently no source of income other than welfare. "I can't believe that I did this to them. I'm no fuckin' good. I'm a lousy motherfuckin' mother. I'm gonna fuckin' pay for this. God's not gonna forgive me."

At certain times during the day, we are allowed to go to each other's cells, which meant that Joanne and I spent a lot of time together. Her natural intelligence and steely resolve attracted me. She keeps vowing, "This will be my last incarceration." When she learns that I am a teacher, she is beside herself with enthusiasm. "I want to learn how to write and talk better, get a degree, go to college, and make something of myself."

"Can you teach me grammar?" she asks.

I agree, and we start grammar lessons the next day. In one of my few phone calls to my support group outside, I ask that someone bring me a copy of John E. Warriner's *English Grammar and Composition*, a book I used while teaching high school English. Several days later, the book arrives. Joanne loves it, starts studying, underlining passages and memorizing grammar rules.

Joanne was a self-appointed caretaker for Tammy, a seventeen-year-old who seemed extremely mentally ill and attempted suicide in jail, which was why she was in the hospital unit. She was in restraints for some part of the day. She acted out by slamming her arms against the bars and screaming, which led to a group of guards coming to subdue her. They hustled us all into our cells and then locked us in. I could never get used to the idea of not being able to get out of the cell of my own volition, even in a fire.

Nearby, I could hear Tammy's screams. She cried out, chantlike, a litany of the guards' actions: "Now they're touching me," she yelled. "They're holding me down," her voice rising in panic. High pitched wails followed: "No, no. Strait jacket. Strait jacket."

One of the male guards shouted angrily, "You're going to max if you don't shut the fuck up." Other inmates yelled from their cells, some of them swearing at the guards, a weird, chaotic, and ominous scene.

Joanne's loud, assertive voice could be heard above the rest as she yelled from her cell, "Don't give the motherfuckers any nuts. That's what they want. They want their nuts."

On another occasion, when the guards forcefully subdued Donna, another incarcerated teen, because she refused to return to her cell, Joanne shouted from her own cell, "We're all God's children." The guards were unresponsive. "Leave her the fuck alone," Joanne screamed. Instead, the screws—the guards, including a few men—pinned Donna to the floor, dragged her back to her cell, and locked her in.

Carol, another inmate close to the action and able to see what Joanne and I could not see from behind our locked doors, could be heard calling: "Joanne, Joanne" her voice rising. "They're stripping her. They're stripping her."

"Here comes the motherfucker brigade," yelled Joanne. Donna moaned. Carol reported. Joanne was rolling it all into an Oscar performance.

I knelt down in my cell to a space with a narrow slot at the bottom of the door. I was not sure what to do, but I tried to hear and see something, anything. I started reading aloud randomly from the Book of Psalms, which no one wanted to hear, but I felt I had to contribute something to the cacophony.

Joanne joined in again, her voice rising above the others. I felt she did a routine for my benefit, but I was okay with it. "God loves his children. You're just like them, flesh and blood. See what they do to you, sisters. Strip 'em, scorn 'em. He's watchin.' God's watchin.' You'll pay for this. He takes care of his own." From evangelical retribution, she turned once again to taunting expletives.

Donna screamed and cried. Joanne kept raisin' and praisin': "The Lord knows His own." She didn't stop, sometimes taking on another tone, admonishment mixed with expletive. "Use some psychology. Use some decency. No. God. I forgot. You're animal trainers. Cat brains, motherfuckin' cat brains."

On my last day at MCI Framingham, Joanne told me with animated, last-chance breathlessness: "I'm gonna get rid of all of the negative shit in my past." She was in earnest. "No more drugs; no more dealin.' I can't do this to my kids any more. Can you help me? You've got to help me. Can you visit my kids? Can you bring them food?"

Joanne's children, who lived in Roxbury with the so-called sister-in-law were ages three, five, and seven. I told her that I would. We started setting up plans.

Meeting Joanne's Children

Shortly after that conversation and while still in jail, I called John Leary, a young friend in the Ailanthus Community. I asked him to visit the kids and their "aunt." He reported back to me when visiting me in jail that the situation was "horrible, the worst

I've even seen." In his twenty-one-year-old life, he had seen homelessness while reaching out to street people and the poor. Yet the utter squalor, misery, urine-filled corridors in a bleak tenement building on Georgia Street in Roxbury, where Joanne's children lived with their caretaker, Christine, struck him as frighteningly extreme.

Eventually, I was released. Joanne and I knew that we would see each other and pledged to stay involved in each other's lives. So, within the week, I set out for Georgia Street in Roxbury to meet the kids and Christine. I had never before set foot in Roxbury, Boston's predominantly black neighborhood.

I fought back fear and nervousness as I walked up the stairs of the smelly, dank apartment building and hesitatingly knocked on the tenement door. The door opened a crack, and three little faces peered out at me through the chain lock that provided a trace of light in the dark corridor where I stood.

Their timid little faces were obscured, so I found myself talking to the chain lock and the tips of children's noses. "I'm a friend of your mom," I said, trying to reassure them. "She asked me to come and visit you. Can I come in?"

In the background, I heard a stern, reproving woman's voice. "Get away from that door!" They scurried away immediately, their fear palpable and my own alarm heightened.

"Open the door," the harsh voice raged. Someone drew back several locks, and the door opened. I stepped into a world I had never witnessed before—a life-changing, devastating world.

The first person I saw was Christine, Joanne's "relative" sitting in a huge, over-stuffed chair next to a mattress without a frame in a dark, unlit hallway, the corridor where she slept.

She chain-smoked and, with every inhale, she seemed to sink more deeply into despair and had trouble breathing. She weighed well over three hundred pounds. Her head was covered in rollers. Spinning out tales of white people's lives and destinies between long drags on her cigarette, she watched a TV that sat on a battered dresser.

A single light bulb hung from the ceiling in each room, and a few broken toys lay scattered about. Christine sat beneath a mawkish painting stapled to a velvet-lined background of an African-American man crying, one tear frozen onto his cheek, his hands in chains. I spotted large cockroaches mixed in with food, dirt, garbage bags, and children's clothes heaped in random piles on the floor. I could actually hear the roaches scampering here and there as I moved through the apartment. Repulsed by the sound of their bodies crunching under my feet, I stepped on a few.

Children's sleeping bags were tossed on the floor, no mats underneath. Christine barely uttered a word to me except an occasional "Uh, uh" or reprimand to a child as she loudly yelled, "Jasmine!" Clothes draped over radiators, which Christine kept touching as if to speed up the drying process with her hands. Some of the clothes were so wet they emitted steam.

Hanging onto each other and evidently afraid to speak, the children followed me. As I moved through the rooms, I spotted a few battered chairs and, on the floor, a torn, stained mattress with stuffing erupting from holes. The youngest child, Christa, three, was adorable, babbling and laughing, thumb in mouth.

I searched for a place to put the bags of food I had purchased and others had donated. The refrigerator was empty, stained with grease and layers of crusted food. A quick check of the oven revealed a litter of newborn kittens.

Christine glared at me with resentment. I could feel her suspicion. I didn't blame her. I wanted to please her, say anything, *do* anything to relieve her suffering.

So, in the pleading, half-scared voice of a defendant before a judge, apologizing, I stammered, "I'll keep coming back. I'll bring more food. I have some financial donations." Christine said nothing.

"I'll be back," I said self-deprecatingly. Christine nodded.

Both Brayton and I continued visits to Roxbury for a year. We picked up the children for weekend overnights at our apartment. Christine occasionally mumbled "Thanks." I learned not to expect gratitude, but it took some getting used to.

We taught the kids some civil rights chants like "I ain't gonna let nobody turn me around . . . " which we all sang loudly in the car. The kids added their own verses with great gusto: "Ain't gonna let nobody smack me again . . . "

Drumming circles suited the theatrical Jasmine. She held us all captive as she excelled at storytelling and chanted: "One day, they put Jesus on a cross . . . " We all followed with faster drumming as Jasmine built her own delightful stream-of-consciousness tale.

We made popcorn, watched movies, went to parks. We missed them during the week, but there were plenty of check-in calls, mainly from Jasmine who, at five, had our phone number and learned to dial it. I'd pick up the phone to hear her say, "Come and get me out of this bug house."

The Children

Joanne's pattern had been to move from apartment to apartment, dealing and using drugs, leaving the children with so-called friends and even losing track of them for weeks at a time. Occasionally when the children visited her in jail, she could get her drugs by having friends hide them in her children's clothing.

I first arrived at Christine's in the middle of September with none of the children in school because, I quickly learned, they had no shoes or clothes except for a few pairs of wrinkled, dirty summer shorts and shirts. Our peace group friends remedied that situation quickly as we began weekly visits with food, clothes, and cash. If we took the children out for any reason, they never wanted to return to Georgia Street. We always felt terrible betrayal in bringing them back.

We had a great rental in Belmont—spacious, comfortable. When Joanne got out of jail at about the same time as her

*Jasmine, left, and Christa, right, finish a meal with
their friend Molly at Boston's Haley House.*

husband, Mark, they stayed with us for several days along with the children. Eventually, our landlord asked us to leave for violating the terms of the lease, which we certainly had done.

The Community Responds to Need

Almost every week for a year, we or others of our Ailanthus team drove the children to visit Joanne in jail before her release. Predictably, when it came time to leave, feisty Jasmine, the five-year-old, always refused, clinging to Joanne and insisting, "I'm not going. I'm not going." She was one determined, fearless five-year-old.

One of the guards arrived to pick her up to move her along. She let out a wail, "Don't touch me. Don't touch me. Get your hands off me. I'm not leaving."

Christa, at three sweet and innocent and too young to comprehend her situation, had seemed unfazed by everything swirling around her. Wanting to be picked up and hugged, she always smiled. Christine favored Christa back "home" on Georgia Street, whereas Jasmine complained of being "smacked and yelled at."

We thought about adopting the children and consulted officials who informed us that the legal process for adoption or foster care took too long, sometimes a year, and would be too complicated with uncertain results. So we tried to keep the children together until Joanne was released.

When Joanne was in jail, Brayton visited her as a confidante and spiritual guide. They studied scripture together as she seemed to be genuinely thirsting for God. She was fascinating to talk to, very intelligent, and with an uncanny grasp of scripture. She and Brayton had a close affinity, and he felt that Joanne added new dimensions to his own spiritual growth.

Once Joanne was out of jail, we arranged low-income housing for her and the children through Kathe McKenna and Haley House, the Catholic Worker community that fostered Ailanthus. Joanne and the kids remained constants in our lives, never far from our reach.

Marriage as a Calling

Brayton

As our relationship formed, Suzanne and I felt in our hearts a nagging restlessness. Conventional jobs, marriage, and middle class professional norms pulled us outwardly in one direction while we slowly moved in a radical alternative direction.

I had developed some proficiency in teaching Hatha Yoga and Buddhist-style meditation, and it yielded some income. Nevertheless, we realized that such jobs held mainly for livelihood, with Suzanne teaching English part time at Bentley College, could not hold us together financially for very long.

We felt that we were neither here nor there but uncertain of how to leap into the unknown.

We had many models and inspired co-conspirators encircling us—Quakers, Ailanthus folks, and the Atlantic Life Community— all speaking to us with one voice: "Leave the conventional world. Build nonviolent community."

Many of us who came of age in the seventies and eighties were dissatisfied with the materialistic lifestyle and meaningless cultural values and expectations that formed us. The experimental nature of the sixties and drastic circumstances of social upheaval, assassinations, and war shaped our thinking while we gained college and graduate degrees we thought would ready us for our adult professions. Armed with career ambitions, many of us threw ourselves into serious jobs for a few years or more. Then we sensed that something revelatory happened as a light shone through.

We could turn our back on it all even with vaunted professions such as The Law or Wall Street and other monetary schemes in business with big futures. I often heard stories like:

"We're leaving the city and going to Vermont to farm and become potters."

"I'm dropping out of this rat race and moving to Oregon to join a commune."

"We're going to Maine to homestead with the Nearings."

Spiritual adventurers were leaving the mainstream work force to travel to India or join a Hindu ashram like Ram Dass.

I vividly remember the support, the encouragement, *the insistence* from peers and others in our orbits that we could just quit our jobs and start living a nonviolent lifestyle full time. I don't remember any real fear about leaving a conventional job or of falling flat on my face and having to limp back to my former job. Promising stories were right in front of us, but the actual leap for Suzanne and me took a few more years.

We dropped out of mainstream livelihood in stages. I went to work part-time for a local Pax Christi office in Cambridge with renowned Catholic author and peacemaker Gordon Zahn while Suzanne taught part time at Bentley.

Is Marriage Necessary?

Then we needed to resolve something closer to home. What to do about our relationship? Should we marry and have children while being pulled inexorably into unknown terrain?

Suzanne didn't see the problem. Our relationship, long-term commitment, and dedication to and love for each other led organically to just getting married and having kids. I wasn't sure. Would a traditional marriage and family life just be another convention that I was determined to resist? Would a nuclear family trap us in a lifestyle of debt to the American way of life?

I ended up trapped in my own fears.

I grew up in a fairly typical twentieth-century, middle-class, white, suburban nuclear family. As a young adult, I was utterly disinterested in repeating my parents' family model of isolation, materialism, and loneliness as the bread-winning husband and father to children in suburban America.

Too many marriages I witnessed, including that of my own parents, had no real spiritual purpose. They used alcohol as self-medication to combat the stress of meaninglessness. The constant pain of discord in my own parents' relationship and failed marriages of friends and family added to my conviction that conventional marriage was not for me.

Yet, I could not ever see myself with any woman but Suzanne. So we found ourselves locked in three years of uncertainty as I continually associated marriage and family with my own memories of suburbia in the fifties. I needed models of marriages and lifestyles that resisted American culture to change this mental block.

My conversion seemed to come almost immediately after meeting Jim and Shelley Douglass and Phil Berrigan and Liz McAlister, nonviolent Christian-based couples living for something more than their family. They were parents raising children under demanding community responsibilities of helping the poor while living active lives of protest with periodic jail witness. We were part of a powerful network of Boston area peace communities whose members helped us discern how to be married and in community. Children and marriage soon became foundational to the community experiment.

A *Quatholic* Wedding?

We were finding our way back to the Catholic Church, not on Main Street but within a communal network of Catholic Christians and Quakers in search of faith. In such small, intentional sub-cultures, we found ourselves drawn back into religion.

Cultivating a daily meditation practice and reading of scripture, Suzanne and I arranged a small chapel space in our apartment dining room for prayer together. Returning to our birthright faith had meaning because we knew something we had not known while growing up Catholic: a foundational faith in the nonviolent Jesus.

It was time for the sacrament of holy matrimony not because we were called to future parish life in the Church but because we were a pacifist community in a Catholic network. Therefore, we didn't feel we had to rely on our local priest and a traditional marriage ceremony. We wanted to design our own marriage, incorporating our new and biological families and expressing our passions and spiritual priorities.

We had become acquainted with Charlie McCarthy. A Boston-area Catholic pacifist and seminal teacher of nonviolence, he helped us craft a powerful vision of a Catholic marriage ritual. We then united the Catholic sacrament of marriage centered on Eucharist in the sacred embrace of the Cambridge Quaker Meeting House.

We learned that the Catholic Church considered the ceremony we created valid but not licit. "Valid" meant, ultimately, a consecrated marriage before God but "not considered licit" or legal within the guidelines of Church traditions, which is to say that Catholics must be married in a Catholic Church by a Catholic priest. We were newly experimenting with choosing Gospel-inspired, ethical forms that cooperated with forces of love. At the same time, we wanted to resist authoritarian hierarchies that coerce and violate the religious freedoms of the faithful.

Monsignor Edmond T. Tinsley, confidant to Bishop Timothy J. Harrington of Worcester and a trusted friend and supporter, said to me when I described how Suzanne and I were married, "You realize the marriage is not licit."

I could feel his gently stated disapproval.

But for us, a more important question emerged. Was God blessing our union? As laypeople embracing our Catholic Church once again, we listened more deeply to the advice of the mystics: *Act according to your own inner voice. Do not be cowed by Church authority* under sway of the Church's most ancient mantra: *We do it this way because that is the way it has always been done!* Too often Church authority is threatened by another authority, in this case the religious experience of the nonordained.

It was stunning to watch our post-Vatican II-Catholic traditions evolving and creating the most unprecedented change in Church history. In this new and unfolding age of the laity, the time was *now* to find a way to become, male and female, priestly, mystical, and ministerial out of our own inner core of religious faith and experience. Sharing a valid-but-not-licit marriage was for me a new way of being Catholic. We wanted to evolve our faith as God demands and let go of the outdated and medieval.

We had asked former Catholic priest Phil Berrigan to preside over our marriage ceremony, thinking that certainly he would not mind "illicit," but he and Dan were, you guessed it, heading for jail and spearheading the first of a wave of antinuclear-weapons Plowshares actions. Liz McAlister, Phil's wife and a former nun, agreed to give the homily, but we still lacked a celebrant. Charlie suggested Father Joachim Lally, a Paulist priest accomplishing impressive work with Hispanic youth in Boston.

Joachim had a tendency to rile his superiors when it came to matters of conscience. When we asked him to risk celebrating an illicit wedding mass in a Quaker meetinghouse, he paused and thought it over a bit. Finally, he responded, "In these kinds of decisions regarding my superiors I feel it is always better to ask pardon than permission." We felt we had the priest sent by God, one willing to risk something for a more vibrant future of a Church yet to come.

Violence of the Law

One more conventional hurtle to marriage remained, obtaining a marriage license, which would make our marriage legal. We were beginning to recognize that the exercise of law is coercive, that legal often means: Obey under threat of penalty of fine or fear of imprisonment.

Why not marry in that spirit of Agape love? At that stage in our moral development, our mid thirties, we saw the state and its laws grounded in the violence of threat and punishment. Law is backed up by penalties meted out for illegal behavior, not in the spirit of the "patience and kindness" of First Corinthians.

The theme of our ceremony was "Love Is Eternal," which we hoped would sustain our married lives. Therefore, we did not request a marriage license. Yes, we would not be legally married in the eyes of the state. But isn't eternal love always patient and kind?

The Wedding Day . . . Is Here!

Suzanne

It was early fall in New England—the sky cerulean blue, late summer flowers blooming, and foliage sparkling. The smell of crisp fall air was intoxicating. We floated in a state of anticipation heightened by the setting of the lovely Quaker meetinghouse, simplicity of the interior space, and generosity of our Quaker friends.

One of my Simmons students created a banner we placed prominently in the front of the Meeting-for-Worship room, a work of art that announced: *Love Is Eternal.* We marveled. What could it possibly mean?

The Vows

Many wedding ceremonies I've attended feel as if the ritual is done to the couple who prefer a church setting for a wedding, although they may not regularly attend church. In our present context culturally, the most prevalent influence, however, seems to be the postmodern secular world with the Church as cultural dispenser of weddings. Most people seem to long for some kind of ritual around one of the most significant experiences of their lives.

After waiting for six years to marry, Brayton and I had plenty of time to ponder the question: What are we called to, together? For starters, we sensed we felt called to be married in the spirit of the Divine Love, Agape. Secondly, we wanted to embrace marriage within community, merging our lives as a couple with that of others, including children. The indispensable direction of our marriage was outward: helping the poor, working to end war and violence, and practicing hospitality.

As we planned our wedding, we decided that conventional wedding dress was not for us. Brayton purchased an Indian style shirt from a Cambridge shop, and I found a dark blue, ankle length cloth dress at Salvation Army. We thought how we dressed and how much we spent on the wedding would serve as a statement of our values and how we viewed ourselves: two hippies in their thirties, finally tying the knot.

We decided on a Quaker-inspired, non-alcoholic, potluck wedding. Liz McAlister, our homilist, attending with her children Jerry and Frida, addressed family and friends, numbering about one hundred. Father Joachim Lally said mass.

I was particularly moved that Liz encouraged us to see our vows as "a sign that despite the ins and outs and ups and downs, the comings and goings of community, people can make it together." She merged community, vision, and marriage. Because frailty and uncertainty were familiar visitors in my life, I resonated with Liz's invitation for all of us to consider "our human frailty before God." After family members and friends spoke, we all headed to the public meetinghouse next door. There we found a sumptuous potluck organized by our elder aunts, Rhoda, Joy, and Norma, who donned aprons to put out the meal and serve it.

My friend Joanne was still incarcerated at MCI Framingham, but we invited her three children to the wedding. Famished and bored after such a long ceremony, the kids sneaked out before it ended, found the wedding cake, and stuck their fingers right in.

Some of our guests came to Brayton and me with the news: "There are some happy kids over there who found the wedding cake and are licking their fingers."

Brayton and Suzanne, top, with Father Joachim Lally celebrate the Eucharist at their 1980 wedding, where Liz McAlister, above with her daughter Frida Berrigan, gave the homily. With guests and Father Lally, Brayton and Suzanne celebrate their marriage, next page.

Agape Beginnings

Suzanne

We embarked on community discussions with several families including Steve and Nancy James, a doctor and nurse team and Baptist missionaries, and Charlie and Mary McCarthy. The Jameses then had four children and the McCarthys eight. Brayton and I were childless and attempting to conceive.

Through our discussions, lengthy discernment led the Jameses to decide, with our full support, on missionary work in Haiti and continued contact with our community efforts. We left our mildly suburban digs in Belmont and moved to Brockton to join the McCarthys.

We purchased a formerly condemned, two-bedroom Cape house, without a clear title, for twenty-three thousand dollars. The house, occupied by a woman suffering from mental illness, hadn't been cleaned in years.

For a year, we painted, wall-papered, and insulated the two-hundred-year-old, previously uninsulated farmhouse. We combined our entire savings, (not all that impressive), plus my retirement money from teaching. We put down twenty thousand dollars and assumed a mortgage of thirty dollars per month from the former owner. It was just about what we could afford with no predictable income. We quickly discovered that a small mortgage or none at all provided keys to simple living survival.

Yet, for me one who loved the classroom and teaching, the transition from my career as an educator with some solid achievement to a nebulous, nevertheless solidly conceived new vocation caused some anxiety. In addition, the house was a disaster, with sinking, rotting floors—a rundown mess. I would have to leave behind notions of even a simple-living, modest home.

When my mother first came to visit the Brockton digs, she was startled by the decrepit condition of the house. She seemed ready to cry. After years of living in deplorable housing situations herself, given my father's unsteady employment as a union carpenter, she had hoped for much more from her PhD-bound daughter.

As she made her way over the planks that covered the mud and water that filled the entrance to the house, she kept nodding her head and repeating: "Oh, Suzy, how could you? How could you?" Her despair and my sadness for her reflected mirror images of what we now knew: our mutually shared dream of social climbing—an advanced degree for me, financial security and a release from the regrets of the past for both of us—were now gone forever.

I was broken hearted for her and me. "How could you?" was an accurate reflection of my own internal wrangling about our decision to move socially downward rather than socially upward. The mess, debris, and amount of rehab work left Brayton, Charlie, and me joking that "Peter Maurin (Dorothy Day's partner in founding the Catholic Worker movement) would *love* this place."

Charlie, Brayton, and I all had teaching backgrounds we could apply to our nonviolence ministry. We felt excitement at striking out into new territory, establishing our base with income that relied on our teaching skills, ongoing resistance work, hospitality, and building community.

Charlie had been a tenure-track college professor of theology at the University of Notre Dame. During the height of Vietnam War protests there, Charlie presented Jesus to students as a radical pacifist. His classrooms filled to capacity.

He left his predictable life of professor after his split with Notre Dame's president, Father Theodore Hesburgh, over expulsion of draft-card-burning students. Charlie entered into a risky unknown: teaching his life's great passion, Gospel-inspired nonviolence. He began holding talks and giving retreats to small groups of people and building a following of like-minded disciples.

On one such retreat, Charlie met Father George Zabelka, a Catholic priest who had blessed the bombing crews of the *Enola Gay* and the *Bockscar*, the American B-29 bombers that dropped atomic bomb on Hiroshima and Nagasaki, Japan, in August,

1945, near the end of World War II. The bomb killed more than 140,000 civilians and ushered in the atomic age. George later credited Charlie for his conversion to nonviolence. During filming of the 1988 documentary *The Reluctant Prophet,* George stayed with us in Brockton.

Directed by Bert Gavigan, the documentary tells how George

Father George Zabelka, left, and Charlie McCarthy take a break from filming a documentary about Father Zabelka, who became a peace advocate after years as a Catholic chaplain when he blessed crews of Enola Gay *and* Bockscar, *US B-29s that dropped atomic bombs on Hiroshima and Nagasaki on August 6 and 9, 1945.*

developed from military hawk to nonviolent peacemaker and examines the concept of conscience, parallels between militarism and racism, ethics of military training, and considerations of war and violence in the Christian tradition.

Concurrently, once in Brockton, Brayton and I developed a base of operation for our own ministry efforts from junior high school through college with a variety of presentations including Confraternity of Christian Doctrine (CCD) and high school retreats, college campus ministry, and parish programs. I became a promoter, teacher, sole person in the "office" (our Brockton kitchen), mother of Teresa, wife of Brayton, community member, homeschooling teacher to four of the McCarthy children, and coordinator of hospitality requests to visit the new community. Stress levels were firmly in place.

I look now at some of the typewritten sheets with white-outs and ancient fonts and realize that when we began, computers did

Guests, including some of the McCarthy children, celebrate the baptism of Teresa Shanley in July, 1986. Charlie McCarthy observes, right.

not exist. Our newly purchased electric typewriter did the job of creating the first fliers for our ministry.

Sometimes, in our effort to sell our product, "the Sermon on the Mount," parish priests damned our program with faint praise. On the other hand, CCD instructors and parish program coordinators, for the most part, welcomed us enthusiastically and none more emphatically than women religious, many orders in the Boston area continuing to support us to this day.

Academics from all walks of life, like David O'Brien from Holy Cross and Michael True from Assumption College, supported and sustained us, themselves participating in protests and encouraging our ministry with invitations to teach in their classrooms and colleges.

One thing we know for certain is that we relied on the support of the Catholic Church. Without countless women religious and laity who were directors of CCD programs; radical and renegade priests; and some bishops, including Timothy Harrington and Bishop Reilly of the Diocese of Worcester—our Catholic community start-up would not have lasted beyond its first year.

As we were creating and promoting programs on peace for students in high school through college, our community life consisted of frequent contact with the McCarthys' children, grown to nine in all and later to be twelve, who lived a half mile down the road.

Charlie, a married priest in the Melkite Rite, presided over the Divine Liturgy in his home. A Catholic expression in the Byzantine tradition that permits the clergy to marry, the Melkite Rite exists in parallel with the Roman Catholic Church. We launched one of our first community projects then with the help of Paul Hood— building a chapel by remodeling the McCarthys' old playroom. The McCarthy family home became in effect a house church where many in the extended community joined us to celebrate the Byzantine Divine Liturgy.

Humorous moments during Sunday's liturgy provided comic relief. Charlie's ornate Melkite robes and stylized singing— many of us not knowing the words or music—together with Charlie notoriously singing off key created a wild scenario for newcomers. In addition, our worship included incense in abundance filling the chapel along with the sound of a clanging censer. Some of the children loved to test their dislike of the unusual setting by coughing and choking, causing them to flee the chapel area.

During our Brockton years, some of the older McCarthy children provided child care for our daughter, Teresa. As a community experiment, Brayton taught scripture, and I taught English to the McCarthy children, who were home-schooled by their mother, Mary McCarthy, in a makeshift classroom in our home.

Intentional communities like the Amish sometimes have boundaries that separate them from the larger society, resulting in their often being pejoratively referred to as sectarian by mainstream Catholics. To some, we were a breakaway sect from the parent church. We, however, remained Catholic, and whatever boundaries we had stayed porous.

Planning the growing ministry and participation of more people in the Sunday Liturgy, we met in Charlie's spacious and cluttered study in Brockton. Children flung around baby bottles and toys and ran in and out to ask their daddy for something.

We greeted the kids, played a bit, and then returned to work—tossing out ideas about faith and practice, drinking cup after endless cup of tea, communing together about everything. We loved the moments of intimacy that developed our ministry goals and solidified our spiritually rich, collaborative friendship with Charlie.

Within one year of our founding, I had amassed eight hundred or so names of those interested in our work in the northeast. I drew from liberal Catholics and Buddhists, peace groups, college campus ministries, and many others. At the completion of our first year in ministry, we had enough support financially to keep four adults and nine children living on the margins with at least a roof over our heads and some food on the table.

The Boston archdiocese director of education, Father Jim Hawker, wanted to hear about nonviolence and offered modest stipends for us to teach high-school youth and adults

Living together either makes you or breaks you. We were all broken plenty of times within our first Agape days in Brockton, as we struggled with financial issues and the arrival of new children in the McCarthy family. Nevertheless, the days moved with energy and excitement that propelled us forward.

Teaching Nonviolence in Catholic Schools
Earning Combat Pay

Brayton

Suzanne and I left our full-time salaried jobs to start the community, but we couldn't live on the meager sum I was making teaching a few yoga classes a week in Cambridge. Charlie helped me land a half-time job at Pax Christi in Cambridge that paid a

During the early 1990s, Suzanne and Brayton lead a classroom discussion at Cathedral High School in Springfield, Massachusetts.

hundred dollars per week. It kept me under taxable income, the only good thing about that kind of pay. Suzanne was making ten thousand dollars a year—also under taxable—teaching writing at Bentley College. Our financial inconveniences were all to the good as we learned the economics of living simply in very short order.

Pax Christi, Cambridge, was established to help promote conscientious objection to Catholic youth. We had a ready-made youth population to teach—students at Catholic high schools in the Boston metropolitan area and beyond, among them North Cambridge Catholic High School and Cathedral High School in Ludlow, Massachusetts. John Leary, Pax Christi gifted staff person and Harvard graduate, worked with Gordon Zahn, scholar, Catholic writer on peace, and co-founder of Pax Christi, Cambridge.

John was like a son to Gordon, who saw in him what many of us who knew him saw: a deeply spiritual young man who gave tirelessly to the poorest of the poor throughout Boston. In his early twenties, John offered presentations on Catholic social teaching on war and peace, including conscientious objection, at Catholic high schools.

According to United States Selective Service law then, the CO position required that, if you were opposed to killing in war as a matter of conscience, such opposition qualified you for noncombatant service if drafted. The Selective Service Board (and the Catholic Church) supported you if you had a valid, documented claim.

John surprised me after one of his presentations by saying, "I feel more suited to serving the poor. I'm not inclined to telling teenagers how to oppose war and violence. I'd rather be home watching *Star Trek* reruns!" Like everyone else I knew, the students loved John, but he was only too happy to hand over the job of convincing teenagers to me. I was drawn to high school students and the opportunity to teach them nonviolent practices.

Most Catholic high schools were co-ed, but during in-class discussions, a culturally accepted speaking-in-public male dominance drowned out female voices. To offset the absence of the female voice, I made certain to call on girls to offer their perspective. Predictably, they had plenty to say but needed space and encouragement. More accepting and inclined to the nonviolent approach to life, girls' measured, reflective tone always quieted the confrontational, point-counterpoint debate style of the boys.

To keep students focused, I presented material not by lecture but by asking what I hoped were timely and probing questions, telling real life stories, sharing my own struggles and history with violence, and getting them to laugh if I could. By teaching them inductively, building on their insights and knowledge about how violence works in their world, I could draw out their youthful wisdom.

I learned the technique from Dr. Deborah Prothrow Stith, who taught a course on conflict resolution at Harvard Medical School entitled, Violence Prevention Program, designed specifically for African-American youth at risk in the inner city. She offered all ten lessons of her program by leading with fundamental questions: "Where do you see violence? What kind of violence do you see?

What is good about violence?" The list of responses to any of those questions was very short. "What is bad about violence?" The list of responses was very long, indeed. After watching her open up teenagers with the respect and care of honest questioning, I wanted to emulate her style.

Following a year and a half of on-the-job training with youth, learning from many mistakes by trial and error, I was ready to leave Pax Christi. Bob Bentley, who funded Pax Christi, and Gordon Zahn, both felt that it was time for me to leave the center. They expected that I would teach conscientious objection exclusively, which I found too limiting. I wanted to teach straight up nonviolence, its philosophy and practice. Bob told me I needed to be "on my own," so I left, compatibly, as I knew Bob was right about my desire to create something that sprung from my passions.

Suzanne had spent fifteen years teaching high school, so we decided to team up and support ourselves financially under the aegis of Agape. Using Gospel nonviolence as our curriculum we taught in classroom settings and offered retreats on nonviolence in parish CCD groups and high schools and colleges throughout Massachusetts and the Northeast.

All Boys High School

One of my favorite impossible challenges was to explain Christian nonviolence to boys in all-male, testosterone-influenced high schools, highly competitive places overvaluing sports, especially football and hockey. All male environments lacked the moderating influence of the feminine and the balance that women provide in an academic setting.

A typical scenario looked like this: A peace-oriented teacher invited me into his or her school to bring a Christian message of peace to uninitiated adolescent males. I had the dubious job of convincing white middle- and upper-middle-class boys of the futility of violence, such as hating, hitting, threatening, or killing.

I hoped, without overeagerly evangelizing, to offer the teachings of Jesus: forgiving, turning the other cheek, and seeking a morally courageous approach to life, especially in violent confrontations with other males. I felt qualified to offer my own experience to such young males because I too, had come of age in a dominantly masculinized and aggressive teenage world. I could relate.

I had been the ideal football-adoring, contact-sport-craving adolescent boy who would have seen no problem in using good violence to defeat bad people. I understood and empathized with them as victims of a culture that nurtures them with violent entertainment and glorifies all forms of violence to resolve conflict.

My classroom experiences often provoked the ultimate in teenage resistance to the countercultural message because the boys in the classes I faced included some of the most talented and decorated football and hockey players in the state of Massachusetts.

I discovered the key to reaching them was never to speak in declarative sentences: Violence is morally wrong. Violence never works. Jesus does not ever use or condone violence, therefore the Christian should not. As most of us did at that age, they resisted moral absolutes that left them no room to come to their own conclusions.

Nevertheless, I encouraged them to consider nonviolent approaches to conflict and differences that troubled them.

A Day at St. John's Prep, Danvers

St. John's Prep football team reigned as the Catholic school football state champ team for years. As a beginner in teaching nonviolence, I will never forget the opposition I met that fall day more than thirty years ago when I began my presentation at St. John's.

I first shared my background and then moved into questions: "Where do you see violence in your world?"

"Everywhere," they replied, a typical young person's reply.

"Give me some idea," I prompted.

"The news, media, school, war, and gangs," some of them clarified.

After puzzling over why we use violence, I moved to a pointed question. "How much violence is too much violence?"

I immediately felt a hesitation compared to the enthusiasm of their previous responses.

"Too much violence is continuing the violence, even after you subdue and arrest a criminal," several of the boys volunteered.

Another question: "What does using violence against a dangerous person achieve?"

Answer: "Well, it can intimidate them and convince them not to mess with you."

"Are there ways to treat dangerous people without using aggression or threat or harm?"

Answer: "No! Lovey-dovey stuff won't work with bad people. Violence is all they understand, and it is the only effective option against them."

No matter the age, most Christians I have met maintain that immovable position: the world contains irredeemably bad people who can only be defeated by violence.

I felt a productive tension mounting. They sensed where I was going: a critique of all violence, but, because I was hearing them out, their own responses expanded their own insights, an exciting

Students from North Cambridge Catholic High School pause near Quabbin Reservoir Gate 44 during an Agape retreat about peer mediation.

teaching process for me. I could feel the process was true, also, for them. I could almost see the wheels spinning in their minds.

"How would Jesus respond to a dangerous person?" I asked. I often detected a pause from the flurry of give and take. "Would Jesus use violence or retaliate?"

More silence, then a reluctant answer from a brave soul: "No."

The problem with bringing up Jesus during discussion with adolescents, especially with boys, is that they know intellectually that Jesus was about nonviolence and forgiveness, but they do not experience his example as relevant in dangerous conflict. Their young faith is too unformed to believe that Jesus's example can be lived effectively in extreme cases where someone can do grievous harm to them and others.

The simple premise that they are Catholics attending a Catholic school does not mean that their moral lives are determined by the teachings of Jesus, whoever they may think that he is. Most young males live in fear of being bullied and feel that using violence against the bully is the only way to stop it. One of the young male teachers present chimed in with the question: "Are you telling the boys never to use violence, that all violence is wrong and makes a person a bad Christian?"

His challenge gave the young men full permission from an adult and respected teacher to oppose the direction of my argument as well as to oppose the nonviolent message. The classroom vibes reverted to a win-or-lose atmosphere.

I backed away and said, "I guess I am not trying to tell them anything but to challenge them to think and not simply respond to violence with violence. Doesn't responding to violence with violence create more violence?"

I tried to review Jesus's nonviolent position invitingly, to keep his moral power in front of them. I clearly recognized that boys in adolescent faith stage were products of the impressions their parents, school, and peer groups offered. What a tragedy that their fledgling faith did not include Jesus models, especially when it came to the extremes of our violence-plagued world.

Is Football UnChristian?

A similar situation arose while I talked with teachers at the all-male Mount St. Michael's Academy, a Catholic high school in the Bronx. The session with the teachers provided an opportunity for us to explain our nonviolent methods and the content we would use when teaching a week-long program to their entire junior class.

After Suzanne and I finished presenting an overview of Christian nonviolence and its implication for teenage boys in that era's violent world, the football coach asked, "I coach the football team at the Mount. Do you think football is violence?" Though sincere enough and asked without hostility, the question stands as one of those questions whose answer you really do not want to blow. By asking the question, the coach risked a total value judgment in a particular answer: If football is violence and violence is wrong, what does that say about me who has given my life to it? What does it say about Mount St. Michael's as a Catholic school and its athletes who are good, maybe even great at football?

We needed the blessings of the faculty to move forward on our nonviolence program for high schools that, with Bob Wegener, ministry team member, Suzanne and I were scheduled to begin. As I heard this question I could feel fear deep in my gut.

"From early childhood," I responded, "I, too, loved football more than anything in the world. I remember the thrill of playing football and the riveting excitement of watching it." I followed with comments that there is something symbiotic about men and football in our culture. "But why?" I asked. "How are we acculturated so that we are led to fantasize about the power of this raw aggression, to be entertained by it, to particularly love the sport's most punishing aspects?"

I complimented the coach for asking such a brave question, understanding as I do, why young boys want the glory of being a football star. By talking about the social prominence of football, what drives its popularity, and discussing our personal experiences, I encouraged him to answer his own question.

I offered to him that if we are truth seeking and transparently honest, it would not take long for us to imagine what Jesus's opinion about football would be. The football coach's civility in our dialogue made all the difference in creating a challenging and productive exchange. Such soul searching and honest questioning is rare among most sports-loving men when facing a threat to their violence-prone world.

A Stalwart Sister and Her Zone of Peace

One of the most strikingly alternative schools I encountered in all my years of teaching was St. Anne's Elementary School in Somerville, Massachusetts. Sister Ellie Daniels, CSJ, the principal, was a small, wiry, lovable, and dedicated woman. She deemed St. Anne's a zone of nonviolence for everyone: students, parents, and teachers. Sister Ellie determined that people would learn in her school under the loving care of Jesus's nonviolence, resolve their problems using wisdom, and learn skills of conflict resolution. Through her personal persuasion, Sr. Ellie convinced her staff to unite around that peace vision for the school.

One evening, I presented the Christian practice of nonviolence to a core group of thirty or so St. Anne's students, their parents, and faculty. After I finished my presentation about the prevalence of violence in our culture and the option of Gospel-inspired nonviolence for home and school, a father of one of the students challenged me: "St. Anne's is located in a dangerous area. Many students in this school have known violence in their young lives. I do not believe in nonviolence, because nonviolence does not work out there." Coming from a parent with adult authority, his was a bold statement of opposition.

A thoughtful silence followed the father's question. Out of that moment of reflective calm came the voice of a teacher. "St. Anne's is a zone of nonviolence. I cannot control all that is *out there.*

What I can influence is in here, this school. We endeavor to make nonviolence work here."

The parent felt understandably overwhelmed by all the violence out there and the immediate need to protect children from it. He could imagine only the stereotype of nonviolence as a passive and ineffective approach to what he perceived as a life-threatening crisis.

The teacher's comment patiently brought the parent back to two essential tasks. First, create a nonviolent ambiance in the school, where everyone is respected. Such a school environment exists for the protection and well-being of the students and staff. Second, learn the principles and practice of a Jesus-centered nonviolence each day you walk into the school zone. Such training will empower students with the tools to de-escalate violent conflict in their inner-city neighborhoods.

If only there were more schools like St Anne's. Why isn't a school that encourages nonviolence the norm for Catholic education?

The Academy of Compassion

The high school that made the biggest impression on me in those first years was Dominican Commercial Academy in Queens, New York. Conducted by Dominican nuns, the school provided one of those rare settings where students and teachers offer more instruction about compassion in a week than we at Agape could ever teach in a lifetime. Nevertheless, for two days Suzanne, Bob Wegener, and I offered programs on nonviolence to the student body of several hundred girls.

The high school served one of the poorest, most drug-riddled, and dangerous sections of Queens. Students and faculty told us harrowing stories of abuse and drugs, including parents' addictions. Most of the teenage girls knew family members and neighbors who had been shot or killed in gang-related crossfire.

Sister Ann, one of the teachers, shared with us that the philosophy of education at Dominican Commercial was not academic achievement first but rather love and protection.

The student body was one-third African-American, one-third Latino, and one-third white. We offered for their consideration the protections of nonviolence, love, and compassion, urging them simply to see the futility of using violence to solve problems of violence.

And what was their response to the propositions we offered?

Seventeen-year-old Tina said, "I do see violence everywhere, in my family and on the streets and sometimes there is bullying in school."

And why do young teenagers use gun violence and why do they bully other kids?

"Because they grew up with gang violence, and they were beaten up by their older brothers and fathers," she said. "Their families have no money."

"Will punishing them with hitting and threatening them or throwing them in jail scare them straight" I asked.

"Never. It will make it worse," Tina assured me.

Experiencing the futility of violence every day, some of the girls miraculously allowed the pain of economic injustice and racism to draw them closer to a loving response, a tough and seemingly impossible journey.

The girls from similar ethnic and racial backgrounds at these inner-city schools didn't tend to challenge me as did the students, primarily male, from all white schools in the suburbs. Those kids invariably asked, "What about Hitler?"

Retaliatory violence had proven futile for the girls because they had seen firsthand its bloody results in relatives and friends shot, killed, maimed, and in prison. Witnessing the repeated sickening spiral of violence convinced them. Some had also seen a street fight involving guns and the inevitable victims. It took just a brief movement of spirit for their hearts to open to faith in nonviolence.

The girls from such nearly all-African-American schools didn't tend to challenge me by asking questions about Hitler and the Nazis. I found it remarkable, that almost to a person, they did not justify the use of violence. A rare exception may have been to prevent a rape or sexual assault.

We have seen how the suffering poor become disciples of Jesus more readily than do the comfortable. Beacons such as Dominican Commercial, like the prophets, taught us that an authentic Christian School is an academy of compassion.

A New Kind of Catholic

Brayton

Suzanne and I were making our way back to Catholicism, drawn by the path of Jesus's Agape love. It took us into the streets, sustained by life lived in community.

During our early years in the Catholic Church, we found few models of faith and action, but we did discover a few powerful and inspired examples in the 1970s. Lay-led movements such as the Atlantic Life Community and the Catholic Worker, joined pacifism, voluntary poverty, and life with and close to the poor.

I observed over the years that rank-and-file Catholics defined their faith in terms of the faith of their parents, based on obligatory church attendance.

Committed Catholics whom I knew well devoted themselves to the sacraments, weekly Eucharist, and periodic sacramental rituals. Aside from sacraments, however, Catholic faith life seemed morally undefined or nonexistent day to day.

Growing up Catholic, I had no choice but to attend CCD classes every Wednesday afternoon. Let out of school an hour early, I obediently attended "the torture hour" as we kids called it, a frightfully tedious, ill-taught religious education.

As a teenager, I could not imagine my religious identity secured solely by attending mass on Sunday and holy days of obligation. My peers and I wondered, "Do we really want this?" My Catholic faith, lived in suburbia, had no relevance as I bided my time until I escaped to college, finally free of mandatory church attendance.

Traveling the questioning path, I did not experience anyone offering me any earthshaking religious choices that made sense. I experienced few if any spiritual or life-altering moments. I kept thinking: Does this Christianity work authentically in our family lives if we are all functional agnostics with a social pull toward upward mobility and no particular reliance on God?

In the 1970s post-Vatican-II era, historic changes suddenly and drastically altered Church life, but, by then, many of us had long since left. Too little, too late.

Could *Catholic* Be Made New?

Some of us in our twenties grew interested in religious practice and curious about world religions. After college, drawn to faith and history and having no particular call to religious life, I began studies at schools of theology. I found the study of religion compelling, loved learning about newly discovered spiritual verities, and couldn't wait to participate in hands-on ministry emerging as a credentialed lay person with religious formation.

Though rarely known at the time, Dorothy Day was probably the best exemplar of the new kind of Catholic. A well-educated, intellectually strong, single mother, Dorothy wasn't called to religious life and vowed celibacy. Rather, she actively originated a religious way of life with a daily practice observably Catholic while living out her identity as a committed lay person in community, serving the poor and protesting war.

I found inspiration in the vowed commitment of Buddhist, Hindu, and Christian celibate religious communities, but Suzanne and I were a married couple wanting children. We desired to live alternatively with others similarly drawn to follow Jesus along a path to Christ consciousness not clearly laid out as it was for yogis and Buddhists on their path to enlightenment.

Our relationship to Church authority and Church tradition grew horizontally, not vertically. Led more by spiritual instincts, we were learning to trust in what was true. Therefore, we saw the necessity to challenge the established tradition of vertical, hierarchical obedience to Church authority and doctrine.

We had no traditions of our own that comprised daily spiritual practice for families and children. Therefore, influenced by the writings of Thich Nhat Hanh and other teachers from the East, we eagerly adapted monastic wisdom and practice in our daily lives. My spiritual beginnings in yoga and Buddhist meditation meant that I started my days with silent meditation, a model that Suzanne and I experimented with—establishing a defined schedule of communal prayer. We began in the morning with the Catholic readings of the day, said a noonday Angelus, and ended our days with evening psalms from the *Liturgy of the Hours,* the *Divine Office.*

We first experienced our regular commitment to communal prayer by taking retreats at Nova Nada, a Carmelite community of men and women hermits living in Nova Scotia. They prayed the monastic schedule that we ended up altering to our lifestyle and taste. Their favorite day was Sunday, the inviolable day of Sabbath rest. We Christians learned the Jewish observance inspired by the creation story. We took our cues from Yahweh, who rested on the seventh day after six days of bringing the created world and its inhabitants into existence.

We asked ourselves and others: How can we bring a daily rhythm of prayer and rest into our lives as family? Should contemplative living be the exclusive practice of the saints and mystics? If we truly wished to live out our calling in following the nonviolent Jesus, would not such a call require daily, even hourly commitments to steadfast disciplines such as had most often been associated with religious contemplatives both from the East and West?

It seemed to me that experiencing a new kind of faith meant a new kind of spiritual practice parallel to that of the local parish. In our early days of community in Brockton, we prayed at home and attended weekly mass in the Melkite Eastern Rite celebrated by Charlie, ordained as Father Emmanuel Charles McCarthy.

Charlie McCarthy, ordained Father Emmanuel Charles McCarthy as a priest in the Catholic Melkite Eastern Rite, leads a circumambulation including Suzanne with Teresa, left near back, in the early 1980s in Brockton.

In spite of the medieval, all-male Church hierarchy, Suzanne and I identified as Catholic. We believed that the Church serves as a powerful agency for good regardless of its terrible sins of patriarchy. Furthermore, I had always believed that when Catholics live their faith straight out of the Gospel, they do so in a profound and compelling way, as did Mother Teresa once at a Harvard University commencement.

In the early 1980s, a group of us from Agape and Haley House attended Mother Teresa's commencement address at Harvard University. Amidst that scene of elite class privilege, the student speaker before Mother Teresa gave a hyperanimated stand-up routine laced with profanity, sexual innuendo, and cynical humor. Her gaze lowered throughout, Mother Teresa sat motionless, rosary beads in hand.

Rising to speak to the upper-crust crowd, her address made her point, as always: "Befriend the poor, and you will know God."

Others shone on other occasions, including Franciscan Richard Rohr, Thomas Merton, Cesar Chavez, Pope John XXIII, Dorothy Day, Sister Joan Chittister, Eileen Egan, and, through the centuries, human icons of Jesus—saints, martyrs, and prophets back to Saint Francis and Jesus himself.

And, then there was Charlie McCarthy. I also had had ample experience in my young life, learning from the great orators of the era: the MLKs, the Malcolm Xes, the John F. Kennedys. Those people changed me with the fire of their words. Charlie's speaking elicited a similar authority. When he opened his mouth, the force of his truth in the name of Jesus changed people, often forever. An old friend first heard Charlie speak at her church and remarked to me, "I thought I was hearing the Gospel for the first time." And he was Catholic, a priest even, a tax-resisting pacifist. What a powerful gift to begin this Catholic nonviolent community with the likes of this prophet for our age.

We were not about to give up on all that tradition without a second look. But—with a prophetic voice for the twenty-first century—we needed to engage in the hard, creative work of adopting an evolutionary form of Catholic Christianity.

Our Church's Original Sin

During Agape's early years when Charlie, Suzanne, and I discussed the Church with a close friend, the subject of women and their position in our Church enraged our friend who, full of anger, stated:

Women in the Catholic Church are oppressed. They can't become priests, they are not even allowed on the altar. How can we have anything to do with this unconscionable disgrace?

Suzanne and I were waking up to the possibility of a Christianity that needed to be different from the past, especially regarding the role of women. As participants in a transformative lay movement, we both felt that it was incumbent on us to be free enough to discern what was true and not true about our faith while having courage to stand on the convictions of our own religious experience. Without apology, we sought to live out what we knew to be true, inclined to listen to the Spirit and to move through the uncertainty of what was beginning to feel like a cataclysmic revolution.

We followed the lead of our brother and sister experimenters in communities serving soup to the homeless, celebrating house liturgies, and resisting violence in the streets. Our close friend and then Jesuit priest, Jack Seery, regularly celebrated Eucharist at the soup kitchen in Haley House. He confided his feeling that "soup kitchens are the only place I can say mass any more. It's here where I experience Jesus." The all-male priesthood with its submissive obedience to traditional Church authority in local parishes rarely spoke to the experience of people on the margins nor to those who served them.

Most parish models failed to convey a sense of trust and confidence in the skill of the laity. In addition, emerging theologies and homilies didn't come near enough to critiquing the culture of violence and greed. While recognizing that the essence of Catholicism was more than governance and obedience to hierarchy, we desired to redefine what loyalty to Church doctrine meant for our lay experience in community.

Priests like the pacifist Georgetown Peace Center director, Jesuit Dick McSorley, and the pacifist bishop, Tom Gumbleton, provided two outstanding examples of priests with whom we shared a common faith. Our alliances with such religious risk takers, socially active men and women committed to lives dedicated to religious vocation, kept our faith strong and solidly Catholic. We were finding our place increasingly on the margins economically and socially with fidelity to scriptures leading us from community liturgies, daily prayer, and public protest to serving those in need in prison, providing hospitality to those out of prison, and working with victims of war.

The Prophecy of Everyday People

By the 1970s, some years after Vatican II, more Catholics read and studied scripture. They found a valued image throughout the Judeo-Christian story in the public nature of faith from the committed orthodox to prophets living faith in full public view. A connection between God and the reader rarely exists in such biblical stories, especially from Jeremiah through Isaiah leading to Jesus and his New Testament teachings.

From Abraham to Jesus, the people in the bible are average men and women, shepherds, fishermen, farmers, prisoners, prostitutes, even everyday bureaucrats—but not the religious elite. The spiritual development of mainstream people, their journey to God, their sufferings and failures constitute the heart of the bible. The original followers leave the lure of wealth and status behind to follow God alone.

Great and revelatory moments for such ordinary people occurred in fields and mountains, in agricultural settings, on lakes, in the desert. Except for the occasional teaching in the temple or in people's homes, Jesus teaches and prophesies on mountain, plain, and sea.

Community formed around and with us while biblical stories spoke to our hearts and turned the searchlight inward. Such self-scrutiny included our Church. Jesus excoriated the hypocritical Pharisees and commanded that they look at themselves first. So, too, like many of our generation, Suzanne and I questioned, the failings and moral blindness of our own Church.

Followers of Jesus tended toward hypocrisy when they strayed from the clarity of Jesus's Gospel. We saw moral demands of Jesus's prophetic message rarely preached or practiced in our American churches. The Gospel we heard, however, was one that revealed the sins of white privilege, demanded a preferential option for the poor, and called us to move away from the violence that protects our privilege and possessions.

We were moving away from a safe Church of comfort and conformity towards dynamic communities of prophetic truth and downward mobility. Gandhi's words cried out a cold, hard truth: "Vast numbers of Christians deny Jesus every day of their lives."

We found out the hard way that living Gospel Truth and not denying Jesus's command to love mercifully comprises a costly and exacting pearl of great price. As kids growing up, we learned from the Church that Catholics were superior to those of other religions, but the Church didn't teach the truth of Jesus, who invites us not to the highest but to the lowest place.

Our sense of Catholic was evolving downward from a comfortable tribal faith to an unconditional compassion where we learn more about Jesus from the oppressed and poor across town than from the person next to us in church.

Finances: How Do We Swing It?

Suzanne

Perhaps one of the most frequently asked questions of people who experience life at Agape can be encapsulated in a phrase: "How do you swing it?"

In reality, even though we voluntarily reduced our lifestyle, we did so realizing that we had the advantages of many others, like Gandhi and Dorothy Day, who had chosen a similar path. We had careers, professional lives, and small savings that made it possible to launch and even sustain, temporarily, the level of existence we decided upon.

Therefore, after slow evolutionary steps of disengaging from a predictable salary with deductions and pension buy-ins, we no longer sought to make enough money to be taxed in support of war but rather to disengage from the salaried world sometimes by living on donations freely given. We set about learning from lawyers who advised tax resisters and from tax refusers themselves how we must live and how much money we could earn to stay successfully below taxable income. We knew that our decision would radically alter our circumstances and have moral, material, and spiritual consequences.

The consultations revealed that we had to be with others in community in order not to exist simply as a nuclear family, an expensive proposition in contemporary America. We sought to share our lives with others who might also voluntarily contribute to the financial base of the community.

For the first five years, our income remained below fifteen thousand dollars a year, the taxable threshold for a family of three. We could survive in part on donations to the community received periodically through bi-annual fundraisers. Tax lawyers advised us that all donations freely given constitute gifts and, thus, are not taxable. Our economic life morphed into a kind of stable precariousness.

Simplicity is not Simple

Our finances required our opting for cheap cars. We drove donated cars and purchased wrecks—some unsafe and others unpredictable.

We lived with donated furniture and clothes or those we purchased from Goodwill and the Salvation Army. I was on a first-name basis with many of the employees of the local Goodwill store, and I called my continual search for cheap household items and clothes Goodwill hunting.

On occasion, Goodwill hunting could go too far. Although I am a pacifist, I determined after the fact, that fighting can be morally correct when it's over an eighty-five-dollar couch at a local Salvation Army, which I staked out and told the manager I would purchase. Shortly thereafter, much to my chagrin, I heard a bunch of college kids oohing and aahing about my great couch as they sank in to its plush cushions.

I panicked as one of them said in a firm voice, "Let's grab it."

I immediately rushed over to claim my couch, explaining to the students that "I saw it first" and "I told the manager." A verbal tug of war ensued. I won the fight and bought the couch, probably worth five hundred dollars retail, and it still sits, after more than ten years, in our living room.

The Agape community had its first home in
Suzanne and Brayton's residence in Brockton, Massachusetts.

"Not very nonviolent, Suzanne," I said to myself later as I shared my experience at Agape with some laughter and a dash of repentance.

Although I embraced the ideals of living below the poverty level, I sometimes had a difficult time with the reality and frequently revisited childhood insecurities about money. Having grown up solidly middle class amid wealthy families, Brayton fared better than I did. Our perceptions about the way to implement our decisions created some stress amid the creativity and challenge of it all. Brayton rejoiced in our frugality while—convinced that God's hand was in it all—I submerged my fears, especially around Teresa's well-being. I tried being positive about rejecting the temptation to consume and store up treasures on earth, something I had never been able to do in my life anyway.

Our loyal, faithful donors had enough confidence in our ministry and serious pursuits at livelihood to provide an increasingly reliable financial base. Added donations from our teaching ministry provided me yet even greater confidence.

Scripture and Jesus became the significant mooring for us as we experienced "mighty deeds, wonders and signs, which God worked" (Acts 2: 22) through the auspices of what we called our angels. Our angels responded to fundraising appeals, many such generous people contributing twenty-five dollars monthly for decades. Other angels contributed larger amounts, making it possible to cover building maintenance and new construction. We also received support from our loyal Catholic community and other faith denominations.

Most simple-living communities rely on a similar committed base of sustainers. Some of us draw the line, as we did at Agape, at accepting or seeking foundation grants or taking money from corporations that invest in the military or big oil or accept Pentagon support. Initially, we didn't seek nonprofit status for Agape because we wanted to avoid accepting a tax break from a government that, as Christians, we have difficulty supporting on many levels.

We paid our bills on time with, on average, between one and two thousand dollars remaining in our bank balance. Yes, it was quite a financial risk not to have any real surplus income, especially in those early years. I'll never forget our first year in Brockton. Worried about how we were going to pay our bills, we left to visit my family in Buffalo only to return and find Christmas cards with hundreds of dollars in donations, a sign that God was with us.

It is truly miraculous and a testimony to the generosity of others but also to trust, sometimes wavering, and grace, often elusive, that we have managed to survive financially. Although our wedding vow to live simply, in voluntary poverty, was never easy for me, I am aware that by the daily standards of economic hardships most people of the world face, our so-called voluntary poverty remains luxurious.

We have always known that unforeseen circumstances could put the entire property—thirty-four acres and two major buildings—at risk for seizure by the IRS. Such unanticipated realities could include a drastic change in the political scene, especially considering the possibility of harassment towards dissidents like us.

Agape operated fiscally as an unincorporated partnership for twenty years before we moved to protect Agape's community property and mission into the future. As a religious, charitable, and educational entity, we incorporated as a 501c3 tax-exempt organization.

What Medical Expenses?

Health insurance became another financial hurdle, a demanding juggling act. If we had not settled in Massachusetts with its free healthcare benefits for the poor, we probably would not have had dependable full coverage.

When individuals or families live below poverty income, the federal or state government covers all medical costs and most pharmaceuticals. We felt morally conflicted not paying into the system. We eased our troubled consciences somewhat by knowing that, outside of institutional frameworks, we served economically poor and disadvantaged families in our midst.

We have offered work and financial donations to the poor who come to Agape looking for assistance and who, inevitably and miraculously, become support to us. For example, a local man who could not abide living in homeless shelters stayed at Agape for six weeks while we assisted him in finding temporary housing. He eventually became our paid handyman.

Millennials and the Risk of Simplicity

We knew that our financial decisions as a community could create a stumbling block for those who wanted to join us. For potential community members, not paying war taxes meant giving up careers and salaries, living on donations, and making do. We did not require tax resistance as we had embarked on it for those arriving at Agape. Most of us have not been raised to bring up our children communally nor to live out of a common pot.

The highly motivated, faith-based young people we have gotten to know well over the years appear decidedly more drawn to the career potential of college and post-college degrees than to giving up such attainments in order to go back to the land. We empathize with their reluctance about living in community and understand their hesitation about the leaps some in our generation took, especially given the world we have handed them.

How scandalous that we raise our children in an unsafe world and then encourage them to go to college, forget the cost, and, upon graduation, end up in indentured servitude with college loans that sometimes take decades—or a lifetime—to pay back. Today's youth experience of never-ending war, mass shootings, compulsive use of social media, and climate change is light years away from my own post-college world. Models of Christian resistance compelled and challenged me to enter into a radical faith and trust in "the power of the spirit." (Luke 4:14)

With such confidence, we want to take scripture seriously and not "store up treasures on earth, where moth and decay destroy." We longed for hearts that now and again might feel "rested and refreshed." (Matthew 7:19-21) Often at Agape, informal evenings and scheduled events vibrate with poetry and music. Even as fine sentiments animate our daily mission, we realize that we occasionally take ourselves too seriously.

In our daily prayer life, we found reassurance in Christ's words that we were digging our foundations deep, but we also knew we needed to enter joyfully into the process. We are a first-generation Catholic lay community, a moral and spiritual work in progress.

Feminism, Abortion, and the Meaning of Pro-Life
Suzanne

Liberation Begins

When I arrived at college in my freshman year, I felt as though my life as a Catholic school girl was over and my liberation was

*Three young women of Buffalo's
Bishop Colton High School, including
Suzanne in the middle, have fun after school.*

about to begin. The winds of change were in the air, and I was intoxicated with a new sense of self, an edgy awareness that something new was emerging within me.

A lot of it had to do with guys, some of whom were friends of my two brothers who attended an all-boys Catholic High School. Although my parents didn't allow me to date even though my older brother did, I managed to steal some flirtatious and furtive looks with guys at the Catholic high school dances for boys and girls that my brothers and I attended.

I learned the meaning of what we called close dancing. I was also reading the classics and delving into political tracts like Hitler's autobiography, *Mein Kampf*. Reading the same book got my brilliant high school friend, Ann, expelled from Bishop Colton High School. Ann refused to renounce having read the book. Subsequently, the nuns expelled her for unwillingness to repent and ask forgiveness of the nuns and her classmates.

Of course, it didn't take long before my early innocence changed into drinking on weekends, partying, and relationships both fleeting and serious. I began to sing the feminist mantras of the sixties and to read tracts by Gloria Steinem and Betty Friedan. Such freedom, I thought—liberation, the pill, sex (that terrible word I had learned early in life never to say out loud), release from bondage.

Suzanne, second from right, attended her senior prom with friends in 1962.

My Catholic girlhood training shaped me so that my eventual dating was defined by the prohibition from "going all the way" and highlighted by a deep and abiding fear of what we young women talked about incessantly, losing virginity. Still, I imbibed the cultural changes around me while developing a deepening sense of self: what it means to be a woman and to find my voice.

I continued to live at home through college. With no money to speak of for extras or even rent, I took three buses each day to get to the State University at Buffalo on the other and distinctly nicer side of town.

I couldn't wait to leave home, yet my ties with my mother were deep and profound.

College, Family, and Taking Stock

As my college years afforded the opportunity to become bolder and more rebellious, I encouraged my mother to do the same. "Assert yourself, Mom. Leave him," I said.

From about the time I entered my twenties, I begged my mother to walk out on my father. Awareness was dawning among my siblings and me that our mother's presumed sainthood for taking so much humiliation from my father and tolerating all kinds of verbal and psychological abuse wasn't all sainthood and qualified at least in part as co-enabling.

I pressed my mother relentlessly, often bringing her to tears, and one time I succeeded in convincing her to take a furnished apartment alone, which was a disaster. I didn't relent but probably should have as much for my own sense of worth as for hers. "Why would you stay in such a debilitating relationship?" I asked constantly. "Just leave."

I begged and pressured. Much of my rant, I realize, had a large dose of self-righteousness and no little personal pain. I evidently wanted to settle the score with my father through my mother.

As we discussed her situation, I began to see my own patterns of codependency and how all of us—mom and children— tolerated male dominance and control. We obeyed, relied on, and sought the approval of our father and the other men in the neighborhood, many of whom were also drinkers.

Influenced by the cultural codes of the time among other women hearing and reading about the feminist revolution, I participated only from the periphery. I found excitement and energy in claiming the language of the feminist revolution opposing patriarchy and sexism. I embraced my gay sisters and brothers in the process.

I also began to see that my existential predicament related to and occurred as a direct result of the repression of my Catholic schooling and, more elusively and amorphously, the Church.

Jesus never factored into the equation, as I had no firm sense of Jesus except for those mystical moments of transcendence in early childhood when I thought I could hear him speak. Doubt about everything, including my home life and the Church where I sought and had once found comfort, threw open the doors of insecurity with no moral touchstone.

What to do About My Church?

Church—the institution and all it represented—became my mantra of rejection of everything Catholic, everything stale and depressing in my life. Leaving provided a pathway into anarchy. Many of my girlhood friends left the Church, an experience I see as a reflection of the moral, ethical, and theological confusion we all experienced. Our sexual curiosity and experimentation led to admonition by priests in confessionals to repent of what the Church deemed our mortal sins, mostly around kissing, necking, and making out. Those prohibitions no longer made sense and even seemed laughable.

My traditional moorings collapsing, I stood helpless before confusion and dread. I was angry that priests, women in religious communities, and others I associated with the Church treated my sexual curiosity as aberrant and sinful. From the pulpit, I heard about the sacredness of marriage and the sinfulness of sex outside of it. The Church said the sole purpose of marriage was procreation, bearing and raising children. No pleasure, no fun— grin and bear it and have kids.

By the time I graduated from college, I still went to church but only on special holy days such as Christmas and Easter. My agnosticism continued after I moved to Boston and lived with roommates for the first time. One of my roommates had several abortions in what she considered her means of birth control.

I felt confused and upset without a firm moral stance on abortion. No one ever encouraged the women in my circles to talk about the secret we whispered about in hushed tones.

Abortion and the Early Stirrings of Feminism

I was also intrigued by the increasing number of Vietnam War protests on college campuses, although I was not immediately drawn to them. It wasn't surprising that in that new sexual climate with birth control pills, abortion, and the publication of the classic feminist text, *Our Bodies, Ourselves*, I faced multiple moral and personal dilemmas never dreamed of in my all-girls Catholic high school.

Abortion and birth control were bigger issues to me at the time than the build-up of troops in Vietnam. Yet, the war loomed too, as my mother scrambled to get her boys, my brothers, out of the draft through our long-time physician friend who wrote letters attesting legitimately to their congenital scoliosis.

Yet, among my circle of women friends, each time I heard of someone having an abortion, I was distressed, but couldn't or didn't want to, put a context to the pain. When we women discussed abortion, our conversations were limited, mournful, sympathetic, or angry. The underlying tone was dark.

A roommate who had an affair with a married man told me that her abortion at three months of pregnancy made her feel despair. "I took a life," she said to me. "Plain and simple. That's what it feels like." She was treated for depression for years after and went into seclusion every year on the anniversary of the abortion.

The Catholic Church's ban on contraception was part of the abortion problem and linked to it. I started to think the way my secular feminist friends did: What right does a male, celibate cleric have to decide what I do with my body? With the Church prohibition on contraception and the birth control pill, abortion seemed like the inevitable logical outcome.

Male and female anticontraception hard liners in the Catholic Church incurred outrage among feminists, an outrage I shared. Ironically, most of the women I knew, so-called Catholics in good standing, either practiced contraception privately, or, like my mother, lived lives of chastity once bearing children became burdensome and oppressive or a medical impossibility.

The sheer hypocrisy of male dominance in the Church and the structures of patriarchy throughout institutions and halls of government caused such anger in women that there remained little space for moral and spiritual questions around the issue of abortion.

Slowly, I began to feel that my body shouldn't be a source of shame. Quite the contrary. I moved from self-condemnation and negative self-image to relishing my looks and seeking out men's glances and approaches. I would realize later that much of my anguish was wrapped up in longing for my father's affection.

By the time I hit my late twenties, I was ready for a deep spiritual reboot revealing itself as restlessness, rebellion, and anxiety. I wanted out of the drinking, partying, promiscuous behavior that would lead to disaster. I wanted meaning.

When Brayton and I met in the mid 1970s, I was reevaluating everything, including the suspended practice of my faith. Once we realized that we were heading toward a lifetime commitment, we had long discussions about the nature of our relationship. At first, it would not be marriage. Many of our friends lived together. Like Brayton and me, they wanted to experience something nontraditional, so wary were we of the stultifying inwardness of nuclear family life.

So we, too, embarked on a path of cohabitation. Yet, I longed for a covenanted relationship. I preferred marriage and children to an arrangement, so we compromised by taking our own vows. We abided by them faithfully for six years without benefit of so-called legal marriage. Our desire to have children, although arriving late in life, eventually changed our view of legal marriage when we entered into an adoption process that required a marriage. In 1986, six years after our wedding, we went to a Brockton justice of the peace and made it legal.

Peace Movement Feminists and Unsettling Issues

During our foray into nonviolent community living, I had my first strong encounter with feminists through peace movement affiliations. In what we then called our women's caucus meetings, some formerly Catholic women whom I had met in the peace movement revealed deep, wounded sexuality and stories of rape, assault, and male oppression.

Among my sister seventies radicals, I got the impression that abortion was not on the table as a topic related to nonviolence. Abortion was then and remains the unacknowledged elephant in the room. Questions about abortion, choice, and reproductive rights still sting in conversation, especially among left-leaning Catholic feminists who may oppose war but are decidedly pro-choice.

The question of abortion became a key factor in my developing feminist consciousness: What does it mean to be nonviolent? What would Jesus have said about abortion? Could I be vocal in my protest of war, capital punishment, and nuclear weapons without protesting abortion?

As a means of livelihood, Brayton and I were then teaching about nonviolence in schools and parishes. In our audiences, many pro-life people vocally expressed impatience and disagreement with our antiwar stance. Some were irate when we either didn't mention abortion or skipped around it. The same pro-life individuals were often strongly pro-military and pro-death penalty.

I was in the midst of a profound dilemma: on the one hand, I didn't believe in abortion. Yet, even in Quaker meeting in Cambridge where we attended regularly for years and especially within our resistance circles, strong feminist voices prevailed with pro-choice or reproductive rights language.

Some in our circles believed in the seamless garment idea, named for the traditional understanding that Jesus wore only a seamless garment at the time his crucifixion. Seamless-garment belief resists abortion, the death penalty, and euthanasia as antithetical to reverence for human life. Those of us who adhered to seamless-garment belief often felt afraid or reluctant to express such convictions to our more vocal sisters. They, in turn, linked our wording with that of Catholic right-wing antiabortionists. Still,

I identified with the radical left, in almost everything but being pro-choice.

I felt insensitive to the vulnerability of women to assault and rape. I realized that some women saw me as narrow, self-righteous, and locked in my own morality. We pro-life resistance women attempted to discuss abortion as part of the larger practice of nonviolence and the sacredness of life from womb to tomb. In so doing, we seemed to become oppressors by falling into agreement with the patriarchal Church.

I remember tense, friendship-ending moments when we women spoke about our sex lives, their consequences, and abortion. I never knew if fierce argumentative moments with some of my friends came from a place of their unrevealed, post-abortion trauma. I couldn't be judgmental and condemnatory, given my own sexual liaisons in those heady liberation days of the sixties and early seventies. Some left scars. I had a fear of the pill, a fear of pregnancy, and a fear of the possibility of turning to an abortion.

We women of the Catholic pacifist left stood vehement in our criticism of the one-issue Catholic Church. Yet, we felt personally somehow sheepish about our own pro-life stance. Within the Church, I saw the hypocrisy of the so-called pro-life movement that endorsed war and promoted it patriotically.

War and Abortion: The Games Catholic Bishops Play

Catholic bishops did not publicly oppose warmaking as definitely as they opposed abortion. Time and time again, Catholic bishops and local priests spoke from the pulpit against abortion with never a peep about war, which I learned quickly, most embraced.

When I challenged any of them to give a token nod in the prayers of the faithful against the killing of women and children in war, they wouldn't budge. A few dismissed me abruptly and walked away.

Catholic Hierarchy's Embrace of the Invasion of Iraq

Catholics nationally overwhelmingly supported the vote of the United States Conference of Catholic Bishops in November of 2001 that embraced President George Bush's war on terror by an overwhelming 167 to 4. The bishops approved Bush's war and "regretfully" approved killing in Afghanistan. Of course, no referendum took place in Catholic parishes on the bishops' statement before or after it was made. Likewise, on the bombing of Afghanistan, the hierarchy ignored the people with no congressional vote.

At the same time, the pedophilia crisis involving Catholic clergy erupted in Boston to the moral condemnation of Catholics outraged that Catholic priests had abused and violated boys (and sometimes girls) with impunity and without censure from bishops. Eventually, Pope John Paul II called the 2003 war on Iraq "immoral, illegal, and unjust," but the sex abuse coverup simmered in the shadows.

The architect of the American Catholic bishops' response to 9/11, Cardinal Bernard Law, embraced the invasion of Afghanistan. Later, Cardinal Law was among the Catholic hierarchy to be disgraced for his handling of the sex abuse crisis in Boston and sent to Rome for a cushy sinecure.

In response to widespread, covered-up Catholic clergy sex abuse, Voice of the Faithful formed, according to its mission statement

- to support survivors of clergy sexual abuse
- to support priests of integrity
- to shape structural change within the Catholic Church

We at Agape made attempts within Voice of the Faithful to draw connections between the emerging, catastrophic pedophilia scandal and Catholic social teaching on war. We asked for clerical accountability for endorsing the war on terror. While war raged and clerical abuse was exposed, Catholics began to oppose the hierarchical model of Church governance vigorously and condemn the bishops' silence around sexual abuse. While bishops transferred abusive priests from one diocese to another without acknowledging clergy abuses, the war on terror—the ultimate child abuse—lay buried in the compartmentalized consciences of a majority of Catholics.

Lay people demanded resignations, prison terms, and accountability for clergy failure to respond to the violence of sexual exploitation of children but failed to call for censure of Catholic bishops who endorsed the shock-and-awe bombing of Iraq. Many Catholics repudiated the pedophilia coverup, but others did not hold the Church accountable for the traumatization, dislocation, and killing of innocent children and families in Afghanistan and Iraq.

As we encouraged Catholics to see war as part of the violence of abortion, the death penalty, and, finally, ecocide, we frequently faced a rhetorical challenge that I began to call the scale-of-evil test.

Pro-life parish people and many priests challenged us with statements like, "Abortion is the worst evil on the scale of evils." They argued that you can't compare war that the Church sanctions as just—often with the rationale that a given war protects the innocent—with killing an innocent, defenseless, unborn life in the womb.

Polarities hinged on the notion that unborn life exists as totally innocent, whereas Church practice justifies taking the life of a killer in capital punishment because the killer had a choice and ignored conscience when making the choice. Therefore, goes the rationale, logic and Church practice justify killing a convicted killer. Plain and simple.

I learned that stating convictions in terms of absolutes escalates negativity around the message of nonviolence. I found the observation particularly relevant when someone asked if I voted and I shared my personal belief as a Christian pacifist that I cannot in conscience vote in presidential elections that leave me obliged to choose between the lesser of two evils.

Many friends, family members, and audiences regard my position as unpatriotic, irresponsible, perhaps even sectarian or outside the boundaries of mainstream Catholicism. Yet, in my understanding of history, most presidential candidates take a conservative-right position, which means pro-war and antiabortion, or they take a liberal-left position, which means reservations about the use of military force and definitely pro-choice.

At Agape, we make Jesus and the Sermon on the Mount our standard. One can't go too far afield staying with Jesus, whom Martin Luther King Jr. called "an extremist for love." But I learned in personal conversation and presentations to large groups that even when offering the teachings of Jesus, timing is everything along with reading and readying my audience for a major moment of insight and transformation.

In my presentations I asked, "When Jesus said, 'Thou shalt not kill' how many *excepts* does he include? Except for Saddam Hussein? Except for our so-called enemies?'" Some listeners shared that the question triggered an awake moment for them as it had for me when I first heard it. Many of us never consider Jesus's definitive moral teaching on violence as relevant to our modern political scene.

I maintain such hard won, much discussed, and prayed about personal beliefs rooted in Jesus and his teachings. I have staked my life on them and have a calling to share. Through trial and error, I realized that by inviting people to consider a different way of thinking, not telling them what to think, made the most sense both practically and theologically.

With abortion, timing and sensitivity seemed especially important. I felt strengthened and encouraged by women who identified as pro-life feminists. They had a spiritually deep and nonjudgmental way of addressing this fraught terrain of abortion.

My seminal reading during the nineties included books by Denise Lardner Carmody, such as *Virtuous Woman: Reflections on Christian Feminist Ethics* and *Double Cross: Ordination, Abortion, and Catholic Feminism* and provided theological as well as social justice grounding for my belief that standing for women means standing for unborn children. Pro-life feminists also recognize mental, emotional, and physical harm inflicted by abortion on women.

Eileen Egan developed a concept called the seamless garment to describe the sacredness of life from womb to tomb. Egan adhered to her pacifist principles and challenged pro-life, pro-death-penalty adherents by observing, "You can't protect some life and not others." Such feminist perspectives on abortion anchored other women and me in a pro-life Catholic perspective.

My beliefs also gained strength through the writing and teaching of Joseph Cardinal Bernadin of Chicago, who supported Egan's seamless garment with his own theme of a consistent life ethic. Bernardin said, "The spectrum of life cuts across the issues of genetics, abortion, capital punishment, modern warfare, and the care of the terminally ill." Having the referents of the seamless garment and a consistent life ethic lent credibility to what I taught.

Nevertheless, I remained cautious on the abortion issue rather than find myself misunderstood, dismissed, or attacked angrily as someone who did not feel the pain of women. Feeling the staggering slaughter of war on a global scale as a priority, I failed to speak about abortion with the same passionate intensity I spoke about war. I usually did not have time enough on the speaker's stand to develop nuanced arguments to link abortion to war without losing my audience.

On several occasions, women of color from economically deprived circumstances shared their resentment of white women becoming their champions for reproductive rights. They saw arguments on behalf of women identified by white women as poor sisters patronizing and an example of female white supremacy. "Who are you to tell us what we can and cannot do with our bodies or that we can't afford any more children?"

I don't feel comfortable with my own failure to introduce the abortion question with progressive, Catholic millennial women in my circles. Often, it seems less that I intentionally neglect the subject and more that I see the dramatic issues of the day such as gender, sexual identity, and environmental issues take precedence. Many women, including me, relegated abortion to a side issue that we didn't address as too sensitive to discuss, an intrusion on a woman's sexual life.

Catholic Identities: Sexuality, Gender, and War

Suzanne

In Dorothy Day's writing in letters, diaries, and in pages of the New York *The Catholic Worker* newspaper, she makes clear the importance of her strong bond with women friends and confidantes. Women peace activists, many of them Catholic, have also immeasurably enriched my life as a peacemaker. Among them was Eileen Egan, a close friend of Dorothy. It was a moving experience to know Eileen in the last decade of her life.

During her eighty-eight years, Egan achieved many peacemaking accomplishments. A journalist, she cofounded the national Catholic peace organization Pax Christi. She dedicated herself to Catholic Relief Services. She introduced Day to her friend Mother Teresa. I came to admire Eileen for her work in the eighties with the United Nations Commission on Human Rights and her advocacy for the right of conscientious objector status for which she lobbied American Catholic bishops while they were writing their 1983 Peace Pastoral, *The Challenge of Peace: God's Promise and Our Response*.

Eileen's efforts with the bishops inspired Brayton and me along with a handful of other Catholic peacemakers to lobby the bishops in Chicago as they prepared the pastoral. With Eileen's encouragement and support, our group fasted and held banners and signs asking for rejection of the Just War Theory and for the expansion of a section in the pastoral on gospel nonviolence. Before she died, Eileen wrote a text about Jesus's teaching called *Peace Be with You: Justified Warfare or the Way of Nonviolence.* Eileen's writing, legacy, and mentoring contributed to shaping my identity as a Catholic woman peacemaker.

Liz McAlister provided another important influence. Wife, mother, resister, and former nun, Liz spent hefty time in prison for significant nonviolent civil disobedience when her children were young. I see Liz as a template of Christian feminism and resistance. I have also found inspiration in the writing and witness of Shelley Douglass, co-founder with her husband, Jim Douglass, of the Ground Zero resistance community in the state of Washington as

Suzanne, Brayton, and Liz McAlister, from left, spoke among presenters at the 1998 Massachusetts Pax Christi conference.

well as the Catholic Worker house in Birmingham, Alabama. One year, Shelley gave a talk at Agape on the feast day of Saint Francis of Assisi, October 4, an annual celebration at Agape. With emphasis on the vantage point of women, she provided context and

Suzanne, left, and Shelley Douglass discuss nonviolence one Francis Day.

perspective on the struggle for nonviolence and a life of hospitality.

In the eighties in several articles in peace magazines, Shelley addressed the issue of male dominance in leadership of the peace movement. She described being elbowed out of key roles in peace actions by men who dominated and served as major spokespersons while implementing strategies that women had often planned. I became increasingly aware of sexism within my beloved peace movement, an eye opener that advanced my understanding of the pervasiveness of gender inequality, often unconscious and hidden.

Elizabeth Peterson became our friend after I met her with her husband, Dave Dellinger. Dave was seven charged with conspiracy and inciting riot at Chicago's 1968 Democratic National Convention. The group became known as the Chicago Seven. I learned of Elizabeth's history as a feminist and peacemaker with steely resolve. She provided for their family on a farming homestead by raising animals and selling bread to provide for their six children and herself while Dave was in jail and traveling the antiwar circuit.

In an evening of deep sharing with Dave, Brayton, and me, Elizabeth confided her feelings of abandonment by Dave during his long absences. Dave wept openly as Elizabeth shared her pain and resentment. When he asked her to forgive him, she patted his hand reassuringly as she said, "It's okay, Dave."

Through Charlie McCarthy, we met Mairead Corrigan Maguire, the Nobel Peace Prize laureate. She invited us to speak in 2000 at the Belfast, Northern Ireland, organizational headquarters of the Community for Peace People, which she cofounded. Mairead and her cohort honored principles

Suzanne, Brayton, and Mairead Corrigan Maguire, from left, reflect on an Agape talk on nonviolence at the Peace People office in Belfast.

of nonviolence and the power of forgiveness as challenging times unfolded.

During sectarian violence often referred to as the Troubles in Northern Ireland, Mairead's sister Anne's three children were killed. Police shot an Irish Republican Army (IRA) gun runner in the head, and the car he was driving careened into the family. Although seriously injured, Anne survived but, suffering from depression, she took her own life four years later.

When we met Mairead, we encountered a woman whose late husband numbered among nine people gunned down at an IRA funeral many years earlier. Under a general amnesty, the assassin, Michael Stone, an Ulster Defense Association (UDA) member, had been released from County Down's Maze Prison that day. Amazingly, calling for reconciliation, the wife of the murdered IRA member forgave Stone. In a moving testimony on a day filled with tense emotions, Mairead summed up her faith in nonviolence in a clear, but quavering voice: "Jesus was naked, disarmed, forever suffering. How could this ever be interpreted as anything but nonviolent love?"

Another example of a woman shaping the world shone in Nancy James, sister soulmate and co-founder of Agape. With her husband,

Dr. Steve James, and their six children, Nancy established a life of nonviolence and service to the poor in war- and coup-ravaged Haiti, where they often risked their lives and those of their children. They maintained regular contact with Agape and visited frequently as spiritual guides from our first days in Brockton through our thirty-fifth Francis Day anniversary celebration.

In the midst of the chaos, hardship, tragedy, and joy of Haiti, Nancy practiced nonviolent motherhood not only with her children, but also with people in Haitian towns and villages. As a registered nurse, she offered ongoing hospitality and medical assistance. Brayton traveled to Haiti several times to support Steve and Nancy by doing small, daily tasks in the local hospital while also giving talks on nonviolence at a seminary in Limbe.

After the devastating 2010 Haitian earthquake, Brayton accompanied Steve and other doctors and volunteers to the Haitian capital of Port-Au-Prince to help treat the injured amid the

Steve James, left, and his wife, Nancy, right, assisted 2010 earthquake survivors in Haiti, where they work as missionaries.

rubble. My first trip to Haiti with Brayton years later was enhanced by our time meeting local people and attending colorful church services with joyful singing.

As Christian peacemakers, Eileen, Shelley, Liz, and Elizabeth helped shape my consciousness. Many others, including Sister Joan Chittister, Jane Sammon, Cathy Breen, Kathy Kelly, Pat Ferrone, and Mairead Corrigan Maguire traveled as peace-movement companions during the daily struggle towards the vision of Gospel nonviolence. We are women rooted in Christ. We are women shaping the world.

Women's Ordination: Roy Bourgeois and Women of Courage

A prominent voice for ordination of women as priests, Joan Chittister has never been officially silenced nor as resoundingly chastised as has another of my favorite theologians, Elizabeth Johnson of Fordham University. In 1996, Elizabeth challenged the Vatican assertion that prohibition against women's ordination came *ex cathedra* as an infallible doctrine. She paid a price for her outspokenness when she taught at Fordham under a cloud of Vatican investigation for challenging the prohibition against women's ordination. Elizabeth, also an outspoken pacifist, and other dissidents became great lights in my search for identity.

In the 1970s, I became aware of the women's ordination movement, secretly ordained women priests, and the Women's Ordination Conference. Father Roy Bourgeois, priest and activist against nuclearism whom I got to meet briefly in the 1970s,

Roy Bourgeois speaks about racism, militarism, and the ordination of women at Agape's thirtieth anniversary observance.

advocated ordaining women. He railed against sexism, militarism, and racism in the Church, which eventually excommunicated him for his beliefs. The Maryknoll order expelled him.

Excommunication did not prevent Father Roy from acting at annual demonstrations against US counterinsurgency in Latin America with arrest scenarios at the Western Hemisphere Institute for Security Cooperation, formerly US Army School of the Americas at Fort Benning near Columbus, Georgia.

Emerging realities and influences led me to meet Jean Marchant, a Massachusetts woman priest. With her husband, Ron Hinderlang, she founded the Spirit of Life congregation in Weston, Massachusetts. I felt alive with new possibilities when I met those brave trail blazers. I emphatically and openly identify with the cause of women's ordination within the Catholic Church and embrace voluminous scholarship that supports it.

A touchstone for my developing beliefs in regard to ordination of women began in the 1980s when I attended a major address by Chittister to more than a thousand Archdiocese of Boston educators. Using the fifth chapter of John's Gospel, when Jesus strongly commands the paralyzed man at the pool of Bethzatha, to "stand up, take your mat, and walk," Sister Joan called Jesus's advocacy for the paralyzed man "a model for ministry in the modern world." Her voice clear and prophetic, she stated, "At that pool, Jesus proclaimed hope through action to the paralyzed, the lonely, and the overlooked. Jesus is calling to all of us, sitting on the sidelines," Joan emphatically announced, "to stand up, take up your mat of docility, and walk."

She then gave a rousing call to the men and women present to stir the waters of protest over America's war-making. She urged them not to sit on the side of the pool and wait but to act—and act now. Many of us rose to our feet in ecstatic applause. Angry and alarmed, others walked out as she passionately continued, "We cannot just sit on the side when generations of those affected by war are calling for our response, to release them from the bondage of violence." She said loudly two or three times in a rising crescendo, "You've got to stir up the waters."

On my feet, clapping and cheering, I was aglow. I had never heard another woman speak so forcefully nor link scripture to resistance at a mainstream Catholic gathering.

Sexuality, Gender, Patriarchy, and War

As the Agape ministry grew and expanded, so did my compassion for gay friends and their struggles for human rights. Gender issues called forth a response as I taught about nonviolence. In our curriculum, we included consideration of human rights issues concerning LGBT struggles. I learned from my homosexual friends, young gay interns, and volunteers who came to Agape. They all spoke of excruciating personal pain and rejection as well as persecution as a group, caused in part by Catholic Church teaching on homosexuality.

We began to make it clear that Agape welcomes all individuals regardless of gender identities. We embrace those of all faiths and those of no faith. We remain centered in our Gospel-based nonviolence and our life as Catholics, but our inclusive community functions in the broadest possible sense.

We encountered a test to the limit of our principle of inclusivity when an eighteen-year-old woman seeking a sex change operation requested a two-week residence at Agape to prepare spiritually for her operation. We consulted psychological specialists who advised us we were likely ill equipped to provide adequate care for someone so young and whom we did not know.

Saying no to the young woman's request for a long-term stay at Agape was difficult but also served as a tiny glimpse into the daily struggle and feelings of ostracism within the transgender community.

Gender issues and sexism became merged in my consciousness as I found it increasingly difficult to find my place as a woman in weekly celebrations of Catholic mass with all-male celebrants. For a time, liberal parishes during the eighties allowed women to preach homilies through sleight of hand by referring to them not as homilies but as "comments by our guest."

I began including topics of patriarchal oppression in the Church, women's ordination, and gender issues relating to war and homosexuality in presentations at colleges and universities. I had progressed well beyond my original awakening to the Jesus of the Gospels and his advocacy for women. In the twenty-first century during my seventh decade of life, I see Church oppression of women and of gay sisters and brothers as all of a piece with male domination in other spheres such as war.

It was no surprise that although Pope John Paul II admirably spoke against war and invoked nonviolence, he also dismissed Father Charles Curran from teaching at Catholic University because of Father Curran's approval of contraception. I also realized I never felt allegiance to the notion of papal infallibility, so the long road to remaining in the Church while feeling in irrevocable conflict with some of its core teachings continues.

When I presented at a Theology on Tap program, part of a lecture series sponsored by some Catholic parishes, a man my age angrily confronted me after I spoke in favor of women's ordination.

"So," he said, "you're against the sacrament of marriage."

I didn't know where he was going with the analogy, but I knew he was casting a wide net. He said that one challenge to papal and clerical authority, especially on a huge issue like ordination, would erode all Catholic institutions, including marriage. He was also concerned that what he labeled my radical beliefs on women's ordination would lead to same-sex marriage, anathema for him.

Homophobia is not an unfamiliar theme to Catholic church-goers. They take their lead from bishops and hierarchs, many of whom adhere to the teaching of the Church calling homosexuality "an objective disorder . . . ordered toward an intrinsic moral evil but not sinful unless acted upon," according to a papal "Letter to the Bishops of the Catholic Church on the Pastoral Care of Homosexual Persons." Although other writings by bishops and Pope Francis have softened the stance with language of acceptance, the question of gay marriage and civil unions stays off the table.

Honoring the Feminine in Our Nonviolent Lineage

For many years, my talks and articles included titles like "Women and War: Reclaiming the Nonviolent Lineage." Over the years, I have attempted to reclaim the lineage of women peacemakers including Lucretia Mott, Sojourner Truth, and Jane Addams.

I also admire risk-taking young women of the twenty-first century, including many women of the Middle East, Egypt, and Africa. Farida Mortada, a lawyer and Tahir Square activist, spoke one year at Agape's Francis Day about the harrowing ordeals of Egyptian women activists during the Arab Spring. Leymah Gbowee, a 2011 Nobel Prize winner from Liberia who founded the Gbowee Peace Foundation Africa-USA, advocates for education for women and girls. Wingari Maathai began the Green Belt environmental movement in Kenya and received the Nobel in 2004.

When Agape sponsored a Francis Day entitled "Listening to Muslim Voices in an Election Year" in 2016, a principal speaker was Nadia Alawa, a Syrian-American, who founded the New Hampshire-based NuDay Syria, which sends supplies to families and children in war-torn Syria. As a community, we support her efforts.

I consider those heroic women and Muslim women throughout the world my sisters. For centuries, women—not all of them Catholic—have raised prophetic and religious voices for truth and resistance against violent power structures.

Agape's Alliance with Catholic Priests

Agape has been nourished by many priests. Father David Gill, our Jesuit chaplain for more than twelve years, led faculty opposition at Boston College to bestowing an honorary degree on Condoleezza Rice, the George W. Bush secretary of state and architect of the Iraq War. Agape held a prayer vigil outside the graduation stadium. Bennett Comerford, Emily Jendzejec, and Becky Perrault, BC graduates affiliated with Agape, carried banners reading "Who Would Jesus Bomb?" into the ceremony.

Other companion priests include Father Fred Enman, a Jesuit, and Father John Sullivan of the Missionaries of Our Lady of LaSalette. John presides at mass during major liturgical times and serves as a spiritual confidante to both of us. A regular at Agape for more than thirty years, he reminds everyone he meets that each of us in our lay Catholic community sustains him in his ordained priesthood.

John sometimes begins mass in our chapel by taking off his priestly stole and laying it across the altar. What is the symbolism for John? "All who are gathered here," he tells us, "are priests." He has sometimes apologized to the women present that they are barred from ordained ministry in the Catholic Church.

Even the area of inclusive language at liturgy seems, after all of these years, elusive. Most Catholic churches adhere to male pronouns without assent to inclusivity of the feminine.

Catholic women have debated the topic of leaving or staying in a male-dominated Church for centuries. Heidi Schlumpf, who teaches at Aurora University in Illinois, addressed the question in a conference centering on women and the Church since Vatican II. She referred to women as "guests in our own house."

She raised the question of whether women need to find a home outside of the Catholic Church. Schlumpf refers to the "benevolent sexism" of the Church, something Professor Barbara Hilkert Andolsen of Fordham says she does not find harmless. Andolsen maintains that, when faced with "moral responsibility," women who stay in the Church may find that such a position "constitutes complicity with evil."

I have thought long and hard about the question, especially as so many young women who come to Agape deal with feelings of alienation from Church structures.

Since we are not part of traditional Church structures at Agape, I have broad autonomy. Brayton and the other men in leadership roles in the community support me in preaching and leading prayer and liturgy. Fortunately, the structure of our community life allows me freedom of faith practice that remains steadfastly within the Gospel tradition of Jesus, who challenged existing structures of religion while paying a steep price for his inevitable marginalization.

I remain steeped in practices that are largely Catholic, as I continue strong affiliation on multiple levels with "our" Church, its Catholic social teaching, and Jesus as the model of nonviolence, to which I have devoted my life.

Death Row Calls Us

Brayton

"We must stand with our African-American brothers and sisters as they continue to be oppressed, jailed, and murdered by government authorities and police." Dave Dellinger, peace activist and nonviolent leader of opposition to the Vietnam War throughout the 1960s, uttered those words.

I heard Dave speak at the University of New Hampshire in May of 1970, a week after the Ohio National Guard killed five students during a protest staged at Kent State University. Those killed were students opposed to the war in Vietnam and the bombing of Cambodia. In New Hampshire, five thousand college students came to hear Dave and Yippee leaders Abbie Hoffman and Jerry Rubin, who urged them to pick up the gauntlet in opposition to the madness of that war.

Abbie, Jerry, and Dave were three of the legendary Chicago Seven, charged, convicted, and later exonerated of crossing state

Brayton greets Dave Dellinger and
his wife, Elizabeth Petersen, at Agape in the 1990s.

lines to incite a riot at the 1968 Democratic National Convention in Chicago. Everyone who attended the UNH rally expected to hear a clarion call to resist the war in Vietnam and incursion into Cambodia, the burning issue at the center of the Chicago Seven trial. A majority of the crowd at UNH, including the speakers, came from educated white classes, so each time that Dave, Jerry, or Abbie spoke, Dave reminded the mostly white audience of the first responsibility of each of them—to stand with our African-American brothers and sisters as they suffered and struggled for racial equality and human rights.

A searing moment in the Chicago Seven trial illustrated Dave's solidarity with African Americans. Black Panther defendant Bobby Seale insisted on defending himself during one of the proceedings. The notorious Judge Julius Hoffman was even more insistent on refusing his request.

Bobby kept up his demands until Judge Hoffman ordered him bound to his chair and gagged. As that scene and the image, so reminiscent of slavery, unfolded to the horror of all observers,

Dave leapt out of his chair and embraced Bobby, interrupting any further effort to silence him. Court officials then dragged Dave, continuing to cry out on Bobby's behalf, back to his chair. When order was finally restored, Abbie Hoffman leaned over and said to Dave, "I thought you were nonviolent."

"I am," he explained to Abbie, "and that means getting between the oppressor and oppressed and taking the blows!"

For me and many men and women of my generation, Dave became a spiritual father figure and mentor. I eagerly followed his career of activism and listened deeply to his nonviolent message throughout the Chicago Seven trial in 1969 and the tumultuous years that followed.

Dave was exactly my father's age, but unlike my father, Dave, was a WWII-era conscientious objector and early civil rights activist with many decades of antiwar campaigns behind him. A passionate, deeply centered resister, Dave epitomized a seasoned, elder voice that a young man like me could trust. Dave and his wife, Elizabeth, became our good friends and visited Suzanne and me frequently at the community during the last ten years of their lives.

In the mid nineties, Suzanne met Dave with Wally Nelson at the Peace Abbey in Sherborn. After Dave's presentation, she mentioned our community and that the main house is named for Saint Francis of Assisi. The information drew an ecstatic response from the ever-exuberant Dave, whose great spiritual hero was none other than Saint Francis himself. We made a date for Dave and Elizabeth to visit Agape.

They trekked from Vermont to Agape many times to speak and stay for a weekend. Dave was our keynote speaker on the fiftieth anniversary of dropping the atomic bomb on Hiroshima and Nagasaki, when he co-presented with several *hibakusha*, Japanese survivors of the bombings.

After Dave's death in 2004, Elizabeth requested that a memorial service be held at Agape and that we spread Dave's ashes at the base of a walnut tree we planted in his memory. She referred to the walnut tree and its similarities to Dave. "My husband was pure protein," she quipped as she placed Dave's ashes on hallowed Agape ground.

As Suzanne and I carry the mission to help the poor as a community in value and practice, we never forget Dave's compassionate pleas for our African-American brothers and sisters, especially when working on behalf of African-American inmates in prison and on death row.

We had a chance to put those convictions into practice a couple of years after reinstatement of the death penalty in the United States. It all began as I drove down Newbury Street in Boston at the end of my work day. I felt tired with hunger pangs peaking, since I was fasting in anticipation of an execution in Florida. I was overcome by a feeling of gut-wrenching dread as I turned on the radio. The newscaster reported, "John Spenkelink was executed in Florida," the first execution in the US since Gary Gilmore had asked to be executed in Utah a year and a half earlier.

Georgia Grants a Stay of Execution

Suzanne

It was a beautiful day in May 1984 when we heard that William Neal Moore, an African-American man who preferred to be called Billy, would become the fifth person executed in Georgia that year. Agape called for vigils, and we fasted at Boston's State House on days of execution with our banner reading "Capital Punishment Is Legal Torture."

On our way home after our vigil, we picked up a *Boston Globe* to check the status of Billy Moore's case. As most stays last twenty-four hours, it felt miraculous to read on page 10 that his execution was stayed until the Eleventh Circuit Court heard his case. At the time, such stays in capital cases usually failed to overturn a death sentence and ended up being another brand of torture, a waiting game for the inmate and loved ones.

I wrote my first letter to Billy that day, and within a week, I received one from him with his explanation of his feelings about being so close to execution:

119

See, the life I live is not my own and God has showed me that
I cannot possess myself and therefore the will of God is all that
matters, so to live or die isn't my choice anymore and to accomplish
the will of God is all that matters in this life. . . . So, this past week has
nothing but a deepening experience for me (seven hours away from
execution) and all those who know me in the depth of Christ.

After he invited us to visit him on death row, I responded that
the trip was long and that we didn't have the money for a plane.
In a subsequent letter, Billy insisted that if we were people of
faith, we would find a way. He encouraged us to raise funds for a
visit. And so we did. Another of Billy's requests was that we bring
Teresa, our seven-month-old daughter. He longed to hold a baby,
as he had not done so for more than ten years.

By then, we learned from Billy and articles about his case that
he had been in the military in Germany and got called back to the
States because the mother of his son, William Jr., also called Billy,
could not care adequately for the child because of her addictions.

Billy returned to Georgia. As Billy remembered the episode, he
spent the first night drinking and smoking pot with a friend, who
insisted that the gullible and penniless soldier accompany him in
robbing his uncle, Fredger Stapleton, who always had money in
his house. The friend gave Billy a gun.

Once Billy entered the house, he recalled, Stapleton heard
him and fired at Billy with a rifle from behind a closed door.
Billy drew his gun and aimed it toward the door. The shot killed
Stapleton, and Billy ran with the cash. Arrested the next day, Billy
was full of remorse. The white sheriff told Billy he would make
sure Billy was executed.

Billy spent seventeen years on death row from the time of his
conviction. Lengthy legal maneuvers and interventions led to
the twenty-day stay of execution and our letters, phone calls, and
eventual visit.

Bob Wegener planned to accompany us, and when we learned
that we could have a contact visit with Billy that could last up to

seven hours, we made our plans. We raised funds, rented a car, and set off with Teresa for Jackson, Georgia, and death row.

It was a long, hot journey with a seven-month-old baby, and I wondered from the moment we made the decision to bring Teresa whether we were subjecting her to a tiring trip with possible illness guaranteed. Just seven months before, within days of her birth, she had had her first open-heart surgery. Teresa surprised us with little crying or fussing during the trip.

When we arrived in Jackson, we immediately saw the gargantuan guard tower at the prison entrance. The turret contained armed guards at the ready, peering out at us from a railing.

Other officials ushered the four of us in. We carried all of the paperwork scrupulously gathered over the days and weeks leading to the visit. Still, we were not certain that we wouldn't be turned away on a vague bureaucratic whim, which people in the know had told us could happen.

Miraculously, we received clearance to pass through successive locked iron doors, each opening accompanied by loud clanging. Wrapped in a blanket, Teresa slept. One of the guards struck a severe note when he informed us: "Death row is in the back of the prison, *way back*," emphasizing remoteness, darkness and isolation.

After a long walk down various corridors with Teresa barely stirring, we sat together in a room. From there, we could see a number of male inmates waiting for permission to join their visitors. Abruptly, we heard Billy's name shouted out: "Moore!"

From old mug shots in newspaper articles and from a few pictures he sent us, we knew what Billy looked like. We had a sense of his angular face and round glasses that made him look studious. Finally, Billy emerged in his starched, white uniform with blue stripes. He looked in our direction and smiled. My first thought was, "What a handsome guy."

We all embraced each other briefly and were led to another room where we would be with Billy for more than seven hours. Almost immediately upon our setting foot in the surprisingly private room, a guard appeared nearby.

drawing copyright by Bob Wegener

Billy Neal Moore holds Teresa on death row.

Billy asked to hold Teresa. They bonded immediately from that early moment through the next thirty years. Billy warmly cuddled and talked to Teresa, illustrating what we later learned about his ever-present gentleness.

Brayton, Bob, and I felt an immediate rapport with Billy as we began sharing details of our trip and snippets of information about our lives. Billy wanted us to go no further, however, until we joined hands and began with prayer, which he led: "Heavenly

Father, I want to thank you for bringing my friends here to Georgia safely." He then expressed gratitude for life, for all that he had been given. We were profoundly touched.

Billy's serenity became apparent as we discussed his case with him. He was on top of the details. Nevertheless, he shared that he had reached a point while doing the legal work alone and filing motions and endless briefs that he could not continue. Billy felt that God had called him to let go of the legal process. I felt I was in the presence of an extraordinary human being, a saintly man. I had difficulty reconciling Billy's composed demeanor with the reality that he had killed someone.

The seven hours passed so quickly that, when officials told us we only had a few more minutes before we had to leave, it came as a surprise and disappointment. Once again, Billy suggested that we pray together. Brayton, Bob, and I were not used to such expressive, personal praying, but we loved it. As I held Billy's warm and reassuring hand, I felt his calm in the face of torture and death. I never imagined that my faith would take me to a place of such extremity.

Meeting Billy on death row transformed us so that, on the car ride home to Boston, Bob, Brayton, and I could barely speak as we realized the limitations of language after what we had experienced. We knew grisly descriptions of electrocution and what it does to the human body. We could not fathom Billy strapped to a chair, unable to move as devastating volts of electricity coursed through his body, causing smoke to rise from the top of his head. No matter the crime, we know execution constitutes retaliatory, premeditated murder by the state, an act of total barbarism that degrades us all.

Run Up to Billy's Execution Date

Brayton

Jack Boger, one of Billy's lawyers, said to me, "We have one of the best cases for commutation I have ever seen." Commutation is a legal decision to lessen a sentence based on its merits. Jack knew his subject well. He had defended many men on death row in the latter 1970s and lost a few to the electric chair in Florida, most famously John Spenkelink.

Billy was blessed with two of the best lawyers available. They represented him *pro bono* for decades. Jack directed the Legal Defense Fund of the National Association for the Advancement of Colored People (NAACP), and Dan Givelbre was dean of Northeastern Law School in Boston. Jack and Dan continually reminded us that our longshot goal envisioned commutation for an African-American man who had confessed to homicide in pro-death-penalty Georgia where the odds are *always* against you.

In July 1990, Dan called to inform us that an execution date had been set for Billy of August 21, not even two short months away. It had been six years since his previous date with execution in 1984. The state of Georgia would finally resolve the case. Georgia could also make a final determination to overrule execution. A five-member board of pardons and parole decided whether his case and the moral caliber of Billy's life in prison warranted clemency. A majority of the board ruled in an up or down vote. If he failed to garner three of five votes, his fourteenth and final execution date would proceed as scheduled the next day.

When we got the news in July, Jack requested we get as many people as possible to write on Billy's behalf to the board. Billy had more than a hundred friends with whom he corresponded. We could tap some of the fifteen hundred folks on our mailing list. The legal team formulated a strategy, simple and hidden from view of the media, to promote Billy's commutation: find influential people, especially in Georgia, and ask them directly and quietly to plead his case to the board with no public gestures or pressure tactics.

Billy's lawyers reminded us, "This is still Georgia." Right off, we managed to land the support of Father Ted Hesburgh, president of the University of Notre Dame. We were down to the week before the execution date. Hundreds of people wrote, prayed, and pulled for Billy to get the 1990 commutation, the third granted by the board since 1976.

The Final Week

I decided to go down and join Dan and the legal team in Georgia a week before the hearing and scheduled execution. We wanted to continue quietly and selectively publicizing his case and gain additional support in Georgia. I stayed with Father Liam Collins, a parish priest in Macon, fifty miles south of Jackson and death row. Liam, a good friend of Charlie McCarthy, devoted himself to nonviolence. He had long publicly opposed the death penalty.

Liam's parish proved a haven of antideath-penalty sentiment, a sharp contrast to the state of Georgia. Those realities gave me quite a culture shock, especially as I hailed from the antideath-penalty Northeast.

After arriving and settling into my digs at the parish, I called Dan to check in. He asked excitedly, "Have you seen today's *Atlanta Journal-Constitution*?"

"No," I told him.

"It has an unbelievable editorial on Billy's case. Go get it and read it," he said.

I grabbed a copy at a local store and flipped to the opinion page with the main editorial headlined "When Mercy Becomes Mandatory."

The opening lines read:

> If there ever was a time for clemency, this is it. In the eyes of many, William Neal Moore is a saintly figure. The execution of Billy Moore would make this world a poorer place. It would be a mark of shame for the people of Georgia. The board of pardons and parole should not let it happen.

I called home to update Charlie, who captured the moment when he said, "Nobody wants to see Billy die, but the machine of death keeps grinding mindlessly on."

The Agape team divided up the labor with the lawyers. We organized the quiet publicity, prayer vigils, and letter-writing campaigns to the board calling for commutation. The lawyers tended to the complexities of legal angles and arguments. We were always in close touch.

I called Millard Fuller, president and founder of Habitat for Humanity and a well-known antideath-penalty activist and lawyer with a nearby office who had represented death row inmates in Georgia. I went to his office to strategize about whom I might contact in Georgia. Millard had read the *Atlanta Journal-Constitution* editorial calling for commutation for Billy and was moved by the strong, clear, and unusual stand taken by the *Journal-Constitution*. He told me, "This is a powerful piece of writing. We should be able to use it to get support."

He then reached for his phone and called Jimmy Carter. Carter answered, and Millard spoke with great intensity. "Did you see the editorial in the *Journal-Constitution* on Billy Neal Moore's execution?" he asked.

They were old friends, and maybe Fuller assumed that Carter would gladly offer to help. Instead, Carter hesitated.

Millard hung up the phone and said pensively, "He only gives his name in support of the wrongly convicted. Sorry. No help will be coming from Jimmy Carter."

Carter's position was unlike that of his wife, Rosalynn, who for months had enthusiastically lent her name to Billy's campaign. As I left his office, an exasperated Millard shared honestly, "Jimmy Carter is wrong on this issue," referring to Carter's longstanding support of the death penalty, especially when he served as governor of Georgia. It has always mystified me how good Christians like Carter who espouse social justice hold such a position and still lived with themselves. Millard, with characteristic zeal, continued to campaign enthusiastically to save Billy.

Four members of Billy's family came to Georgia to be with him during the final days, including his father, James; his sisters Norma Jean and Regina; and his nephew Brian. We went to Ebenezer

Baptist Church, Atlanta's largest Baptist church, to share an evening of prayer with fifty or so friends and family who had come to town to give their all to the final hour.

At moments, our prayer together felt like a southern black Baptist revivalist meeting with shared deep, spontaneous petitions and testimonies to the lives of the forgotten poor on death row. We all came for Billy Neal Moore, a man with absolute trust in God. The prayers of Billy's family were fervent as they beseeched, "God of Mercy, break these eighteen years of prison chains. We beg you Lord, set Billy free." We prayed for Billy's victim, Fredger, and all victims of murder.

Billy's case was conducted methodically, professionally, and sometimes joyfully with zero overconfidence or prediction of likely outcome. Although his commutation case remained strong, the lawyers maintained a legal straight face because their defendant was an African-American man convicted of murder in Georgia.

Dan called to inform us that Jesse Jackson had scheduled a press conference in Atlanta at seven the next Saturday evening to support commutation for Billy.

"Go to the Sheraton in Atlanta, find Jesse Jackson, and ask him to please cancel his press conference," Dan instructed firmly. Dan and Jack felt that Jackson's public persona was too controversial in Georgia and could even hurt Billy's chances. Every move by our team was below the radar of high-profile press coverage.

I drove to the Sheraton and waited two hours in the lobby for Jesse, who never showed up. Billy's team had made several attempts by phone to discourage any public statements by Jackson, and, undoubtedly, they had gotten through.

"Imagine," I thought, "not wanting Jesse Jackson to champion your cause to save an African American from execution." We antideath-penalty activists from the north had entered a savvy world of legal strategy and trial-by-fire politics about capital punishment in the Deep South. It always made good sense to take counsel's lead, I figured.

On Saturday afternoon, Liam celebrated mass for Billy on the grounds next to the maximum-security prison where Billy sat awaiting execution. The presence of Christ in the Eucharist was offered in the name of all of the condemned just days before Billy's scheduled execution that apparently nobody wanted. The holy words of mercy and the sacred ritual offered urgency and solace.

In the final seventy-two hours before execution, a guard attended Billy twenty-four/seven in his ten-by-six-foot cell with the electric chair visible to him only twenty feet away. Because the condemned die penniless on death row, often without close friends or family, prison guards discard their belongings, including the usual white starched uniform with blue stripes. Instead, on death watch inmates each wear an orange jumpsuit, designated attire for execution. Death-watch inmates receive three prison meals daily until the last day, when they get to "enjoy the meal of their choice." Electing to fast for the ten days leading up to his execution date, Billy declined all meals.

A Call to India Might Help

On Saturday, Suzanne and John Dear, a friend and activist priest who knew Billy well, joined me at Liam's parish to offer three more days of organizing before the board's hearing on Tuesday, the day before the execution date. Attempting to save a person from the chair with just a few days to go leaves you with the feeling that you can never do enough. Love for Billy propelled us to keep scheming creatively to locate the right influence at the eleventh hour. John had a good friendship with Mother Teresa, and it was the eleventh hour. "Should I call Mother Teresa and get her support?" he asked. We decided to call Calcutta.

"Hello, Mother. This is Father John Dear." John's booming voice was just audible enough to be heard by Mother Teresa in India, even if they had a less-than-ideal phone connection.

After he explained his reason for calling, Mother Teresa told John she would be happy to be on record as being against the death penalty, especially on Billy's behalf. However, she was unable to call from India but suggested that John convey to the board of pardon and parole that "They can call me."

We were all aware that frequent attempted interventions by Pope John Paul II and Mother Teresa in scheduled executions had never stayed an executioner's hand. The board could theoretically choose to call Mother Teresa without it being known to the public. But why would the board call India to speak to Mother Teresa? We were sure board members knew exactly what her request would be.

Concerned that Dan didn't want a big publicity splash about Mother Teresa at the eleventh hour, I phoned him.

He surprised me by saying, "You guys are too much," followed by loud, hearty, stress-releasing laughter I had never heard from him. Not certain of any positive outcome, he passed Mother Teresa's phone number along to the board. It couldn't hurt. Many of us felt convinced that Jesus was present in the countdown, especially in this joyous interlude with Mother Teresa joining the team.

That evening just before dinner, we turned on the evening news. At the top of the Atlanta news, a sensational story unfolded. The chairman of the Georgia Board of Pardons and Parole had called Mother Teresa in India. She had advised the board to "live in the spirit of pardon" and to "do as Jesus would. Pardon the prisoner, Billy Neal Moore."

Seeing the television report made an exquisite ending to our five-year campaign to help save Billy's life. Everything seemed in place. The hearing that could commute Billy's sentence from death to life would take place the next day. If it failed, then on to the US Supreme Court in the eleventh hour.

Billy's Last Day on Earth?

The days before an execution include powerfully symbolic moments of last visits. Suzanne, John, and I joined the privileged few to meet with Billy, who was eerily relaxed twenty-four hours from death if the board declined commutation. We chatted as if at a reunion with an old friend.

On the tenth day of his fast, Billy remained as composed as ever. Then again, ever since 1984, he had believed that God would intervene. I recalled the spring morning in May the day before Billy's second scheduled execution. On death watch, he read Psalm 118, Verse 17, "You will not die but live and proclaim the works of the Lord." Billy believed God spoke to him directly in that scripture and reassured him he would not lose his life to the state of Georgia.

As we had what we imagined would be our final, unlimited visit with Billy, I looked up to see a woman smiling and waving energetically through the window of our visiting-room door. It was Murphy Davis, longtime antideath-penalty activist from the Open Door community in Atlanta.

She knew the good news. A guard abruptly brushed past her into the waiting room and announced, "Moore's case has been stayed by the Supreme Court of the United States for thirty days. This visit is terminated. All visitors must vacate the prison immediately."

Absolutely no one on the defense side predicted a Supreme Court ruling. We hurried out the door and immediately drove across town to the hearing of the board of pardon and parole. The entire seventeen-year case could be resolved in the next few hours.

We entered the hearing room with the proceedings already in progress, our buoyancy palpable from learning of the Supreme Court stay. However, the elevated tone changed immediately to somber reserve as we observed expressions of Billy's lawyers at the defense table. Their demeanors spoke to the heavy burden carried by those who defend the condemned, mostly pro bono with win-or-lose, life-or-death stakes. I imagine that when it comes right down to a verdict, lawyers for the defense often feel that the outcome depends entirely on them.

Several character witnesses absorbed our attention, beginning with Bishop Nealon Guthrie of Rome, Georgia, a born-again,

African-American preacher man. Soon after the court sentenced Billy to death seventeen years earlier, Bishop Guthrie arrived unannounced at the prison. He came to bring Jesus to Billy, preaching, "Billy, you are loved by the God of mercy. You are forgiven." The Reverend baptized Billy in a prison bath tub. That baptism was the conversion moment for death-row-inmate William Moore.

Sara Farmer, niece of Fredger Stapleton, Billy's victim, also testified. Sarah talked of Billy's "deeply repentant character." She added that "in spite of the fact that he killed my uncle, I always felt there was something special about him." She and her family never had difficulty forgiving Billy. "As Christian people, it was in our nature to do so," she humbly testified.

Billy Neal Moore carries Teresa at Agape after his release from Georgia's death row.

For six years the Stapleton family had publicly petitioned for Billy's clemency. Another niece, Mary Ann Neely, wrote in the clemency petition, "My family never wanted Billy Neal Moore to die. He still writes to us. He is a truly changed man." Leading up to the hearing, the Stapletons made it known that they were pleading for pardon, parole, and ultimately, release from prison. Their reasoning? Billy Neal Moore was no longer a threat but would be an asset to society.

Their public advocacy broke precedent with every capital case any of us had ever heard of. Victims' family members pleading for release of their loved one's murderer? In most instances, the prosecution effectively manipulates victims' family's cries for justice to win a death sentence. The Stapleton family broke the mold with their anguish for Billy, a pure and tender mercy.

After three hours of testimony, board members adjourned to consider their ruling. The half hour or so it took them to decide was agonizing, a *tempus vierge*, the notion that just before the instant of dawn comes the darkest moment of night. As the imminent decision loomed, we imagined the worst outcome.

I glanced over at the defense counsel table. Billy's lawyers appeared stalwart and ready.

When the board emerged from deliberations, Chairman Wayne Snow Jr. took the floor to address the hearing. "The decision is unanimous in favor of clemency," he said. Chairman Snow added that Billy would have to serve twenty-five more years before parole consideration.

The courtroom erupted with shouts of joy and spontaneous song, "Amazing Grace, how sweet the sound . . . " A clear and utter victory over senseless state vengeance, clemency for Billy had triumphed as an irreversible legal fact.

After Suzanne and I embraced Billy's father, he exclaimed, "I think it came out . . . beautifully!" Billy's father knew something of incarceration, as Billy had spent his childhood visiting his dad in prison.

Billy had set a record as the US inmate with the longest stay on death row. Now he set another—the first confessed murderer to receive a unanimous decision for clemency by the Georgia Board of Pardons and Parole.

They took Mother Teresa's advice after all.

Attempting the Impossible: Nonviolent Childrearing

Suzanne

As Brayton and I navigated our way through the beginnings of community, our desire for children, and the prospects of starting a family late in life, we struggled medically for more than ten years unable to conceive a child. After a decade of fruitless attempts to have a biological child, God gave us the child of our destiny, Teresa Ellen Shanley. Over the years, our exploration of overseas adoption proved too costly—twenty thousand dollars, not including travel to the foreign destination. Catholic Charities required anywhere from two to four years for prospective parents to qualify to adopt. With both of us in our late thirties, we felt that such a long wait wouldn't work.

Our dear friend Patrick Davis, a social worker and member of our Brockton worship community, suggested we begin to explore adoption through the state Department of Social Services (DSS), since reorganized as the Department of Children and Families (DCF). Patrick said he would get word out through his affiliations that we would welcome what was called an open and identified adoption, where we knew who the child's biological parent or parents were and they knew who we were with some degree of option to contact each other.

Dealing with the state agency meant taking a required course to certify us as foster parents. We immediately began the course with other potential foster families or prospective adoptive parents. The possibility of our receiving a newborn child seemed slim, as I was forty and Brayton, thirty-eight. Thus, when Patrick called to say he had a friend whose sister would soon give birth and could not care for her child, we felt the answer to our prayers.

Eventually we learned the problematic nature of the medical and psychological history of our potential child's birth mother. We also found that our as yet-to-be-adopted, unborn child had a serious heart defect detected in utero, that would, no doubt, require open heart surgery at the child's birth.

After much prayer, meeting doctors, and feeling urgency and anxiety, we committed ourselves to go forward with excitement and purpose no matter the outcome. We hurriedly prepared a room for our then-unnamed baby while we waited during six weeks of paper work, meetings, and visits from DSS. We had to complete many documents before we could bring the child, identified as "female," home.

We put euphoria on hold as we learned the baby who could be our child would enter life with a possibly life-threatening condition.

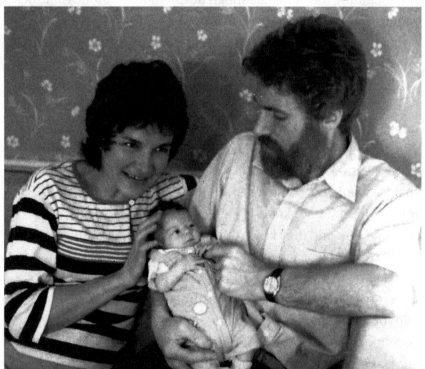

Suzanne and Brayton welcome Teresa on her first day in their Brockton home.

Her neonatal cardiologist informed us that she might not survive. Apprehension and worry became our companions together with the sense that, if our child lived, her birth would signify God's anointing. We spent much time in earnest prayer with the McCarthys, Jameses, and others in our extended community.

As we settled in to the idea that the child could be ours, we moved in the direction of calling the baby girl Teresa. With that name, we called on the feisty mystic, Saint Teresa of Ávila, a woman of strong character who renewed her Carmelite order in fifteenth century Spain during the Inquisition.

When we visited baby Teresa for the first time in the hospital, we immediately fell in love with our tiny daughter. Weighing little more than five pounds when we first laid eyes on her, the child who would become our Teresa had her head shaved for intravenous lines in veins near her skull because tiny veins in her arms would not accommodate needles. We had never experienced such terrain of acute physical necessity. After six weeks of daily visits to Teresa, we brought her home to Brockton with us. Teresa survived thanks to a defined drug regimen and a full calendar of follow-up hospital visits.

Teresa proved delicate in every way. We sat for ten minutes at a time just looking at her in our Brockton house chapel, all the while repeating to ourselves, "She is ours. I can hardly believe it." In the midst of such excitement, community-building with the McCarthys, and the sleep deprivation common to new parents, we decided on a July baptism for Teresa in the McCarthy chapel.

Nonviolent Parenting: No Punishment?

As Teresa grew and her health began to stabilize, we realized that traditional methods of discipline such as time-outs and spanking along with punishment in the form of consequences wouldn't work for us. Brayton and I shared the instinct that, with what we were discovering, we had to incorporate nonviolence into our childrearing.

Surrounding infant Teresa at her baptism are, from left, Brayton, Suzanne,
their niece Megan Ruane, Teresa's godmother holding the baby;
their nephew Robbie Mendlewski, Teresa's godfather, and
Father Charles McCarthy, who baptized her.

I worked long hours with Brayton to advance the ministry of
our new community life, raise funds, and foster outreach while
caring for a sick child.

Early on, Teresa had a routine that involved waking her every
four hours for medication, a demanding regimen on little Teresa,
Brayton, and me. Friends came to the rescue by offering child-care
time and respites. My limitations humbled me. My tone with
Brayton often became harsh, and I felt like a hypocrite espousing
the peace I couldn't practice.

Homeschooling Education: Easy on Paper

As Teresa grew, Brayton and I studied homeschooling options
and met with nearby parents who home-schooled. When Teresa
turned five, we learned that she would require special education
programs in a more conventional setting.

The reality, then, meant that Teresa should function in the
world, which jeopardized our hope for avoiding, at least to
some extent, conventional experiences of war toys, television,
retaliation, hitting, and yelling. On the other hand, we had a

great circle of friends who similarly committed to countercultural values, including no Barbie dolls. Several of the mothers in our Hardwick circle agreed not to provide Barbie dolls for our girls because of the inherent Barbie depiction of women as sex objects and other stereotypes. Most of us avoided the Barbie explosion until one Christmas when well-intentioned relatives purchased Barbies for Teresa and other girls in her circle.

Shortly thereafter, other mothers and I agreed that we would treat the Barbie test in creative ways. As the girls played with their Barbies in our Francis House living room, together we created a homeless shelter where the Barbies donated their clothes. In our elaborate drama, some of the Barbies fell on hard times and had to live in the shelter with other homeless Barbies. The girls seemed to love the role plays.

We were vegetarians and had publicly identified the community as vegetarian, so by default, Teresa became a vegetarian. It didn't always work out so well. For example, when Teresa began school, her tofu burger sandwiches caused her embarrassment and humiliation. Most of the other kids had meat sandwiches. She felt isolated and bewildered by our choice for her diet.

Also, since Teresa attended schools for children with different intellectual abilities, the vegetarian diet became a constant drain on her. As she got older, she resented it more and more. We realized we had to compromise. We agreed that when Teresa was out, she would make her own decision that soon led to her regular meat eating.

The compromise came years after an incident that took place when Teresa was five. A local author invited us for a home-prepared dinner with plates of cheese, meat, and other foods available. Teresa, dressed in an adorable outfit to suit the festive occasion, ran up to the table, checked out the chicken, and then cried out, for all to hear, "Meat, Ma. Look, Ma, meat. They have meat!" She proceeded to reach with her tiny hands for the contraband as everyone around us looked on with attentive amusement.

Teresa, left, in purple jumpsuit, white shawl, and checked apron,
performs with other children skit about Saint Francis of Assisi
taming the wolf of Gubbio in a dramatization at Francis House.

Television created another big hurdle. Ninja Turtles were in and violent movies, like *Rambo*, the rage. Teresa began to want to watch what her friends watched, which we believed constituted a steady diet of violence.

In her teen years, Teresa felt separate from her friends, an isolation we felt was too much for her. We had to remind ourselves that self-serving short sightedness sometimes clouded our best intentions.

Aggressive, Violent Childhood Play and How to Respond

Many families in Ware, where we lived during the construction of Francis House, experienced unemployment, teenagers dropping out of school to become parents, and drug use. Although we paid close attention to the backgrounds of Teresa's friends, her friendship circle included a girl her age whose family often punished by hitting and yelling.

While visiting Teresa at our new residence in nearby Hardwick, the child, Jennifer, bit Teresa without warning. I wasn't far away when I heard Teresa shrieking. Her skin hadn't been broken, but the severe incident alarmed me. Teresa sat on a bed crying with Jennifer next to her looking very guilty. Testing of the nonviolent parenting model officially clicked in.

As Brayton and I spoke with the girls separately, we discovered that Jennifer didn't understand why she bit Teresa nor did Teresa. Even though they were very young, we asked each child how she imagined the other child felt. They both seemed pleased with themselves and reconciled, likely wanting to get the laborious process over with and begin playing again.

We called Jennifer's parents to them of the incident. We told them we had dealt with it. The dad, Michael said that he would be right over.

Jennifer's home life was rough, but we didn't anticipate her father's response as he entered the house and, without any greeting, demanded, "Where is she?"

I tried to mollify him by explaining that we had negotiated a truce between the two girls. He ignored my comment. "You just can't bite someone," he said heatedly.

Speaking in low tones, I followed him. I repeated his name and suggested, "They're only kids. Jennifer apologized. It is okay."

As her dad entered the bedroom where the children were now playing, Jennifer cowered in a corner of the bed. I tried to reassure her. Her father cut me off, yelling at Jennifer, "When we get home, I am going to bite you harder than you bit Teresa."

In a split second, all of our delicate negotiating caved in as the father quickly hustled his child out of the house. I never learned the outcome of his threats. Our repeated calls to the parents went unanswered.

Violent Spousal Abuse and Its Aftermath

We liked Jennifer's parents, a young couple, and felt close to them. Many years before the biting incident, however, we knew of risks to everything about their lives. We had lived in a basement apartment below theirs in Ware before moving to Francis House, and we had witnessed their interactions.

The wife, Crystal, had confided in me that she experienced bipolar disorder, and by her own account, her behavior was often erratic. We suspected that they both might use recreational drugs. The husband, breadwinner in an assembly-line job, oozed stress.

One evening, we heard shuffling, crying, and pounding on walls directly above us. Though we suspected a physical confrontation, we couldn't be sure.

The next day, as I drove down the street with Teresa strapped in her car seat, I spotted Crystal and stopped the car. When she came up to the window, I saw bruises on her face and a blackened eye. In her demure and self-effacing way, she said softly, "We got into a fight."

Crystal agreed to pursue temporary shelter, and I arranged for a meeting with people we knew who ran an overnight shelter for battered women, the location and whereabouts kept strictly confidential. In the meantime, Brayton met separately with Crystal's husband, Michael.

The nun supervising the shelter advised us that, if there was hope for reconciliation, "at all costs try to avoid a restraining order if the husband seems reasonable. Once police are involved, there is little or no chance for reconciliation."

We met with the couple for hours over many days. We explained time-honored steps of reconciliation and tried to get each of them to see the perspective of the other. Brayton guided them in a couples' mediation. Gradually, trust took hold, especially between Brayton and Michael. Michael and Crystal reconciled until the next confrontation.

Abortion and Its Aftermath

For a time after we left the apartment and moved into Francis House in Hardwick, we didn't see or hear from Michael and Crystal until Michael showed up at our doorstep to inform us that Crystal was pregnant. Crystal had been romantically involved with another man whom they both assumed was responsible for her pregnancy, though neither of them was certain. There had been no paternity test.

Michael, outraged and hurt, insisted that Crystal have an abortion. "Only then," he emphatically stated, "will I entertain any notion of saving this marriage."

We learned that the other man, mentally unstable and handicapped, had nothing to recommend him as a potential father. He apparently had no knowledge of the pregnancy. In the meantime, Crystal sought shelter with us as Michael continued his unwavering stand. Brayton and I agreed to become involved in a mediation between Crystal and Michael. We encouraged Crystal to see her pregnancy through to adoption.

We realized the tragic complexity of considering abortion as we intimately shared recollections and counsel with women who had had an abortion or who, like Crystal, contemplated one. Acknowledging raw emotions felt by women facing such predicaments raised more immediate challenges than presenting a lecture in defense of the preciousness of life at all stages

While living at Agape, Crystal pinned an ultrasound image of the unborn child to her bedroom wall. Through Brayton's skilled counseling and the couple's perseverance, at least the situation didn't escalate. We began discussing the possibility that after the baby's birth, we could facilitate an adoption.

Daily, Crystal professed her increasing conviction that she did not want an abortion. She strongly objected to encouragement that she received at every level in the medical world to abort the child. Crystal repeatedly stated that nurses and doctors really pushed hard for her to abort. She said they reassured her that, in the long run, an abortion would be the best option for keeping the family intact. Some of it made perfect logical sense, except for my conviction that adoption provides an alternative to abortion which the clinic did not present.

After working on the possibility of an open adoption and reassuring Crystal that she could stay long term at Agape, we left for an overnight presentation. I had an ominous feeling. When we returned, her clothes were missing, her room was empty, and the ultrasound image gone. She left a note saying that she and Michael had driven to Connecticut for an abortion.

A miracle didn't occur. We had the experience of trying to save a life and lost, which brought us face to face with the realities of sexual, physical, and psychological abuse sitting in the shadows, waiting to be exposed.

A Final Note

Teresa's life unfolded with confusing and heart-wrenching scenarios not uncommon in many families with a teenager. As I reflect on our resolve never to hit Teresa and not to use force or coercion in manner or speech, I have no qualms. But years after the fact, I began to wonder if, perhaps, we should not have

*Teenage Teresa, center, worked with children in the
Domincan Republic to build houses.*

enforced a vegetarian diet nor restricted movies as much as we
did. We tried to focus on the positive, but in a world of upward
mobility, our downward track made little sense to our young
daughter. Now, as an adult and mother doing her own parenting,
Teresa seems to agree that nonviolence makes sense. "I really
appreciate that you did what you did, Mom and Dad. I think you
did the right thing," she said.

Yay for one small victory.

Community life presented tough choices for a child who didn't
do well with large numbers of people, frequent guests, interns,
weekend groups, and retreat work at Francis House, which was
also Teresa's home. On the other hand, she met many people and
encountered wholesome, humane, and even sacred points of
view. Many young women interns helped shape Teresa's attitudes
in the most remarkable and positive ways towards what it means
to be a woman.

The reality demonstrates that children may not readily embrace parental life choices, especially when they go against the grain of culture that immerses a child outside of the home. Nevertheless, we have grown as a family into a warm, loving relationship.

Now that Teresa has her own daughter, we find ourselves revisiting the themes of Teresa's younger life. Olivia proudly shares with anyone who will listen, "Grandma eats Tofu Pups, no hot dogs. Grandma doesn't eat doughnuts. No chocolate milk."

With tremendous satisfaction, she says to me, "We're organic, aren't we, Grandma?" Family members report that Olivia refuses hot dogs at family gatherings, so we see early signs of a brainwashed vegetarian.

Nonviolent parenting means that at least we made an attempt to live our lives with children within the community structure with an emphasis on compassion, love, and forgiveness. When I get out of line now with Olivia and miss the nonviolent mark, she says, "I forgive you, Grandma."

Is This Lay Monasticism?

Brayton

"This is my favorite prayer," Casey Stanton, college senior at the University of Notre Dame in Indiana, enthusiastically proclaimed as she entered the Francis House living room at noon after a full morning's work in the Agape garden. Casey, a summer intern, gathered with others in the community for a short meditation just before lunch. "I have grown to love this moment of silence in the midst of the busiest and most demanding work time of our day," she shared.

The Catholic mystic Catherine de Hueck Doherty wrote, "Rural is quiet, and quiet is holy." Most people who come to Agape, especially the young, associate quiet with peaceful. Visitors and interns have a special need for the quiet because their worlds are so jammed with noise, speed and stress.

I think back to an experience I had in the late 1980s while on retreat at Eastern Point House of Prayer, a Jesuit retreat house in Gloucester, with some nuns from the Sisters of Saint Anne. After a yoga session I led during the retreat, I commented on the nascent Agape vision of prayer, voluntary poverty, and nonviolent witness.

"Your vision is of true lay monasticism," one elder nun remarked. "Lay" I assumed meant ordinary, a nonordained Christian responding in community with avowed disciplines to life's ordinary daily demands.

The monastic idea has its origins in chosen, disciplined rhythms of work and prayer dating at least to the Christian practice of Saint Benedict and his followers in the sixth century in Europe and to far earlier dates in Asia. Therefore, stopping a rigorous workday at noon to share a moment of silence and meditation interrupts demands of earthly work, a practice I had experienced in monasteries throughout the world. The noonday Angelus, a prayer to Mary, the mother of Jesus and a traditional Catholic daily practice, provides a sharp and intentional break from earthly routine.

Such a moment of prayer presents a spiritual challenge to the idol of constant work, incessant multitasking, and the drive always to be doing something. Our work days condition our habits as we lose ourselves in a frantic daily steeplechase headed into the oblivion of unremitting deadlines.

Most of us greet the alarm clock and caffeine as our first experiences of the day. We commute to work, then leap into the vortex, a time-is-always-money to-do list driven faster by the reminders that we are always behind.

Jumping Off the Merry-Go-Round

Dave Hammer left a life of climbing Manhattan's corporate ladder to intern at Agape. With high school and college groups, he shared the story of his daily routine as a rising star in a prestigious accounting firm:

Each morning, there were twenty minutes from alarm clock to catching the train to work. My breakfast was a milk protein drink. That breakfast took a mere ninety seconds to mix and drink down, preparing me for my ten-hour work day, a tightly wound series of financial accounting meetings all over metropolitan New York. Each day, I had to see too many clients in too short a time. My job was to reassure my clients that, yes, you still have lots of money.

Dave, who didn't enjoy the job as much as he did the expectation of regular pay raises and the assumption of a steady climb up the ladder, summarized his moral blinders on the fast track: "Reflecting on how I felt about where my life was going was never part of my day." At Agape, despite hard work, he had time to reflect when he oversaw Agape's prayer schedule in the midst of the demands of our work day.

Like Dave, many who come to Agape want to leap off a world spinning out of control. In the American workplace, we find reward for losing ourselves in goals we know we can't make with any equanimity, in a money chase we can't seem to stop.

Suzanne and I established a pray-three-times-a-day schedule even during our building projects. Stopping community activity for a moment to pray means a radical reorienting to God lest we lose ourselves in work. Capable of succumbing to our own demands of incessant activity, we at Agape experience the same stresses as the folks downtown.

Paul Noreau came to Agape as a thirty-year-old, hard-working intern. Most of Paul's six-hour work day at Agape centered on physical labor—wood cutting, mixing mortar, lifting heavy stones, and landscaping. A college graduate with a degree in philosophy, Paul loved to ruminate on life and spent most of his free time reading spiritual and philosophical classics. He often regaled us with potent quotes from great thinkers.

Arriving for prayer one evening, he complained that, in order to pray in the evening, he had to interrupt his nightly reading of works of spiritual masters. I identified with the philosopher's untiring quest for the best ideas and was tempted to sympathize.

Then I remembered the genius of the monastic way and the wisdom of mystics. The whole point of a communal prayer schedule is to stop whatever you're doing and turn toward God. So, I leveled with Paul, "We can lose our way every day doing our own thing, so we need to be brought back. One essential purpose of evening prayer is to interrupt your reading."

Mystical Knowing

"Nothing in all of creation is so like God as stillness," Meister Eckhart emphatically states. Christianity's much-quoted spiritual master utters his words in the thirteenth century as mystic, preacher, and Dominican priest.

Since the 1970s, two trends within organized Christianity appear. First, vocations to religious life have declined dramatically matched by a similar decline in church attendance across all Christian denominations. Second, some nonordained men and women, like me, began attending divinity schools to study theology, develop spiritual practice, and prepare for lives of service and ministry. If God exists and can be known, all the faithful, especially ordinary people of faith who may never have considered the idea of stillness, should experience the contemplative silence Eckhart proposes.

Trappist Thomas Merton, a cloistered monk and wisdom figure, offered many occasions for spiritual formation through his writing on nonviolence and social activism. Guiding peace activists grounded in a contemplative search for God, Merton writes from the monastic perch with language crafted to help activists understand our often driven selves. He writes:

> If our life is poured out in useless words, then we will never hear anything in the depths of our hearts where Christ lives and speaks in silence . . .those who love God necessarily love silence also . . . they fear the noise that takes the sharp edge off every experience of reality.

By the time I graduated from St. Anselm College, I almost exclusively associated silence, mysticism, and looking within with Asian religions. The more I was pulled toward Christianity, the more I found contemplative disciplines also had a rich tradition within my own Catholicism.

As a married couple, Suzanne and I found contemplation accessible through the Carmelites, the religious order of Teresa of Avila and John of the Cross, both dedicated to mystical revelation and silence.

In the summer of 1985, the year before our daughter, Teresa, was born and three years into Agape's formation, Suzanne and I spent most of a summer in silence on retreat as caretakers at Maine's Nova Nada, a Carmelite community of men and women hermits. We spent forty days in solitude, housed in single hermitages among others similarly situated.

As a typical Catholic growing up immersed in the values of suburbia, I was never encouraged to take extended times of silence. No youth groups at my parish went on retreats. Later, however, many young adults began to find a life-altering oasis of silence in monasteries and Buddhist, yoga, and Catholic retreat centers. At Nova Nada, Suzanne and I broke our silence periodically for daily communal prayer, Eucharist, Sabbath socials with occasional guests, and the appearance of visiting priests and nuns.

Axiomatically, we adapted experiential lessons gained from contemplatives, their theology, and their practice to our family lifestyle and community schedule. We returned home with a desire to approximate hermitage solitude, determined to make mystical stillness part of our too-demanding lives. Recognizing that our daily routine wore us down, we left longing for a deeper, truer peace that comes only with a daily spiritual practice.

Hermitage for Householders

Agape is planted in the rural quiet of central Massachusetts, a perfect environment for grounding in silence and solitude. Sister Pat McGowan, close friend from Nova Nada, visited Agape a few years after we built Francis House and helped us to locate a site for a hermitage. Walking the land behind Francis House with us, Pat became our spiritual dowser as she called out to me, "Here's a good spot."

For a year and a half, volunteers, guests, and friends with carpentry skills assisted in constructing a twelve-by-sixteen-foot hermitage with cathedral ceiling and meditation loft. The hermitage accommodates its visitors for a comfortable stay in solitude for an hour or a week.

The word hermitage derives from the tradition of monastic life. The word monk arises from the Greek *monos*, literally meaning "alone," and refers to one—a hermit—who seeks God alone while existing in a solitary environment. Such a person must break with the frantic motion of the human herd while existing alone but bonded with a contemplative community that supports the individual's journey.

As co-founders of Agape, we believed we were at a juncture in Catholic history that pointed to evolving notions of monos and hermit. Those terms must include spiritual seekers who are single, married men and women, and all people who juggle work and the demands of family life.

Life at Agape, especially for community members, can be locked into overdrive. In ascending the hill to the hermitage behind Francis House, the climber agrees to forsake the inner tyrant that enslaves the individual's thinking mind with a call for constant doing that rarely allows the urge for quiet to surface.

As I have attempted to live my life in a more awake and aware state, being increasingly attentive to the present moment, I realize the burden of the inner tyrant—my own mind. Buddhists call such spiritual observance mindfulness, cultivating a more receptive, nonjudgmental watchfulness of what is happening within me and in front of me.

Too frequently, I get lost in my favorite thoughts, fierce opinions, and reactivity. Fidelity to a steady awareness of where my mind is taking me offers protection from toxic anger, unfair judgment of others, and that aggression my thinking too often reveals.

I often hear others speaking of their yearning for relief. They say:

"I need to get away from all this work."

"My family is driving me nuts."

"This world is going to hell."

My ability to be aware demonstrates that the desire to escape constitutes a need to be free of myself and my own fixed ideas of just about everything.

A ladder provides the way up to the hermitage loft.

The Agape hermitage, a sanctuary of relief from the heat of personal frustration, has attracted people over the years who request time to spend a few days alone, to get a break from themselves! Our deep spiritual instincts inform us that for compassion to grow within us, we must allow ourselves time in the quiet.

Out of Our Minds into Our Hearts

As I walk up the side of the hill to the hermitage, I encounter impressive rock-hewn boulders whose massiveness stops me in my tracks. I reach the hermitage door that, once opened, yields a complete break in routine. Stillness. I choose to be in a place apart, void of normal twenty-first-century distractions, media, computers, phones. I'm free from incessant demands of keeping up.

One leaves a world of time-driven accomplishment in order, simply, to be. I recognize that I am a human being, willing to be watchful in the quiet and to listen. Inevitably, God speaks in and through me. I am likely to hear divine utterance through the natural world.

Agape's hermitage borders the Quabbin Reservoir watershed in the deep New England woods. Crossing the threshold into the prayer hut is enough doing for now. I am content to leave ten thousand things behind, to be still and confident in the oneness of things.

The poet William Butler Yeats writes, "We can make our minds so like still water." Solitary silence is a meditative force that Yeats says enables us "to live for a moment with a clearer, perhaps even with a fiercer life because of our quiet."

Each morning as dawn breaks, I walk up the hill and settle into the quiet before the day's demands begin. Enveloped in natural-world silence, I rest with my good friend, the hermitage, in whose daily counsel I gratefully partake.

We didn't build the hermitage only so that we could rest inside its walls and then return to the world more mindful, better-conditioned resisters of evil. We didn't build it solely to have a place

Agape's hermitage shines in the summer forest.

to pray or to petition God. We didn't build the hermitage for any purely utilitarian reason.

Inside the hermitage walls, I feel loved. I simply sit in the presence of divine love.

The Foreboding Desert of Silence

Being alone in the woods may manifest a desert where inner demons demand their say. "If I went to your hermitage in the woods alone, I would imagine the eyes of all those animals out there staring in at me," said a close community friend after we built the hermitage. Our friend has probably seen too many horror movies.

"I have *never* been alone," said a mother of five who lives every waking moment for her maturing brood.

"Being alone in your hermitage is something I am just not ready for," confided a deeply spiritual seeker.

When we stop and gaze into the inner land of our souls, the result is not always serene. Raised as an Afrikaner in apartheid

South Africa, Bobbi Louton spent three of the coldest January days of the year in the hermitage. She found herself speaking to her compassionate God throughout the stay. Later, she wrote an account that resonates with the prayer of saints over the centuries:

> I crave relief, abstinence from my needs and burdens, wants, and dependencies both good and bad. I want to recognize which dependencies enslave me.

At night, when the prayer hut is dark except for her small candle, she writes:

> I lean against the rough cross on the wall, feel the size and fit of it with my arms. Will you really bear the weight of these things for me?

Those on retreat sometimes intensify the experience with fasting or reduced food intake. Bobbie limited herself to bread, cheese, honey, and water. Throughout her stay, she continued her divine soliloquy:

> There should be so much joy in meeting our needs, the sheer goodness of you who made things to be this way. In the prayer loft, I kneel at the window, looking down on the woods out to the hills far away. I know you see me like this always even when I do not see you.

As we end our time away in solitude, we retreatants know the necessity of taking home insights and revelations heard from God. During her last moments of a weekend in the hermitage, Susan Arraje wrote:

> I am reminded of those with whom I live and work, God's temple defiled by poverty, mental illness, drugs. The solitude and grayness speak to me as I return to my ministry. The hermitage is an instrument that bridges the two lives.

Unlike the hermit who lives in solitude, we followers of Christ leave the desert stillness to walk with the prophetic Jesus back into the streets, the suffering ghettos, and the strife-and-war-ravaged world to be signs of peace.

Back to the Land!

Brayton

I was thirty-seven and Suzanne, thirty-nine, when we decided to go back to the land. Up to then, neither of us had ever planted a seed in the ground nor pounded a nail into a piece of wood. We had spent our lives in urban apartments, coming off five years of living on the outskirts of Brockton, a medium-sized working-class city south of Boston. Our skills—or lack thereof—did not prepare us for our rural plunge. No way. We may as well have been rocketing to Mars.

We were products of World War II parents and their generation, the first to produce an almost exclusively male, middle-management, and corporate world. Many of our fathers sat in their offices on the phone or planning business strategies with their colleagues. Like me, my father never pounded a nail, was raised by the Shanleys, a millionaire-New-York-City-restaurateur family, formed in high society hospitality and groomed to appreciate the finer things of life and to earn a living by managing others.

As Suzanne and I considered going back to the land in the latter twentieth century, we knew that such a choice meant forsaking our professional lives for working the land, which for a time looked and sounded pretty romantic. Nevertheless, we knew that we were entering into a new terrain that would demand some real, daily, physical toil.

Leaving the city to practice the rural life of homesteading became a crash course in house design, building and repair, gardening, land clearing and landscaping, and a physical life and pioneering effort traditionally meant for people half our age. Our forsaking upward mobility and surviving by the work of our hands made us feel like modern-day throwbacks to American pioneers but with a major difference—we had modern tools and equipment.

Our decision to live on the land and from its bounty was similar to beginning Christian community itself. Motivated by those whose examples inspired and energized us, we could not have known when we started out that our desire for simple living, would eventually cost what T. S. Eliot calls "not less than everything."

Growing up in northeast North America, I was intrigued by the stories of the first wave of societal dropouts in the 1960s and

1970s. These were folks who had begun their young professional careers chasing the American dream of money and status and armed with business degrees from elite schools, some ending up on Wall Street. In their late twenties or early thirties, many such social climbers became disillusioned with the chase and decided to leave it all, grab what savings they had, and flee to somewhere rural to live the simple life.

Those back-to-the-landers were often young and inexperienced countercultural, antiwar, anticapitalist, all-purpose contrarians who wanted to build an alternative society within the network of wholesome, rural, peace-loving communes.

I learned more about the history of rural Christian community when I took Religion and Socialism with Harvey Cox at Harvard Divinity School. The course covered the successful, enduring nineteenth-century Jesus-Movement commune—the Oneida community in rural New York. Founded by John Humphrey Noyes, Oneida aspired to be a model of the "total Christian life." Three hundred people lived a self-sufficient bible communism and supported themselves making silverware that became the world-famous Oneida Silverware. I learned that the Oneida community lived and thrived for forty years.

I began to imagine my life dedicated to Jesus, which seemed impossible to do alone or within what I considered the typical contemporary lifestyle.

Ready to Make the Plunge

By the mid-1980s, Suzanne and I found land in central Massachusetts and were ready to purchase thirty-two acres. Our close friend Bob Lueders coined a name, "Bootstraps Nonviolence," for our community project to identify an economically viable community built literally from the ground up. What we faced as novices was daunting: land clearing and building a three-thousand-square-foot main house structure with no experience in any of what we eventually called homesteading.

Friends and supporters gather to bless Agape land in the late 1980s.

Before our move, I had been reading Helen and Scott Nearing's books *Living the Good Life* and *Continuing the Good Life,* described by the authors as how-to guides for "living simply and sanely in a troubled world." The Nearings went back to the land in the 1930s and developed a model of radically simple house building.

Shortly after Scott's death, Suzanne and I made a pilgrimage to Maine to spend an afternoon with Helen. We thanked her for their extraordinary lives as we readied ourselves to build our own community with their books serving as gritty manuals of pacifist, pragmatic, bare-bones simplicity.

Clearing the Land

With an interest-free loan from my Aunt Rhoda, we bought thirty-two acres of land in Hardwick, a quiet farm town in central Massachusetts. The purchase was less than a thousand dollars an acre, a price that clearly came from heaven given the unjust and unaffordable cost of real estate for most property in the Northeast in the 1980s. Two major tasks loomed: clearing the land of dense hardwood trees and putting together a crew of skilled carpenters to plunge into our daunting house-building project.

By April 1987, we had the makings of our team of builders. The entire project was headed up by Bob Wegener, an active member of Agape's teaching ministry and antideath-penalty efforts. A skilled architect who graduated first in his class in the school of architecture at Notre Dame, Bob rejected a certain, lucrative career in mainstream architecture to work consistently in firms dedicated to low-income housing. Bob blazed the trail for Agape's original structures with his considerable skill and respect for design collaboration. Gathering in our nascent dream of what would become the first community house, he drew a sketch of what became Francis House, the four-bedroom, three-thou-sand-square-foot main structure.

Needing a head carpenter to work under Bob, we thought of Dan Lawrence, a former Trappist monk, whom we knew through our antinuclear weapons work. I couldn't call Dan at that moment to invite him into the project because he was serving a two-month sentence at a county jail for a protest at GTE, a high-tech weapons manufacturer in Westborough.

I wrote a letter to him in prison asking if he would be interested in serving as head carpenter, to which he responded, "Let's talk in a month or so when I get out."

Upon his release, he looked over the Hardwick work site, pounded a few nails, and said "I'm in." His requested recompense— $3.50 per hour with room and board—testified to his Trappist adherence to the vow of poverty. We had never seen nor could ever have imagined the likes of his almost complete indifference to money.

Alden Poole arrived next on the team. He and his wife, Janet, already long-time Agape and Ailanthus supporters, had both spent time in the county jail protesting nuclear weapons at Draper Labs, the MIT think tank that made guidance systems for weapons of mass destruction. A jack-of-all-trades carpenter retiring from more than twenty years of teaching journalism at Simmons

College, Alden had framed a few homes in his day and built a complete summer home for his family of nine children. Recently freed from what Dan Berrigan called "an all-expense paid state scholarship" at Middlesex House of Correction in Billerica, Alden selflessly agreed to work two days a week while traveling four hours round trip until we completed this first Agape dwelling.

Wayne Petrin, Dan Lawrence's closest friend, agreed to be our electrician. He was an unreformed career peacemaker fresh from a recent stint at Worcester County Jail as a result of his opposition to nuclear weapons. Except for thirty-year-old Bob, Wayne fell in with our over-fifty, semi-retired crew of offenders for peace.

Then there was me, totally unskilled at building anything. Convinced of the Nearings' notion that leaving conventional, urban life in middle age (no less) made sense, we stepped up to learn a completely new way of life. Our team stood ready to start construction, but first we had to clear dozens of trees, build a gravel road, and dig a foundation hole making way for the first Agape building.

Ignorance Is a Dangerous Bliss

I readied myself for the most dangerous project of a lifetime. With virtually no experience, I showed up on our land with a chain saw I had never used with the expressed purpose of cutting down massive oak, maple, poplar, and ash trees.

I purchased the chain saw, and on my way to the land, I stopped by the home of Dave and Kathleen Legg, old friends and supporters of the community. Dave, who had years of chain-sawing experience, walked me through the basics, the dos and don'ts of safety. Trusting Dave's skill implicitly, as he knew carpentry and had built his own house, I figured a forty-five-minute primer from Dave would qualify me to begin.

I arrived at the site, took a deep breath, begged God to save me from an early end, fired up the saw, and proceeded to cut what would eventually be a hundred or so trees. As a saving grace, Bob, who also had limited experience with chainsaws, joined me periodically. Unlike me, Bob had become accustomed to power tools and building, and nothing seemed to scare him. He generated contagious confidence.

Teresa, Suzanne, and I moved into a two-bedroom apartment in Ware, a ten-minute drive from the building site. Dan soon joined us in our tiny flat, and for the next eight months, we lived together. With what floor space we had in the two-bedroom digs along with ample space for pitching tents on the land in Hardwick, we hosted hundreds of volunteers, both skilled and unskilled, for the next nine months.

Fine Art of Design

Suzanne, Bob, and I mulled over the function and scope of our first building, imagining together a domicile that would comfortably accommodate up to six people. The first structure was to be a main lodge among other smaller out buildings: a thirty-by-thirty-nine-foot square-shaped house, a story and a half high with four bedrooms, two bathrooms, and most significantly, a large living room space where people could gather.

We chose to construct the building of stone and wood, natural outcroppings of our wooded New England land. Bob added passive solar emphasis with primary windowpanes on the south side and two-story cathedral ceiling for light and heat. The sheer excitement of first imagining, then designing and eventually building a main house that future community dwellers would occupy was intoxicating. The image came to me of cowbirds, the only bird that lives in nests built by other birds. Here at Agape, we were living in an extended community whose members were designing and building a communal nest to exact specifications: a place to raise children and serve the needs of others.

As we talked back and forth, we asked ourselves: "How do we want this place to feel?" *Feng shui*, the ancient Chinese language of design translated as "wind and water," was becoming known within the building world. The term refers to the Chinese art of positioning objects or structures so as to harmonize with spiritual forces. Related to the Taoist balance principal of yin and yang, the philosophy of feng shui holds that we all have the capacity to feel balance or absence of balance, especially in living spaces.

During the design process, Bob introduced me to Christopher Alexander's theory of creating a "pattern language" that forms ancient building design patterns, some that Alexander claimed can be traced to the African savannah. In his study of how humans live within their structures, each pattern meets a specific daily need. Alexander maintains that the most wonderful places in the world are made "not by architects but by people."

After wondering over what the building would be, our conclusion was to build a structure that a stranger walking into would recognize as carrying a sense of home. Experiencing the right balance of assembled spiritual forces, any newcomer could feel welcomed and loved.

We were ready to build!

Greg McDonald, Dan Lawrence, Bob Wegener, and Doug McDonald lift the main oak carrying beam during 1987 construction of Francis House.

The Barn Raising

First day on the job included Bob; Matthew Stone, the fifteen-year-old whom Suzanne found in an alleyway in Ware; and me. Al Mueller, another peace activist from nearby Connecticut, and my thirty-year-old cousin Leo from New York City came on board later in that first week. For the next nine months from June to February, several hundred people dropped by to help. Some came for an afternoon; some stayed for a month. Our Collie Maggie was the only one who lived full time on the building site.

Because I had never been around building projects, I was not ready for the full-throttle stress of twenty-four/seven demands, nor did I expect the intense excitement and joy that happens when you watch a building go up. The change in landscape is a daily drama. Our crew of carpenters appeared to perform sleight-of-hand magic, the primal elegance of a building forming before our eyes.

Alden immediately named the experience "our own Amish barn-raising." Consider the fact that Alden, Dan, Bob, and I actually built an entirely framed wall flat on the first floor and then lifted up the entire structure! Our horizon had its first aesthetic, a wall of a house actually made with the work of our hands. It was heart pounding, an unrepeatable moment that bonded and charged us up for the construction trials that lay ahead.

The building site began to hum with the sound of nails pounded into wood, saws buzzing, and carpentry directives shouted above the din. Our end-of-the-day ritual was to pause and gaze at the work of art in progress. From each other, we were learning the life skill of housebuilding, a common proficiency only a hundred years before.

We called in two more of our expert builder friends, Daniel Sicken and Mark Korban, both nonviolent disciples and activists from Vermont. Mark and his son Jonathan put in the top-floor skylights, and Daniel built the pine walls in the kitchen. The

Dan Lawrence, head carpenter, frames the Francis House kitchen.

memory of who built what room has become a permanent and indelible part of the Agape narrative. "Remember when you put up that wall?" "How about the skylights you figured out how to insert when you were sixteen?"

Positioned on the lowest rung of carpentry skills, I became the general contractor without portfolio. It fell to me to hire subcontractors, purchase all materials, run them to the site, and of course, pay for everything. Alden, always the worry wart, asked, "How do you pay for all this?"

"Oh, it's easy," I responded. "I just don't ever keep an account balance."

So up went the first floor with the help of Neal Mongold, George O'Neil, and Kitty Ryan, Bob Wegener's architectural school classmates from Notre Dame. The handicraft of that tall barn-like Cape had the texture of natural surfaces—wood walls and a stone veneer foundation.

Bob Thiefels, a professional carpenter and old friend from our early Boston peace activism days, arrived to help out. He and Dan Lawrence taught me how to frame walls and put up pine wallboards. All of the wood was locally milled, the first floor built with oak trees cut and milled right from our land. We were learning from one of our environmental movement's greatest thinkers, Wendell Berry, who said, "Think locally, act locally." We always looked to consume everything homegrown and to purchase as much as possible within a fifty-mile radius.

My cousins from New York finished the first floor and readied themselves to put up the main-girder oak beam. The crucial support for the entire middle of the house-a sixteen-foot, eight-by-eight-inch oak monstrosity—took all my cousins, Greg, Bruce, and Doug McDonald, to lift, a brutal heft, with Dan and Bob helping to complete the task. Raising the main girder lift was our

Brayton, left, and Dan Lawrence raise the second floor wall.

pacifist equivalent to raising the flag at Iwo Jima. All the family and community carpenters lifted a locally grown oak beam for peace, an iconic moment of the entire project.

We then moved to building the second floor, but we needed stairs to get us up there. Bob was the only knowledgeable one for the job. Usually the man you can count on, Bob labored long and hard to get the stair framing right because of a complicated measurement and cut. Three times it came out wrong, and for a day or two, the building rhythm that reflected a certain momentum was seriously on hold. On the fourth try, he succeeded. Unusually calm about building deadlines and stresses, Bob appeared relieved that he, head architect and building supervisor, was no longer stalling the project.

Wayne Petrin, our electrician who worked closely with Bob for months, called it right when he turned to me and said, "Bob has a meditative personality." Not finding too many centered people in building supervisors like Bob, Wayne was amazed that anyone could juggle architect consultation, carpentry, and building supervision so easily.

Bob also became quality control manager for the work of dozens of amateur carpenters and unskilled volunteers. Imagine, I thought, getting all this done with a "meditative personality." That was Bob.

Living without Debt

Even though we had a perfect record of paying cash, up front for everything we bought, we were ineligible for a housing mortgage because neither Suzanne nor I had ever taken a loan except for my college loan twenty years before. It was just as well, because the etymology of mortgage, rooted in Latin, means contract of death.

Our entire venture was made financially possible when Bob and his wife, Tara, offered to buy our previously condemned Brockton house. How is that for community? In solidarity with us, Bob and Tara took the risk and began their newly wedded life in our former Brockton house.

Suzanne's nephews Robbie and Dave Mendlewski work with the crew to build scaffolding for the Francis House roof.

Upon sale of the house, the IRS took five thousand dollars to address the long-standing lien for our refusal to pay war taxes. Our resistance had not resulted in total victory as the IRS ended up with some dollars for war. We did, however, succeed in communicating opposition to war, and our refusal to pay voluntarily made it a bureaucratic headache for the feds to get the unpaid taxes.

Because of the generosity that provided free carpentry and general volunteer help, we were able to build an impressive community house on the cheap—maybe half the average cost of a conventionally built house. We appreciated a supportive network of believers in the common good behind us.

In September, Paul del Junco joined us from Toronto to assist in the urgent task of completing the second and third floors, including full roof and shingles. At the same time, Suzanne did a bit of matchmaking behind the scenes when she suggested that Jo Connelly from Haley House in Boston join us for a workday. A relationship immediately blossomed, as we all observed Paul and Jo move from building partners to friends to very close friends. Suzanne observed with no little pride, "They're holding hands."

Alden, who had an ear for worksite scuttlebutt, heard from reliable sources, "It's not a question of whether but when they'll get married." We noticed how, ever so gently, work slowed down around them. A year later, Paul and Jo were married. They were our first community marriage, an Agap-eros moment!

The Last Gasp: Raising the Roof

The high wire act of building roof rafters was next. Dan and Bob constructed a twenty-five-foot scaffold from the second floor that could carry two people. One person held and positioned an impressively heavy two-by-twelve-foot pine rafter forty feet in length and the other nailed each rafter in place. At first, only Bob and Dan volunteered for the breathtaking job until our nephews from Buffalo, Dave and Rob Mendlewski, showed up. Those strong, strapping teenagers were eager to climb the wobbly planks to brave a forty-foot drop to the ground and toss danger to the wind.

The last of the fall volunteer teams were friends, Sister Kathleen Deignan of the Congregation de Notre Dame and Father John Giuliani from the Benedictine Grange, a liturgical community in Connecticut. They arrived with two community members, a four-person volunteer crew to help make the building winter ready. Almost every crew that arrived had little to no actual carpentry experience. Either Dan or Alden offered speed training on how to measure and cut. As head carpenter Dan managed quality control. The inevitable mismeasurements did slow us down at times, but we marveled every day about a house built on the good will and sweat of amateurs. Our Grange friends ended their days at the building site with a prayer of thanksgiving "for this community of love within the stunning beauty of the deep woods —the poplar, oak, maple, and ash trees."

By November, we had been working for six months with three floors framed in, weatherproofed and waterproofed windows installed, and roof finished. It took another three months to complete inside finish work including walls, doors, plumbing, and electricity. The house was, finally, livable. By mid-February Steve James, Agape's co-founder from Haiti, helped Suzanne and me move into the habitable but unfinished barn-like house during a classic New England snow storm. Once inside, we lit the old wood-burning stove, looked around, and felt the blessing of the precious work of so many hands.

People arrive at the Francis House opening on the first Saint Francis Day, 1989.

167

Living in Each Season as It Passes

Brayton

Lillian, Agape's spiritual mother, urged, "Isn't it time to start the garden?" A gardener herself, she always supplied the community with her once-in-a-lifetime raspberry jam every summer. She jump-started the Agape garden by donating several young shoots from her well-cared-for raspberry bushes that would become our first perennial crop.

It was 1990, two years since our moving into Francis House. We were overdue to embark on the third pillar of a homesteading life: first, build the house; second, cut wood for heat; third, grow our own food. We felt uneasy knowing that we were in our early forties and had never planted a seed into the ground. But residing as we did in central Massachusetts, the historic farm belt of New England, we felt emboldened to practice gardening since we lived alongside so many farmers.

By the 1990s, gardening was evolving from America's number one hobby to organic farming as ecological necessity. We were entering a time of seismic change in agriculture; the New England family dairy farm was dying out, and farming had to be re-invented. Although small organic farms and community-supported agriculture (CSA) were poised to inherit some of the former dairy farm land, rural New England was in crisis. We wondered how we could protect land from being sold off to become suburbs?

I was a committed vegetarian since attending a yoga retreat in 1973. Experiencing a rebirth of body and mind after ten days of meditation, hatha yoga, and vegetarian eating, I was on my way to a brand new life. The yogis informed me that the human anatomy was made for plant food due to certain anatomical facts: digestive enzymes in the mouth and stomach coupled with our grinding teeth and long and complex small and large intestines made for elimination on a twenty-four-hour cycle. Our entire human digestive system was designed to break down plant food.

Cats, on the other hand, are classic carnivores. Killing prey with ripping teeth, they immediately eat the raw meat and, in an hour or two, digest it completely and eliminate. So it was no wonder to the yoga practitioners that I felt so good. I was eating what my body was made for.

In six short months after I began my new diet, I lost thirty pounds by simply eliminating all that meat, beer, sugary junk, and processed food. Swami Satchidananda, who founded the Integral Yoga Institute, instructed me that the spiritual life and practice has to start with diet because Americans are so desperately unhealthy. When you go toward wild animals, they run away from you. No need to chase them, trap them, shoot them. Let them be. Observe the apple tree, how it grows its fruit and the apple naturally falls to the ground as gift. Following a vegetarian diet is in noninjurious harmony with nature.

Another important fact that is not harmonious with nature: in the US, sixty billion animals are raised for slaughter for meat every year, ninety percent of them heartlessly on factory farms. Chickens are trapped in one-square-foot coops; pigs and cows are penned up and force-fed with hormones to grow more quickly for bigger profit. Agribusiness animals are killed as things with neither reverence nor respect.

And what is the scariest fact of all? No federal laws protect factory farm animals. We can treat them any way we wish. They are without legal protection. The tortured, helpless animals are among the most abused in the world. Therefore, in the ahimsa spirit of non-injury, vegetarianism is for the good of the land, our bodies, and our right relationship with animals.

It is longstanding historical fact that growing organic food provides the best food for the lowest price, cheaper even than our beloved fast foods. Suzanne, others in the community, and I had to learn the ancient life skill of farming from local friends, because we city folk knew virtually nothing about growing our own.

Raised Bed Revolutionaries

We cleared our first thirty-by-thirty-foot garden plot. The soil had not been worked in more than a hundred years, so we had to bring in workable top soil and organic fertilizer in order to get a start. Our land had not seen significant vegetable farming since the Civil War era. Then, ninety-five percent of American people were engaged in some form of agriculture. As we began to sow our first seeds in 1992, we were one among only three percent who were directly involved in agriculture. Why do we outsource our food production to corporate agribusiness? No wonder we are so full of diabetes, heart disease, and cancer.

Rich Bachtold, our local Agape community member, came from a southern Illinois dairy farm family. From his lifelong experience, he instructed us how to prepare soil and plant the crops in raised beds. Another local friend, Chris Greene, a longtime grower, suggested we buy our seed from Fedco Seed Company in Maine. Growers in our small New England organic farm network refused to sell fungicide-treated seeds or offer genetically engineered products and boycotted all Monsanto

*Brayton, Teresa, and Rich Bachtold, from left,
sow seeds in an Agape raised bed.*

products. Our current ecological age did not encourage us to let up when it comes to resisting tentacles of corporate America, especially those entities selling food.

With our organic seeds in hand, we plunked down fifty bucks for soil amendments and planted our first garden of broccoli, peppers, Swiss chard, carrots, lettuce, radishes, beets, and cabbage. Miraculously, a few crops even survived and proved edible.

We began to grow our own food and learned to eat like rabbits. The radical vegan healer Dr. D.J. Scott once told me, "If you want to run like a rabbit, you have to eat like a rabbit!"

Our Hands in the Soil

As we immersed ourselves in working the soil, the essential desire to farm could strike us as utilitarian: that is, we have to eat. However, living close to the earth and working the earth with our hands always evoke closeness to the divine. Jesus, lived within the rural culture of family farming, frequently preached parables of sowing and taught using familiar analogies of plants growing in nature.

The smell and touch of soil have sensations of intoxicating purity. Hale, wholesome, and holy are three names of the sacred that come to me as I dig into the earth. It is not a surprise that, as year followed year in the Agape garden, not one of the interns or volunteers ever complained of the long hours of garden labor. I have always gotten the impression that Agape's vegetable gardening tasks filled a void in many of us and proved more satisfying than driving to work and sitting all day, even at a job we enjoy.

The mystique of growing connects me with the providence of the divine. Plants are primarily green and luminous, the color of life, drenched in fecundity, the promise of abundance with the simplest touch of seed to soil and . . . just add water.

Growing has also taught me great lessons in simplicity. We work every stage of the emerging garden by hand. Shunning fossil-fuel machines, we turn soil by hand shoveling, a quiet and sometimes monotonous but necessary toil providing all-natural

Agape interns and volunteers, including high school students from Springfield, work together in the Agape gardens.

work for the body. Daily digging shows us that, if we want simplicity, we have to start doing simpler things.

We fertilize by using composted weeds, kitchen scraps, and fallen leaves from our trees. The new disciplines took years to perfect. Our organic method came to us thanks to the spiritually evolved techniques of the German mystic Rudolph Steiner and his biodynamic methods. In the growing process, we return all organic material from the homestead back to the soil to complete a regenerative circle. All garden- enriching materials are best taken from the same land, void of any toxic store-bought chemicals.

When the garden soil was ready, the drama began. With Rich's guidance, we dug a shallow trench, gently dropped seed into it, covered it with soil, watered, and waited. A week went by when

Sheila, one of our interns, came in from an early morning stroll in the garden and exclaimed, "The peas are up!" Her excitement proclaimed a childlike happiness in the exquisite mystery of the soil's fertility.

A few weeks later Geoff, a college intern, yelled out to the other gardeners, "The beans are in!" By mid summer, Margaret looked to the south side of the garden and exclaimed: "Tomatoes are turning red!" The long hard toil yielded to garden pandemonium. Growing instantly returns the wonder of experiencing nature in action.

Loving My Garden Enemies?

Soon enough we expanded to a hundred-by-hundred-foot garden with three hundred plants. It's a little like having thirteen kids: good days for sure, but worry-filled days, too, often laid low with unavoidable bad news.

A few years back, I walked into a bucolic June morning garden to find most of the broccoli, cabbage, and cauliflower plants eaten. "Oh, no," I yelled as anxiety began to overtake me. "A woodchuck."

Nathan, a former intern and a regular visitor at Agape, joined me in getting to the bottom of it all and puzzling over what to do. Advice came in from my local, old-timer farming network: "Just shoot them." I prefer the noninjurious, ahimsic way, so I bought a Havahart trap that catches the pest alive. Faithfully, we found a new home for our offender somewhere twenty-five miles away.

I also purchased thirty plants to replace those ravaged. The next day, Nathan came in from the garden to share more bad news. "More plants were eaten," he announced. "Even some of the kale is gone."

Rage mixed with violent fantasies filled both of us so- called vegetarian gardener pacifists.

"Oh, this is going to be very hard," Nathan confessed.

Impossibly hard, I thought as I angrily sped to the garden store to buy thirty more plants.

"If you do not want to kill the woodchuck," my pest control expert Tom informed me, "then I certainly would not try to catch him with the peanut butter that you are using. For bait, you must use one of your young juicy broccoli plants, because that is what they are eating."

"What?" I moaned. "More plants need sacrificing?"

I called Bruce Davidson, earth-spiritualist friend and co-founder of Sirius Community, a local eco-village. His suggestion: "I have the best results praying and meditating in the garden when animals ravage our plants."

His advice did not exactly qualify as the quick-fix solution I hoped for. But I knew prayer would quiet my agitated mind, as I was desperate to be rescued from my days of fear and loathing at the one animal on its way to eating the entire garden.

Employing only spiritual weapons, Nathan and I began every workday meditating near the woodchuck living under our garden shed a short thirty feet from his favorite vegetable plants. The next day, it devoured only ten plants.

White-hot anger burned a little less due to the enhanced mindfulness.

"The woodchuck is an innocent, beautiful, and hungry eater," I repeated to myself, "who like me has every right to exist."

A week went by, and we continued to meditate near the woodchuck's home. It ate only a few more plants, and I managed to replace them.

My efforts at self-control and the stark awareness that my own anger at losing my garden, row by row, was deadlier than pesticides, modified my aggressive edge.

The woodchuck was often sighted just after sunrise checking out the broccoli. "Oh, this is very hard," was Nathan's daily lament. Although "hard" was the painful truth, the woodchuck also supplied us with an essential lesson: how to care noninjuriously for garden-destroying critters.

Chipmunks Are Not Cute

Soon I noticed the bean and corn seeds were not germinating. They are usually quick sprouters and easy to grow. I checked the corn bed and discovered that every seed I had just planted was gone, eaten by overpopulated chipmunks. Hundreds of corn, pea, and bean seeds were consumed or stored in their nest. The rapacious animals were seen digging trenches into the greenhouse and then ravaging my little cabbage and melon seed in germinating trays. "This is insanity," I muttered.

I called Bruce back and asked, "How do you stop chipmunks from eating vegetable seeds?"

Having recently experienced chipmunk overpopulation, he suggested, "Buy a fifty-pound bag of sunflower seeds and cast them where they are nesting. They will prefer this seed to yours." He cited a German environmentalist's research that suggests that, due to climate change and ecological decline, animals in the wild are living on inferior vegetation. Feasting on garden and sunflower seeds constituted their superfood.

I ran out and got sunflower seeds and fed the chipmunks more generously than our birds and, sure enough, they quit eating my vegetable seed immediately, evidently preferring the high-end protein. But did it mean that next year I would have twice as many chipmunks looking for a free lunch?

Two days later, I checked my trap and, after three weeks of agony, I found a twenty-pound woodchuck in the trap. The prodigal son's father could not have been any happier. But Tom, my pest control guy, was not happy. "When you let that woodchuck go," said Tom, "you'll be sending it off into someone else's garden."

Nonviolent ethics requires never-ending scrutiny. Hard as we try, no perfectly non injurious act is ever completely possible on this side of the grave. I complained to my friend Pat Tracy of my garden woes, and he reflected, "What would life be like if everything worked out perfectly and every garden was a worry-free masterpiece?"

I am reminded of the permaculture design philosophy that recommends, "Turn problems into solutions. Hardships inspire

Bruce Davidson, co-founder of Shutesbury's Sirius Community,
coached Brayton on management of backyard pests.
Hood's up on the Sirius vegetable diesel car, behind Bruce.

creativity. We are continually confronted with insurmountable opportunities!"

With more experience, when we head into the fall harvest season, a gem of Thoreau's about sustainable growing comes to mind: "Live in each season as it passes, breathe its air, taste its fruit."

The New England garden cycle places us in intimate contact with the land in four distinct seasons. Beginning in snowy, below-zero February, I order my seeds. By the March thaw, I start seedlings and plant lettuce in the greenhouse. With a crew of April volunteers, we start direct-seed planting in the garden. By the middle of May, the college-rural-immersion groups arrive for a couple of weeks to turn and fertilize the soil and plant a hundred different varieties of vegetables.

The deep heat of summer months offers a feast of tomatoes, corn, basil, squash, and peppers, to name only the favorites. Fall is the harvest season, the time of completion and gratitude as we freeze and can surplus vegetables that will feed us until the following June. College summer interns do most of the work.

As I gaze over the last remaining harvest, I anticipate that the Brussels sprouts will delight us all the way to Christmas Eve dinner. In the deep dormant winter frost of January, soups of homegrown beets, pumpkin, butternut squash, and potatoes will warm us. Eating from the garden is a yearlong reassurance that God often does provide the sweetest provisions!

Living with Difficult People

Suzanne

We lived in a basement apartment with a fluctuating number of volunteers who slept on the floor in the small, economically depressed, rural town of Ware. As I pushed eighteen-month-old Teresa in a stroller, I noticed a young man slumped against a nearby corner curb. As I got closer, I realized that he was a bare-chested, unkempt teenager.

Hesitatingly, I passed by him thinking, "You can't stop. You have Teresa. May not be safe." Nonetheless, I turned around quickly, as I moved Teresa and the stroller close enough to see the young man's soulful, deep brown eyes, red rimmed, apparently from crying. He didn't say a word, just stared blankly. Shabby, shirtless, and dirty, he had a heavy chain tied around his waist.

"Are you all right?" I asked.

"No," he mumbled.

"What's your name?" I continued.

"Matthew," he whispered, his voice barely audible.

After inquiring if he was hungry and receiving a wordless nod of no, I asked if he would like to come home with me. I received a nodded yes. Once back at the apartment, I watched over Matthew as he amused Teresa and ate sandwiches. Eventually, he appeared more relaxed and confided that his older brother had beaten him up. He also announced with great seriousness, "I need to make some money."

Then, out of nowhere, Matthew blurted, "Do you want to meet my mother?" Of course, I didn't want to say no, and so we headed out to meet Matthew's mom.

Immediately walking into Diane's presence, I realized that she is Native American. That day, she had a reassuring, Mother-Earth smile with ample figure to complement it. The furniture in her apartment, located in the section of town known for drugs, was ripped and soiled. A pile of dishes sat stacked, unwashed, decaying food on and around them.

Our conversation included an agreement that Matthew might come the next day to pick up a little work at the Agape construction site, and we would pay him. Diane seemed pleased.

Later visits to their apartment with food and money revealed multiple residents, including many children and not enough beds, explaining the mattresses on the floor.

After a month's stint at our construction site, Matthew became increasingly involved in criminal activity that led to arrests and time in jail. Diane worked at Agape for about ten years and became a real helpmate to me and Agape staff. She cooked, cleaned, and prepared the house when college students came for retreat. Diane was indispensable, a key player in the early days of the community and building its base.

We've Been Robbed

Brayton

I ran my customary after-work errands, including a bank stop in town at our local Country Bank for Savings. I needed to ask for an account balance after realizing that something was seriously wrong with the Agape checking account two thousand dollars in arrears.

The teller checked recent records of withdrawals only to discover that someone had cashed a two-thousand-dollar check a few days prior. I didn't have to think too long to figure out who this someone could be. "I'll bet it was Pete," I said to myself. Hidden cameras record pictures of every transaction, so we instantly saw the evidence—our young friend Pete Stone cashing an Agape check.

Pete is Matthew Stone's youngest brother, who, like Matthew, is mentally challenged with language and intellectual disabilities even more severe than Matthew's. Like his parents and five siblings, Pete lives on Supplemental Security Income (SSI) benefits. Agape provided Pete and his two brothers, Brendan and Matthew, some bread labor and a sense of community. Their assistance, in turn, was invaluable. We needed them.

When I returned from the bank, I noticed a few checks missing. For people marginally employable and on the financial edge like Pete, stealing is a way of surviving. Yet, the entire family, including the parents, often assisted us at the community. We had known them for decades, watched five of the kids grow into adulthood, and accepted the fact that our relationship often felt unsettling and complex.

The theft presented an immediate legal dilemma, as the bank had to proceed with a police report, including details of who did what and when. The bank manager assured us that our loss was covered, but we felt it was our responsibility to inform Pete that we and the bank knew about his theft and to remind him of his responsibility to pay off his debt to the bank.

We decided to seek Pete out at his small apartment building, home to those as poor as he is, including, we were told, local drug users and small-time traffickers. Suzanne insisted we show up unannounced in spite of the fact we couldn't predict the danger we might find. I had more reluctance than Suzanne, so I followed her lead.

We arrived early on a weekday morning, but Pete was not home, so we began knocking on neighbors' apartment doors to find information about his life and whereabouts. We decided to be as nonthreatening and reassuring as possible and to state that all we wanted was to talk with Pete.

Rural barrios and inner-city ghettos were not unfamiliar to us, so the hallway of Pete's building had the anticipated smell of decaying food and the stale air of cigarette smoke. We started down a corridor, knocking on doors as we went along. To our surprise, almost each time we knocked, someone answered the door and greeted us, usually warmly. Within a few minutes, we seemed to have attracted a hallway full of tenants eager to talk, friendly, and even animated. We greeted the single moms and young couples eager to share their impressions of Pete and to confide spontaneously about their own woes.

Pete's neighbors listed their sicknesses, legal run-ins, or problems with absentee landlords in their dilapidated apartments. In that moment, we found ourselves among marginalized twenty-somethings who lived on the edge of poverty simply because they were born there.

Sharing what they knew about Pete, people were honest with us. We were not the police. The poor we have known are always wary of the cops, and there would be no trust if we acted upset or ready to report Pete. We made it absolutely clear that we did not plan to press charges as we inquired about Pete's well-being. After all, we had known him since childhood, cared about him, and wanted to help.

We bid goodbye to the coterie of Pete's friends, seemingly sincere and real as they reassured us that Pete would return but they couldn't be sure when.

A Compassionate Cop

Our next stop was the Town of Palmer police station down the road—a small, rural police headquarters—to discuss the police report of the theft. Officer Williams, a warm and friendly man already familiar with the Country Bank report, greeted us. We informed him of our long and committed relationship with Pete and that we promised not to press charges nor did we wish him arrested. We felt an immediate connection to the officer as he leaned in and listened with interest and sympathy, more like a social worker than our personal stereotype of a policeman. We were amazed that what became immediately apparent was that we could work together in Pete's best interest.

Having seen him often biking around to odd jobs in the neighborhood, Officer Williams knew Pete. Like many in his family, Pete couldn't afford a car or had a license suspended for failure to pay fines. He bicycled everywhere, ten to twenty miles in a day if necessary.

Officer Williams had a feeling for Pete's plight—a simple, struggling soul trying to live like an independent adult in spite of his severe challenges. Certain that any time in the county jail would not improve him in any way, we requested that the police not arrest Pete or charge him with a crime. Imagine our astonishment when Officer Williams agreed to all of our requests, and in addition he agreed to keep an eye on Pete, whom he was likely to see around town soon.

We were mutually dumbfounded by each other's responses. Pete had stolen from us, but we sought no punishment for the crime. The police officer with a gun on his hip, hired to protect the public, seemed in perfect agreement with us that what Pete needed was steady paid work, not more jail time. He was already on parole, and he could land another six months for the current violation.

Although Pete's theft clearly violated his parole, neither Suzanne nor I nor, more unbelievably, Country Bank pressed charges. Pete was about to receive a most remarkable alternative sentence as the violated parties and the police chose to look the compassionate, nonpunitive, other way. We shook hands with that most amazing cop and agreed to keep in touch as Pete's life continued to unfold.

A few days passed before we returned to Pete's apartment and found him there. He admitted everything. His emotional life and mental struggles prevented him from expressing remorse except for the look of guilt on his face. A heartfelt apology, we knew, would have been too much to expect from him.

Pete's lack of emotion flowed from a childhood of abuse, bullying, and mental illness. Because Pete lived his life on the defensive and in fear of punishment, he had no inclination toward apology or admission of wrongdoing that would have undoubtedly increased his sentence in a court of law.

We didn't want to leave without reminding him that he still owed Country Bank two thousand dollars. He listened intently, but we knew that his daily survival struggle and the constant pain of rejection left him emotionally incapable of making commitments. Still, we reassured Pete that if he ever needed help, especially in an emergency, we remained open to assisting him.

My greatest fear in our work is of being worn down by the Petes of this world—not of becoming cynical, just sometimes feeling exhausted and overwhelmed. Our world produces and then neglects so many Petes, and my instinct is to protect myself from their overwhelming demands.

Three months went by. Then Palmer police informed us of a court hearing regarding Pete's parole status. I went to the hearing as a character witness to meet with his parole officer and check on his legal status. As I drove down Route 9 headed for the East

Brookfield Courthouse, I spotted none other than Pete Stone himself standing on my side of the road hitching a ride.

I picked him up, and he filled me in on his life and status with the court with his halting, innocent, almost giddy enthusiasm. After we arrived at the courthouse, I met with court officials and Pete's parole officer to finalize our involvement in the case. With no formal charges, there were no violation of parole, future imprisonment, nor official record of felony theft. The great Agape heist never reached the status of a crime.

Ten years after the incident, I ran into Pete, who shared with great pride and enthusiasm that he drives his own car, pays rent in a local apartment, and works full time as a paid farm hand.

The Pete Stone story shines as a test case for true rehabilitation. All four people of social and economic advantage—the bank officer, Officer Williams, Suzanne and I—were the first to be rehabilitated.

Healing the Violence of Prison

Toward the end of our first year of building Francis House, we got a call from Phyllis, a female chaplain for the men of Massachusetts Correctional Institution-Norfolk, a medium security facility where I had been teaching a program on nonviolent conflict resolution for the inmates. She informed me that an inmate named Mike was to be released on parole after a twelve-year prison sentence. I had gotten particularly close to Mike during the six months I met and worked with the men at the jail on how to reduce violence in that most violent of institutions. The call came as a total surprise as Mike was not up for parole for another three years.

His crime was bizarre and horrifying. It unfolded as he was being tried on a misdemeanor when Mike showed up for the court hearing with a concealed handgun. He started shooting randomly around the courthouse building. Thankfully, no one was killed or wounded, and he got a twelve-year sentence for his potentially lethal outburst.

The chaplain explained that Mike had forty-eight hours to find a place to land, and typical of most parolees, he had zero dollars in his pocket. We had no experience taking former inmates into the Agape community after their release, but we did know that a good transition was key in helping inmates break the cycle of prison-parole-prison.

When Mike's father was informed that Mike was to be released on parole, he filed a restraining order. My guess is that Mike probably didn't have one visit for the ten years he was in Norfolk, a familiar burden for those doing hefty prison terms for violent crimes. Their crimes often result in severing of family ties and contacts.

Our decision to take a newly released inmate with a violent background and prison history was fraught with difficulty. We discussed whether Agape as a community could shelter a homeless and desperate man, risking personal safety and possibly that of our child, Teresa, as well as jeopardizing the safety of others who lived at Agape.

Almost every family I observed throughout my entire life, including my own family, prized security and safety first. Growing up, I had never met anyone who would even consider visiting someone in prison, much less invite that person home upon release from prison after committing a violent crime.

Here we were at Agape, a community of seven years, inspired by Matthew 25, "I was a prisoner and you visited me." We felt inclined to respond to Phyllis's request: "Can you take Mike in?" Still, the unknowns were total, and Teresa was just five years old. Phyllis reassured us that housing would be for twenty-four hours or, maximum, forty-eight, which gave us some wiggle room . . . not a long stay, with Phyllis's pledge to support the entire process.

Still, we had to calculate the risks, and as with all moral dilemmas, that one was not destined to be a neat and clean either/ or decision: either we never invite a poor and wounded person into our home and community because of potential danger or we do so and inevitably risk possible harm to our daughter, college students, and interns who live with us at Agape.

I had known Mike for a year and saw no red flags in his personality when it came to aggression. Phyllis had counseled and befriended him for five years and insisted that Mike was not a risk for violence. I trusted her convincing tone. We wanted our decision to be a Gospel response to "house the homeless," but we also saw the need to be vigilant about ego calling to heroic impulse and willed blindness. We knew that if we took Mike in, we would have to watch him closely. Brand new at this, both Suzanne and I felt ungrounded and wary. It took a week of discernment to be confident that the move was appropriate and safe. We decided on the forty-eight-hour, go-with-it option, with Phyllis at the ready.

Mike had been in prison for a decade. When he arrived at Agape, we were finishing building Francis House. Life at Agape was a rude awakening for someone with Mike's personality-a born talker and thinker and not inclined to physical work of any kind. Overweight from an unhealthy and sedentary ten years in prison, Mike's body had become the scaffolding that held up his over-active brain. He was reluctant to work on our dawn-to-dusk building project. He eventually helped me put up a few wooden walls that called for measuring and cutting.

However, I treasure a lasting image of Mike, a burly forty-year-old man hauling gigantic oak logs out of the deep woods, securing our supply of heat for the coming winter. Satisfaction was written all over his face one summer day when physical rigor caused sweat to pour down his brow like a healing cleanse. Lifting the mighty oaks had to be a great stress reducer, a spiritual release from his lifelong pattern of just talking and thinking all day and not getting much done.

But like a few other male former inmates and homeless who lived with us at other times, Mike was reluctant to work on a daily schedule. After years of nothing to do but watch television and banter with the men, Mike suffered from fear of work, of being told what to do, and of "not knowing how to do anything."

Mike's fundamental contribution on and off the building site involved acting as court jester. Well read with a razor-sharp intellect, he delivered nonstop real-life commentary, peppered with hilarious one liners. He didn't possess a verbal pause button even when working.

He loved political satire. One of Mike's serious interior decorating proposals? Place life-size murals of Arnold Schwarzenegger as the Terminator and Sylvester Stallone as Rambo on the eight-by-ten-foot main bathroom wall to guarantee, in his words, "Better shock value than reading magazines while we do our business."

He and Teresa enjoyed each other's company, and one of his favorite activities was to teach her some of the silliest classic sixties songs. Teresa loved to hear him belt out, "oo-ee-oo-ahh-ahh, ting-tang, walla-walla-bing–bang." They both danced, with Teresa memorizing these inane, catchy lyrics. Watching him with Teresa, I sensed his comfort with a child and imagined all of the harsh judgments he had likely received from adults, especially his father.

Dan, our carpenter, resided at Agape and accepted Mike as a housemate. Suzanne found Mike difficult. He wore her down, especially after the initial forty-eight hours turned into a week, and then one month followed another.

Because of Mike's broken and violent life and the extremity of a long jail sentence into his late thirties, he had a hard time trusting people enough to tell the truth about himself and his past. We discovered after he left that he had fabricated a Vietnam combat veteran history. Feigning sadness, he shared the false story with me while I taught him in prison. He sounded convincing enough, and I readily accepted that his service might explain his mood swings from manic talking to depression.

A central issue emerged around Mike's residency with us and recurred repeatedly over our years in community: When a person is invited into the community out of need and extremity, how much mental and emotional illness can we handle? Mike's nonstop talking and perpetual, seemingly obsessive-compulsive movements led Suzanne to conclude that she could no longer continue to live in the same community with him.

Suzanne had expected Mike to move on after the first week, and it became two months. Unity around living with difficult people is always the most challenging task in community second only to disagreements around money.

It was Suzanne's strong view that "We are not a therapeutic community." I sensed her desire to relate to people who live in community as contributors to the process. Unstable people who display chronic, emotionally draining patterns of relating and who are unlikely to change make for ongoing turmoil and stress in community.

Everything in the message of Matthew 25, "I was a stranger and you invited me in," inspires and compels us to open our community door to those who knock. We saw the Gospel relevance, but in Mike's case, Suzanne felt obligated to "stretch and stretch and stretch" beyond what we were capable of. Such are the excruciating demands of open-door hospitality.

Such dilemmas revealed a hidden fact to me about living with others: I too am difficult to live with, my love is more conditional than I want to admit, and I tend to hide that fact by denying it when I feel unmanageable feelings brewing inside.

So, although I sense Mike benefited from his time at Agape while contributing as he did to community life, we found other lodging for him in nearby Worcester. Eventually he ended up with friends in Canada who had a bad experience with him, including theft and other borderline behavior.

Like others we have known with broken histories, Mike fell completely out of contact, no doubt wandering from place to place. When folks like Mike disappear, I always assume the worst.

After his departure and after a much-needed rest, we prayed for Mike's well-being and for our ability to grow in acceptance, especially of the wounded ones among us. We continue to be guided by the God of Matthew's Gospel who tells us: "What you did to the least of these you did to me." (Matthew 25:40).

Invasion of Afghanistan and Iraq

Suzanne

September 11 shaped the thoughts, prayers, and actions at Agape and other nonviolent communities in ways unique to the enormity and scope of the devastation. We petitioned and marched to forestall invasion and retaliation. Many peacemakers waded in the murky waters of guilt, blame, and complicity in the build-up to disproportionate military response. The nation was in trauma as images of fellow citizens jumping out of windows and of New York towers burning dazed the country into a period of prolonged mourning and fear.

In the dark post-9/11 days, it seemed possible that massive global protests could temper escalated US rhetoric of preparation for bombing Afghanistan (even though no Afghans had been involved in the catastrophe). The rubble of the Trade Towers buried any hopes of avoiding bombing as Bush's build-up to all-out military response became increasingly more evident. Pleas of millions throughout the globe for nonretaliation evaporated into Bush's denigrating words as his adherents called massive numbers of people in world-wide resistance and especially here at home "focus groups."

Bush stonewalled humanitarian concerns in a horrifying prelude to the March, 2003, Shock and Awe blitzkrieg of Iraq almost two years later. Reporters covered the Shock and Awe campaign as if it were a video game, with breathless commentary on the glow from the fires burning people and buildings in Baghdad. For the most part, the government ignored, vilified, or censored pacifists. Much of the nation, including the press and religious spokespersons, seemed bent on revenge either overtly or by the complicity of silence.

Shortly after and leading up to the October 7 bombing of Afghanistan, peace communities all over the country rallied and met with Muslim and Arab sisters and brothers. We at Agape wanted to lend sympathy and support to the Muslim community in Massachusetts as fear and anxiety about attacks on Muslims escalated. The press reported daily incidents of Islamophobia.

We held an open, public forum at Agape after calling together extended community members while we invited imams and Muslim community members from the greater Springfield, Worcester, and Boston area to speak about their faith and predicament as we listened and offered support. The evening of Compassionate Listening to Muslim Sisters and Brothers took place in the Francis House living room packed with more than eighty people. The atmosphere was charged with outrage, despair, and a sense of powerlessness.

One local imam, voice quavering, spoke about holding his children's trembling hands as they walked in their community and he escorted them to school. With good reason, his children were afraid of being attacked. Many in local Muslim communities were keeping their children out of school. We all had heard from a general or a member of the administration of the US intent to bomb Afghanistan. It reminded us of the threat from the Vietnam-era US general Curtis LeMay, who said, "Bomb them into the Stone Age."

We at Agape were taking the unpopular stand that, as nonviolent Christians, we were holding to Jesus and the Gospel of nonretaliation. Like Dorothy Day and the Catholic Worker after the US entry into WWII, we would not be moved from what Dorothy called "Our Manifesto, the Sermon on the Mount." Jesus didn't present a conveniently disposable set of principles when war breaks out. He acted on and modeled for all of us the consequence of adhering to a doctrine of radical love: suffering, maybe even death, but certainly, refusal to cooperate.

From the late seventies, we adhered to Gospel nonviolence, nonretaliation, compassionate listening, dialogue, and resistance.

Why would we abandon Jesus after 9/11? Why would we abandon his teachings and our adherence to them after the singularly worst terrorist attack on American soil? Some, especially prelates in the US, did just that. We knew a deep, personal, collective moral response was required from religious pacifists. We began calling our peace community friends to garner a consensus on what to do.

Immediately after 9/11, Pope John Paul II was reported to have paced like a caged lion, so opposed was he to the invasion of Afghanistan on October 7, 2001. During that post-9/11 period, Agape sponsored a trip to Assisi, Italy, home of Saint Francis, our nonviolent saint/mentor and patron saint of ecology. In Assisi in January 2002, seven peacemakers from Massachusetts—including us—joined the Pope in his Interfaith Day for Peace along with representatives of all the major world religions from throughout the globe.

The timing seemed obvious to us. Pope John Paul II opposed the invasion of Afghanistan, so we traveled to support him and stand in opposition to the already-ongoing blood bath named the War on Terror by the George W. Bush administration.

We leafleted tourists and locals with fliers that read, "The prophetic call of Jesus through to Saint Francis does not call us to kill our enemies but rather to love them." The Assisi police could not have been more cordial.

We carried our vigil to Vatican Square in Rome where, after an hour of protest with our large banner reading, "We US Catholics to our Church Say No to War on Terrorism," the Vatican police called a halt to the witness.

With its pulverizing precision bombs, the US claimed to save Afghanistan from the Taliban, thus exposing the great lie of redemptive violence. Cardinal Bernard Law, chairman of the International Peace and Justice Committee of the American Conference of Catholic Bishops, functioned as a major power broker in the war games. Ethical relativity, which he and the Vatican unsparingly castigated when applied to abortion,

Agape vigils in Assisi to say, "No to war on terrorism."
Vigilers include, from left, Suzanne, Sister Irene Comeau, Cornelia Sullivan,
and Brayton, who stands over the word "Catholics."

women's ordination, or issues of sexual identity and morality, became the hypocritical sine qua non when applied to post-9/11 ethical stumbling over war. We are a pro-life Church except in the case of invading another country and applying standards of just war to such an invasion.

In his pastoral message, "Living with Faith and Hope after September 11," Cardinal Law pledged his allegiance to the war machine when he said, "We are in solidarity with our president in prayer and in love of our country." Further, as one of America's foremost prelates, Cardinal Law underscored his willingness to smoke out the "evil ones" by whatever means necessary. In other words, when all is said and done theologically, the ends do justify the means.

So, what does pro-life really mean? Not much except ongoing ethical relativity, over which American Catholic bishops rail and pontificate. Parishes nationally passed out pamphlets asking parishioners to sign cards condemning abortion as they exited Catholic churches. No such cards were visible in the condemnation of bombing Afghanistan and Iraq. In fact, many Christian leaders from across the religious spectrum delivered carefully nuanced homilies in open support of pulverizing Afghanistan and Iraq. Others wrapped the horrific deeds in a blanket of complicit silence.

Meanwhile, body-piercing fifty-thousand-pound Daisy cutters, grotesquely described with detached monotony by gloating generals, blew apart our cave-dwelling so-called enemies and any civilians who happened to be in the trajectory of an errant "smart" bomb.

The Birth of the Catholic Call to Peacemaking

At Agape, we pondered our response nationally with Pax Christi, Catholic Peace Fellowship, Quakers and other peace organizations and communities as the challenge became startlingly clear. We had to issue a call for our Christian churches to "come back to the teachings of Jesus."

Jesus took his message of unconditional love to Jerusalem, so too we nonviolent Christians needed to take our message of nonviolence to our Catholic bishops and fellow congregants. We realized that a national call to nonviolence would be met, in some quarters with derision and dismissal. Our treatment would not be different from that of Jesus: "They laughed at him." (Mark 5:40)

Thus, momentum grew for what we saw as a need for an unambiguous proclamation—a definitive, unapologetic statement from Catholics who adhered to nonviolence. We encouraged friends in other faith communities to do the same or to sign our document which we named the Catholic Call to Peacemaking. Edited and eventually endorsed by Pax Christi New England and Agape, the document represented hundreds of other constituents.

Through a coalition of Catholic religious orders and groups dedicated to peace and justice, we created and published a nonviolent manifesto eventually signed by more than two thousand peacemakers nationally and internationally. We included a call that asked the question, "Will our hearts become large enough as Christians to embrace Jesus who will deliver us from the violence of revenge and give us the courage to pray for those who hate us?" (Matthew 5:44)

We encouraged signers to take the message symbolically to Jerusalem, to their local churches, as many in the peace movement were doing nationally. One example of such an effort was that of Paul McNeil, a member of Agape's mission council from Spencer, Massachusetts, who stood at a table across the street from his parish to ask for signatures on the document we had christened the Catholic Call to Peacemaking. Without signing, fellow worshipers streamed past him. Some angrily ignored him or muttered under their breath as they walked by.

Not all responses were negative. For example, Father Henry Donoghue of St. George's Parish in Worcester, with the assistance of John Paul Marosy, also a member of the Agape mission council, printed the Catholic Call in the church bulletin. The Jesuit School of Theology at Santa Clara University in California signed on through the efforts of Father David Gill, a Jesuit and Agape's chaplain. Brothers Philip and Daniel Berrigan signed as did Liz McAlister. Hundreds of women religious joined the call. The Catholic Call to Peacemaking evangelized Gospel nonviolence, by prophetically requesting the rejection of war while United States Catholic bishops affirmed the bombing of Afghanistan with "regret" on November 14, 2001.

The vote among bishops was a shameful 167 to 4. Long-time pacifist and friend of Agape, the Melkite bishop John Botean whose mentor Charlie McCarthy assisted in crafting wording of the call, became, along with Roman Catholic Bishop Thomas Gumbleton of Detroit, singular voices of dissent among disgraceful support. Bishop Gumbleton publicly queried his fellow bishops in the US, "When we discuss violence elsewhere, we urge a return to negotiation, not to violence. Why, then, aren't we applying this standard to the US?"

We intended the document to be used as a teaching tool in colleges and universities and other Catholic institutions. We knew that our little effort would not have a definitive impact, but our intent was clear: "Thou shalt not kill" does not admit to exceptions.

Father Bryan Hehir, America's defender of the just war theory, meticulously articulated the muddled, contradictory, and ancient distinctions of just war. He offered qualified support of the invasion of Afghanistan and Iraq as "just but unwise" and guided many theologians into the same ethical quagmire.

Witness at Holy Cross Cathedral in Boston

On the Feast of the Holy Family in December, 2001, Pax Christi, Agape, the House of Peace, and others in the extended Catholic community carried a banner to Boston's Holy Cross Cathedral that read, "Would Jesus Bless the Bombing of the Holy Families of Afghanistan?" We knew that Cardinal Law would be presiding over mass there and had the full intention of confronting him. A handful of about twenty of us stood in front of the cathedral as people streamed in for mass. As people walked past, we carried framed pictures of refugees and victims of American bombing making mostly futile efforts to pass out copies of the Catholic Call to Peacemaking.

John Schuchardt of the Ipswich, Massachusetts House of Peace, Tom Lewis, and Father Emmanuel Charles McCarthy, from left, hold a banner in front of Boston's Holy Cross Cathedral in December, 2001, during the Christmas season and soon after the US invasion of Afghanistan. The banner reads, "Would Jesus bless the bombing of the Holy Families of Afghanistan?"

We had discussed the possibility of interrupting the mass by kneeling on the altar with our banners but decided, instead, that some of us would attend mass and approach the cardinal afterward while others stood vigil outside where a phalanx of reporters from various news outlets showed up, cameras ready.

Mass over, Cardinal Law strode down the aisle in his medieval paraphernalia including a crozier, pointed satin hat, and flowing floor-length gown. A group of us approached the cardinal as he greeted people in the rear of the church, crozier in hand.

I could barely contain my rage as, with others, Brayton and I approached Cardinal Law. As if to amplify my displeasure, in a matter of days, the *Globe* Spotlight team accused the besieged cardinal of covering up sexual abuse of minors by many priests in the archdiocese.

Brayton engaged Cardinal Law first and thanked him for condemning the death penalty in several public forums in Boston.

photo copyright by Skip Schiel

Brayton engages Cardinal Bernard Law at Boston's
Holy Cross Cathedral and encourages him to urge the
Church to condemn all war.

The cardinal seemed pleased as he leaned in toward Brayton to grasp his hand. Brayton followed with, "Now isn't it time that we as a Church condemn all war?"

Law drew Brayton's hand into his chest and said, "Please read the catechism." Cardinal Law played a major role in promulgation of the *Catechism of the Catholic Church,* according to his obituary in *The National Catholic Register* and served as chairman of the Bishops' Committee on International Policy.

I responded, "I *have* read the catechism on war. It contradicts the teachings of Christ." Cameras clicked and buzzed. Seemingly rattled and eager to flee, Cardinal Law started moving away. That night, local television stations highlighted the action at the cathedral. Agape's phone began to ring off the hook with invitations from right-wing radio talk show hosts seeking to interview us to invalidate our position.

Ray Flynn, former mayor of Boston, Bill Clinton's ambassador to the Vatican, and a Dorothy-Day-inspired Catholic, called Agape. He interviewed Brayton for his radio talk show on Boston's WRKO and clearly endorsed Agape's antiwar position.

Witness—Invasion of Afghanistan and Iraq

Leading up to America's invasion of Iraq, we at Agape with many friends and area peacemakers held weekly vigils in nearby small towns of Barre, Ware, Spencer, and West Brookfield as pick-up trucks resembling covered wagons and boasting American flags on poles, drove by us. Some drivers shouted, "Kill 'em all."

While we vigiled in Ware, one man walked over to us and asked menacingly, "Why are you here?"

"We are opposed to the invasion of Iraq. We think there is a more peaceful way," we replied.

Fuming, he moved closer to us and said, "I'm gonna kill you. I'm gonna kill all of you."

As the US invasion of Iraq became more certain, we received a call from Dot Walsh and Lewis Randa of the Peace Abbey,

Suzanne, left, and Brayton, right, flank the Peace Chain 18 antiwar witness at Natick's Biological Chemical Command Center in Natick on March 22, 2003, two days after the US invasion of Iraq.

Sherborn, Massachusetts, inviting Agape to an arrest action in nearby Natick at the US Army Soldier and Biological Chemical Command. The witness was scheduled for March 20, the day that the US unleashed the incomprehensibly evil, Shock and Awe saturation bombing of Baghdad.

The very existence of the US Army Soldier and Biological Chemical Command Center in Natick underscored the lying hypocrisy of our invasion of Iraq. The facility, in Boston's backyard, was orchestrating our country's research and design of weapons of mass destruction and biological warfare.

We decided on a simple civil disobedience scenario. Each of the eighteen of us planning to risk arrest would carry chains through Natick Center to the gates of the United States Biological Chemical Command Center. We dubbed our group the Peacechain 18. In our prayer ritual observed by police in riot gear, we looped our chains around each other's arms as we crossed the line onto base property after the police read a no-trespass order.

Together with supporters who did not risk arrest, we intoned prayers from every faith tradition as we scattered pictures of wounded Iraqi children before us on a red carpet we placed on the ground to symbolize spilled blood.

We were arrested and booked on trespass charges.

Meanwhile, the war criminal, the US vice-president, Dick Cheney, called the invasion "one of the most extraordinary military campaigns ever conducted."

On Trial

The trial phase of our witness at biological chemical command was preceded by a moving walk of defendants and friends through downtown Natick. On June 26, 2003, in the antiseptic tedium of the courtroom, five of us fully expected jail time of possibly up to a month. We had decided not to pay a fifty-dollar fine nor to accept Judge Sarah Singer's offer of community service, which we acknowledged with gratitude as we reiterated that we were all already engaged in community service as a way of life.

We were shocked and relieved when Judge Singer, whom we learned had gone to Boston College, refused to send us to jail. Rather, her legal response was "Continued without a finding."

Unintended Consequences:
Arrest on Day Three of the Iraq Invasion

It was an unseasonably sweltering spring day. Brayton was on his fourth day of water fast with many others. With insanely moderated regularity, media coverage of scenes of death played out on the airwaves with instant replay of the burning of Baghdad and little or no resistance from thousands of Iraqi troops eviscerated by our bunker-busting bombs.

On the third day of the invasion, March 24, just two days after our arrests in Natick, we joined in a walk with several thousands of peacemakers. The walk was later reported as one of the largest protests in the country at the time with opponents of the war

Brayton and Suzanne, left, with monks and nuns from the
New England Peace Pagoda of Leverett, Massachusetts,
risk arrest on March 24, 2003, at Chicopee, Massachusetts,
Westover Air Force Base to protest the March 20, US invasion of Iraq.

streaming in in all directions to Westover Air Force Base in Chicopee, Massachusetts.

Our sixteen-year-old daughter, Teresa, had mixed feelings about her parents being arrested two days earlier in the Natick protest. Nevertheless, she traveled on bus trips to DC and New York with us for massive protests and proudly announced her antiwar views and reported her parents' arrest at school.

Teresa wrote an article for the Agape newspaper *Servant Song*:

My parents were going to a protest witness, and they picked me up after a sleepover at a friend's house and couldn't take me home because they were going to speak at the rally. I didn't want to be there. I was feeling tired, and I don't like to be forced to be at anything. When the protest began, I started to feel much better about supporting the atmosphere.

Then I saw my dad walk out the gate to where the police were. I started to get nervous. Then, before you know it, my mom was in the crowd of the people being arrested. Then I saw (Agape) interns David and Michelle, my friends, joining in. I thought, "Oh, my God. What is happening?" The scene was very intense. There was drumming and a line of police giving orders.

My first thought was "Oh, my God, who is going to bring me home?"

Then I spotted Simon, another intern and friend, and he said, "I think I'll be driving you home."

We learned that, to feed the voracious war machine in Iraq, equipment and personnel were being flown in cargo planes we could see overhead. The shipment included laser-guided tanks and soldiers in forty-pound protective gear—some of it made, we learned, at Natick where we had recently been arrested.

As we approached the crowds at Westover, we joined with a chanting, flute-playing, youthful, orderly crowd as it eventually grew into two thousand. I was struck by the solemnity of the participants. My grief and sorrow were heightened by the steady chanting of our soulmates and family of friends since the seventies, Sister Clare Carter and Gyoway Kato, Shonin, of the Buddhist New England Peace Pagoda. Kato stopped drumming and pointed to the violated sky.

We walked with Kato and Clare toward the line of police at the base entrance. A mixture of tension and purpose filled the air. We knew that many had pledged to be arrested. A large number of officers casually stood guard near the stage area where a permit had been granted for speeches and songs.

The sound of hundreds of feet hitting pavement and the Buddhist chanting underscored America's depravity. Well-orchestrated affinity groups moved forward for preplanned risking of arrest to weave a web of resistance, linking and binding each other with colorful yarn.

Sensing the drama of the moment and seeing Brayton in the distance, I hurried back to ask friends from the House of Peace and the Peace Pagoda. "Should we join? Should we sit down in front of the police?"

Interns Simon Doolittle and Jeanine Heing, from left, wait with Teresa, right, for her parents after their arrest at Westover in March, 2003.

We all agreed the time had arrived. Kato pointed his drumstick towards Brayton and said, "You lead. You begin."

The Jesus prayer accelerated, as did my heartbeat, as we approached the police line. I felt profoundly the rightness of our spirit-led spontaneity. Looking back from my kneeling position next to Brayton, I spotted David Hammer, Michelle Carty, and Jeanine Heing, all former interns at Agape, their youthful faces etched in sorrow as they knelt to join us.

I searched the crowd for Teresa, hoping to catch a glimpse of her before I would be arrested. Turning around from my kneeling position in front of the police, I finally spotted her. She looked apprehensive and nervous standing next to Simon, our intern. I thought, Teresa! Then I lost Teresa's face.

In the *Servant Song* article, Teresa comments:

> I heard the police say, "You have ten seconds to move, or you will be arrested."

Then I looked over and saw my dad and mom being taken away. I had a surge of violent feelings because I wanted to keep my parents from being arrested. I had no control over what was happening. I am still proud of them for being arrested, but in the future, I suggest they wait until I'm older and I have the choice of joining them or just leaving.

Aftermath

Many courtroom appearances with pro bono lawyers prepared us for a jury trial for the Westover action. The trial dragged on for a year. Finally, the ten of us arrested in our group came to trial and were found guilty of trespass. Again, a sympathetic judge refused to sentence us. We all went free, but the world had changed. Nothing would be the same again.

The Children of War

Brayton

I was working on some stone masonry at Brigid house, our straw-bale second residence at Agape, when Jeanine Heine, a former intern, came up to me excitedly and said, "Sabah and Omar want to come to Agape's Francis Day." She filled me in on the Iraqi family's story.

Jeanine had met Zahara, a young Iraqi activist who was living in the US. Through Zahara, Jeanine was introduced to an Iraqi family, Sabah Kader and his four-year-old son, Omar. Sabah and Omar were residing at Boston Children's Hospital, where Omar received treatments for burns over sixty percent of his body, the direct result of an American attack on the family's vehicle when they lived in Iraq.

In 2005, the four members of Sabah's family were traveling with another Iraqi family in Mosul, when American soldiers attempted to stop the van at a checkpoint. The US military began firing on them.

Sabah opened the car door to pull his son Ali from the wreckage and was shot by American forces. He then returned to rescue Omar, who was sitting on his mother Suad's lap, and pulled him from the burning van. Again, Sabah was shot. One more time,

Mahatma Gandhi's grandson, Arun Gandhi, left, spoke at
Agape's Francis Day in 2005. He converses with, from left, Ahmad al Hadidi,
Sabah Kader, and Bob Thiefels.

he turned back to rescue Suad from a car engulfed in flames. He
could not save her. Sabah has hundreds of pieces of shrapnel
in his back that cannot be removed, thus resulting in medical
complications and continuing hospitalizations. The US attack on
their country killed and injured tens of thousands of innocent
Iraqi civilians.

We finally met Sabah and Omar during Agape's twenty-fifth
anniversary Francis Day celebration featuring Arun Gandhi,
grandson of the Mahatma. Up the driveway came Sabah, Omar,
and their good friend Ahmad, an Iraqi doctor who arrived in the
US on a Fulbright scholarship a few years before Sabah and Omar
arrived. Sabah was a friendly-looking man with a gentle smile
speaking only rudimentary English.

With his warm smile and engaging way, Ahmad had the
advantage of perfect English, having grown up learning the

language in Iraqi schools and then studying in the US. We spent some time introducing ourselves and orienting the family to the Agape Francis Day scene, a beehive of activity with hundreds of people milling around.

Then Omar walked toward me. A handsome four-year-old, he had piercing brown eyes and a determined gaze. He grabbed my hand and insisted, "Come with me." His hand grip felt firm despite his missing thumb and pinky finger, his palm tight and swollen with scar tissue. I was completely taken by such an unusually assertive four-year-old boy.

We immediately bonded as he demanded my full attention insisting we look for frogs in the Agape pond.

A year after Sabah's arrival in the US, Omar and his father were joined by his ten-year-old brother. Ali had been living with family in war-torn Iraq while waiting to be reunited with his dad and brother. They all lived together in a small one-bedroom apartment

Omar, left, and his brother Ali dance at Agape with members of Sal Y Luz, a group of Dominican young adults from New York City.

at John Leary House, an apartment building for the poor under the auspices of Haley House and named after our good friend John Leary, who had died suddenly more than twenty years earlier.

A year later, Kathy Kelly, founder of Voices in the Wilderness who has spent years visiting and aiding people in Iraq, joined us for a Francis Day dedicated to Jewish, Christian, and Muslim dialogue and reconciliation. Through her connections with people assisting war-ravaged Iraq, Kathy knew Sabah's family.

What I remember most vividly that day is watching Kathy spending every moment of her free time playing with Omar and Ali. Kathy ran with them, round and round in circles, then pushed them both on our swings as they all laughed in delight.

Over the next two years, Sabah grew close to us, reminding us often, "You are like my family. You *are* my family. We miss our own family back in Mosul, but we can never go back. There is no medical help in Iraq that can compare to America. I need special care that I can only get at Mass General." As a result of the shrapnel remaining in his body, Sabah suffers from bacterial infections along with painful emotional trauma. Combined treatment of Omar and Sabah may take years, Ahmad informed us. "Omar will need ongoing burn treatments and plastic surgery that he can get only in Boston where the cost is covered."

Sabah often shared how he missed his late wife, Suad, but without any observable bitterness towards us as US citizens, the agents of his misery. His biggest battle was fulfilling the role of single father to his two wounded, demanding boys. Nothing in his cultural background as an Iraqi working-class family man prepared him for the hands-on role he now had as a full-time single parent with unrelenting responsibilities.

He found himself a refugee in the country which was responsible for his sorrows. Trauma-stricken himself, Sabah continually found parenting overwhelming with Omar's frequent surgeries as well as his own hospitalizations. I was struck by the fact that Sabah never expressed even a hint of angry resentment towards us, his adopted family.

Through it all, we felt the privilege of being family to Sabah, his boys, and Ahmad, who acted as both brother to Sabah and uncle to the boys. Ahmad, too, had a family in Mosul, Iraq, and he often said, "Sabah is like my brother."

Neither Sabah nor Ahmad felt it politically safe to go back to Mosul after we of the US blew the social and political fabric apart into a murderous civil war among Shia and Sunni Muslims. Ahmad felt it could be life threatening for them to attempt a return to Mosul, with its radical anti-American sensibilities, especially after having lived in the US. They all decided to continue their stay in Boston and pursue American citizenship.

Fire Is My Friend

Suzanne and I traveled with Sabah, Ali, and Omar to New York City for a Christmas weekend. We all stayed with Tom Wilhelm, whose home overlooks a breathtaking stretch of Hudson River north of Manhattan. We had spent a full and exhausting day seeing holiday sights and Rockefeller Center, drinking in the magical but often dizzying New York Christmas scene, and enjoying the warmth of Tom's living room. Christmas carols were playing throughout the house while Tom prepared dinner. Life on that festive December day was unusually good. The family was at peace.

I began to bunch up newspapers to throw on the andirons along with kindling wood to start a fire in the fireplace. Omar had seen me light many bonfires and wood-burning stove fires at Agape, and the minute he saw me grab the matches, he began his usual incessant pleas. "Let me light the fire," he said. "Please, please. Come on."

It had become his job at Agape to light the wood stove with my supervision, and he had plenty of opportunities to ignite big blazes in the fire pit with me and others at Agape's special events. Today, as on other occasions, I guided Omar's hand, my hand on top of his. "Please, Omar—very careful now." With Omar's burn history, I was alternately intrigued and concerned at his

"Fire is my friend," Omar observes at the door of Agape's wood-burning stove.

fascination with fire. Was it trauma pathology, an unhealthy fascination with fire, the very flames that once had almost destroyed him? Was he tantalized by a fantasy of another conflagration?

"Why do you like fire so much, Omar?" I asked. His response was mystifying.

"Fire is my friend," he said. "I feel good around it—excitement."

"You are not afraid of being burned again?" I asked.

"Nope." Omar was always honest, direct, and did not hesitate when dealing with difficult emotions.

I pushed a little. "Do you remember the attack on your family in Iraq?" I sensed an opening and asked, "What happened?"

Omar told the entire story of bomb explosions, gun sounds, and fire with perfectly clear and articulate confidence void of high emotions or reticence. With pen and paper in hand, he sketched a picture of the attack as it unfolded. In the middle of flame, gun sites, and bombs falling, he placed his family in a van with a huge ball of fire surrounding it and taking up nearly the entire attack scene.

He drew a helicopter with one pilot and another figure in the rear seat. "That's me," he said, in a matter-of-fact tone.

His mother was gone, his father had rescued him from the burning van, and he didn't know where his brother Ali was. He penned in the helicopter and described some figures in the drawing as military personnel who took him from Sabah's arms and airlifted him to the local military hospital unit nearby.

Omar was transfixed, seemingly in a state of awe while telling his story. Unwittingly, we found ourselves in a variation of play

Omar's drawing invokes the US attack on his family.

therapy, where a therapist introduces objects of play—dolls or puzzles—to encourage traumatized children to relive what they have experienced. In the rapt stillness of the story of drama and bravery, Sabah and Ali sat motionless without comment as they listened to Omar's every word. They provided only knowing glances of sympathy.

He seemed to want to convey to us how he was not afraid of the pain he experienced, as if he announced, "I can tell you this story. I'm in it. I'm here."

Omar: Suffering of the Innocent

Suzanne

I met Omar when he was four, and I felt I was encountering Jesus. I remembered the passages about the suffering servant in the book of the prophet Isaiah in Hebrew scripture. Those passages have moved me deeply over the years as a prefiguring of the tortured Jesus.

I experienced Jesus standing before me in the innocent suffering of a child of war. Omar's ear was burned off, and the left side of his face drooped from many plastic surgeries. College students who met Omar at Agape also felt compassion when seeing him. They commented, "I never really knew what war can do until now."

When he was eight, Omar and his dad, brother Ali, and family friend Ahmad, came to our Cape Cod rental during our annual summer break. At first, everyone was filled with excitement and good energy. But the minute we hit the beach, Omar became anxious.

Walking with him on the beach at Sesuit Harbor in Dennis, I was mildly annoyed by Omar's sullen mood. He was asserting himself aggressively to get his way. "No, I'm not going there. This is the rock I want to climb. I'm staying here."

I have learned, over the years, that such a firm "No" is Omar's survival mechanism, a way he has of ordering his world over which, given the tragedy of his days, he has little say.

Eight-year-old Omar strode ahead of me on the beach, irritated, unhappy, his skinny, defaced body vulnerable and ravaged. He kicked the sand, head down amid stares and curious glances as people registered, "Whoa. This is bad. This kid is really burned. A fire?" Everyone who looked turned away quickly. Omar saw it and knew it. None of the beachcombers would likely guess his are the scars of war.

On that splendid Cape Cod day, we Americans sat contentedly with our coolers, umbrellas, and wealth. Yet, we supported the invasion of Iraq by large percentages. We are responsible for Omar's seared off ear. This is why despair and guilt covered me like the rainy afternoon fog on Slough Pond.

In biblical terms spoken of in Isaiah, I know that Sabah and Omar are "bowed down."

I wanted to retreat from such thoughts on that summer day. I wanted Omar to enjoy breathtaking beauty as boats cruised beneath the causeway stirring up the magnificence of wave and ocean. Yet, he refused to climb the gigantic jetty boulders, a favorite sport for kids. Keeping his distance from me, Omar walked further and further away so that we were beyond the range of other beachcombers. His head bowed low, his chin nearly on his chest. It amazed me that he didn't fall.

Impulsively and angrily, he kicked up sand. The sun beat down. It was hot, and he refused to wear a shirt. His scars must have hurt and burned, yet he insisted, "No shirt." I didn't understand. I didn't ask.

My rage at the world, at the people on the beach, glowed irrationally. I imagined myself stopping each staring person and screaming at them, "We did this. You and me. Us. We bombed his country, took over his city, and shot his father in the back. We did this!" Once again, Isaiah instructs and moves my understanding:

> Oppressed and condemned, he was taken away,
> and who would have thought any more of his destiny?

When he was cut off from the land of the living,
and smitten for the sin of his people. (Isaiah 53:8)

Sabah is a beautiful name, as soft and gentle as the man who owns it. Sabah and Omar are my friends. They are all Jesus to me. Sabah, so harshly wounded, seems beyond comprehension to submit to his fate in the foreign land of his oppressors. "Like a lamb led to the slaughter/or a sheep before the shearers, he was silent and opened not his mouth." (Isaiah 53:7)

I watched Omar struggle with his absent left toe to position his feet on a bogey board. He tried, fell off, and tried again. Omar continued with anger and grit navigating his life in the same way he sought to balance his body on the bogey board.

Omar is someone we might "turn away from" as Isaiah prophesies. (IS 52: 13-53: 12) A "bruised reed," he is not in the streets loudly proclaiming his affliction. His suffering is hidden and indicts our complicity in his disfigurement.

*Sabah and his boys plant a tree for Suad, his wife and their mother, at
a Francis Day observation dedicated to reconciliation of
Palestinians and Israelis.*

A Song over the Land

Only the song over the land yields blessing and commemoration."
—Ranier Maria Rilke, *Sonnets to Orpheus,* 19

Suzanne

Earth mysticism is central to our lives on the thirty-four acres of lush and compelling woods that comprise Agape. Rich Bachtold, Agape's mystic poet in nonresidence, wrote a dedicatory poem to Agape for our tenth anniversary in 1992. Rich described Agape as "a healing vision" that "sows sacred seeds in the world," thrusting them "in the midst of a barren, soulless society."

Though Rich's earthly voice is stilled, he keeps us focused on the eternal realm where he dwells and which he realized so eloquently in his poetry.

Yes, our Hardwick world is luminous and poetic. We have been awed by a moose walking past our breakfast window and lumbering up into the garden. When Teresa's bus driver came to pick Teresa up, we asked her if she wanted to see the moose footprints.

"Yes!" she gasped in disbelief. Retracing the journey of our unearthly being filled us with awe.

One morning at dawn, a bear lumbered up the driveway in view of Carl, our campus minister from Iona College in New York. Carl approached me in his pajamas, breathless at the sight of a brown bear purposefully striding on all fours towards our garden shed. We watched as the bear, drawn by the scent of the five-gallon jug of vegetable oil we used for our grease car, bit a deep hole into the container, raised it over his head, and sucked out the remnants of the grease. Satisfied, the bear continued to make his way up the hill behind the house. Such preternatural creatures are mysteriously beckoned by the almost life-size statue of Saint Francis of Assisi that graces the Agape porch.

The beating heart of the earth is alive in every prayer circle and bonfire on this Quabbin land, named "many waters" by Nipmuc Indians. We are privy to many hands touching the soil to become the garden that will feed us from the spring equinox to the winter solstice. The sacrificial wood of the trees reminds us of how such a

Arun Gandhi prepares to lead singing in the Agape chapel.

living force of nature offers itself to warm those in the community gathered in the deep winter months. In our chapel, constructed with trees from this land, we experienced the mysticism of hearing Arun Gandhi, grandson of Mahatma Gandhi, singing "Lead Kindly Light," Arun's grandfather's favorite Christian hymn.

Another of our departed earth mystics, Bruce Davidson, prayed over a mighty oak tree we had considered cutting in the front of Agape property. Conversant with the language of trees, Bruce spoke to the Agape oak and asked, "Is it your wish for us to take you?"

"Only in reverence," Bruce heard. Bruce and the oak remain with us, speaking powerfully still, one of them from the other world and one from the circle in front of Francis House.

Dark Beauty

We mark advent evenings at Agape with the candlelit Francis House interior. I remember a time when seventy individuals

213

emerged into unprotected cold. We encircled the hand-hewn tree-stump seats in the large fire pit. Always breathtaking in its splendor, that breath infused us, imprinting its life-force in our souls. I wrote

> . . . twenty degrees below zero.
> Beauty descends
> from that cosmic place/of interbeing and time/that is not time.
> . . . Now, the stark birches
> stand watch over
> the fire circle with its stumps
> where hundreds have stood
> before roaring logs
> to look up at cold bursts of stars.

As we walked in procession to Francis House, we chanted into the night, "Maranatha. Come, Jesus. Maranatha."

The solemnity of the season lit people's faces that night as it always does.

The Feast of the Patron Saint of Art

Brigid, patroness of poetry and hospitality, whispered to us through the centuries from her monastery for men and women in Kildare, Ireland. Bequeathed to us by the monastery caretaker in memory of our visit to the Brigid enclosure, a stone from her bell tower has become a keystone of the hearth in the Agape straw-bale house.

Walking in silence into the still night, we lit the passageway from Francis House with luminary lanterns to the straw-bale house, named after Saint Brigid. We stopped to create a prayer circle under the winter sky. Then, our voices called out into the darkness,

> Brigid, Keeper of the Hearth, kindle us. Beneath your mantle, gather us, and restore us to memory. Mothers of our mother, foremothers strong, guide our hands in yours. In this tired world, remind us how to kindle the hearth, from dawn till dark, from dark till dawn.

Some seventy of us walked to the door of Brigid House, where a statue of Brigid stands on the threshold, waiting, dressed in a long

Celebrants of Saint Brigid's feast day gather at a February bonfire at Agape.

robe. We knocked and called out, "Midwife of Mystery, open the door." Once Brigid allowed us entry, we heard the lively music of the Celts played by Fred and Rose Higgins. Fred himself, Scottish stonemason, helped build Agape's Saint Brigid home.

The undulating stucco interior of straw bales reverberated together with the crisp songs of mandolin and guitar. We honored the poetic angles of the architecture, inspiring a line from my tenth anniversary poem, "We build a house to hallow the hearts of those who enter." We know that beauty is the antidote to violence and fear. Our community homestead reflects the art of green living.

Our lives are dedicated to poetry and song. Lady Poetry compels us to internalize the words of Wendell Berry, who says, "My most inspiring thought is that this place, if I am to live well in it, requires and deserves a lifetime of the most careful attention." We pay attention. Our attention leads to ineffable mystery. Saint Paul writes in Ephesians 3:7 of the fruits of focus, as we apprehend "the unfathomable treasure of Christ and of throwing light on the inner workings of the mystery kept hidden through all the ages in God, the Creator of everything."

Some inner workings Saint Paul observes shine through to the world in the experience of the young, like Samantha Leuschner, who writes:

> Although my time here has been short, I feel connected and welcomed to this place. Here I have been able to contemplate the conditions of the world, the wonders of the world, and the tragedies of the world. Being among the trees, the nature, and the wildlife allows me to see how I—we—are all part of this extraordinary circle.

Like most of the young people who come to Agape, Samantha senses nature's imprint on the soul life of Agape's rural rhythms. Through such imprints, we are upheld to persevere and to serve our distraught human race.

Gathering at the Sacred Fire

We were destined to witness on our thirty-fifth anniversary, the culmination of our years of reciting native prayers,when Chief Arvol Looking Horse of Standing Rock in Dakotas came to Agape for Francis Day, 2017. He joined us at the sacred fire, lit and watched over in native tradition, inspiring my response.

Chief Arvol at the Sacred Fire, 4:30 am

We walked as if in a dream,
flashlights guiding us to the
Sacred Fire where, yesterday, hundreds sat
transfixed in timeless surrender
by fire and breath, we held each other
at the center, love rising,
tobacco smoldering,
Mini Wi Coni, Water is life.
Chief Arvol speaks, intoning, keening
a Lakota prayer
on this Nipmuc land, after thirty-five years,
Agape blessed by the nineteenth keeper of
    the White Buffalo Calf Pipe.

The blessings continue as we move into Agape's uncharted future. The solitude of rural quiet and welcoming stillness, the call

Francis Day 2017, "Listening to Native American Voices," includes attendees, top, around a sacred fire with Chief Arvol Looking Horse, seated in a chair, and a Mni Wiconi (Water Is Life) prayer and procession, above, led by Beatrice Manase Kwe Jackson, right, wearing a red shirt and black skirt.

of wild and primitive coyotes from the Agape back woods, and the hooting of night owls console and enrich the seeker of peace.

An aspiring young Jesuit novice, Garrett, who spent time in contemplation at Agape, wrote:

Nighttime in the hermitage on the hill. A muddy path and a thick, tall section of woods led me here, grateful for a headlamp. I write in yellow light until bed. The winds sweeping the whole forest—bare of trees of spring. Japanese Zen trail. Salamanders. So ambivalent.

Always with us is the paradoxical darkness of poetic truth juxtaposed against inconceivable oppression, weighing us down, making us cynical, unresponsive, and hard. In her poem, "Mass for the Day of St. Thomas Didymus," Denise Levertov speaks eloquently of the paradox. We insist on summoning beauty. We call out to the saints of poetry and mysticism: "Journey with us on this jagged terrain of resistance and light."

And so, we at Agape call on you, Beauty, your presence, to save us. The glory of God calms the fear of our timid hearts, shining, always radiant. As the poet Levertov continues:

"O deep unknown, guttering candle, beloved nugget lodged in the obscure heart's last recess, have mercy upon us."

Race, Class, and the Millennial Generation

Suzanne

Once we arrived in central Massachusetts, we began our college teaching ministry in earnest. Initially we launched a retreat entitled "Come to the Quiet: the Spirituality of Nonviolence" advertised through college campus ministries in New England and New York. Students and faculty were increasingly drawn to a sustainable faith-based community dedicated to growing its own food, living in a straw-bale house built by community members, and tapping into solar energy. Also included among these features was Agape's compost toilet. Our goal was to lessen our carbon footprint on the planet.

The retreat offered college students, faculty, and campus ministers an introduction to a program and lifestyle that integrated gospel nonviolence with radical environmental stewardship. Our focus on interfaith outreach extended also to those with no faith affiliation who often referred to themselves as spiritual. During such retreats, many students forged meaningful, long-term relationships with like-minded peers and continued their contact with Agape. Eleanor Maclellan of the Society of the Sacred Heart who served as Boston College campus minister, brought BC students for successive years. BC was one of the first colleges to sign on for the retreats.

We were also invited to speak at BC. On one occasion in the eighties, while Brayton and I were giving a presentation on peace for a student group, an elderly, unshaven, and scruffy-looking man strode into the room. He muttered a few words; then, suddenly and fitfully, he stretched out his more-than-six-foot frame on an empty couch. Both Brayton and I thought, Ooops. Now what? Maybe he was mentally ill. Maybe homeless.

Brayton continued his presentation about Gandhi, citing one of his gems: "One of the greatest disappointments of my life is the hard-heartedness of the educated class." The seemingly troubled man bolted upright and exclaimed loudly, "Oh yes, oh! That's it! That's it!"

As it turned out, we were in the presence of the intellectually gifted author, theologian, and Benedictine monk, Sebastian Moore, with whom we eventually became friends while he taught at BC in the nineties. A well-known spiritual writer and mystic, Sebastian delighted in bringing BC student groups on Agape retreats, where he stayed very much in the background. He wrote poems about the experience and, with theatrical enthusiasm, shared them with the group.

Shortly after the invasion of Iraq, I facilitated a discussion with members of the Reserve Officer Training Corps (ROTC) and other students who had traveled to Agape from Erie County Community College Campus Ministry (ECC) in Buffalo, New York. Using Jesus's teachings on enemy love, I encouraged the young would-be soldiers to express their views. Predictably, they endorsed bombing Iraq even as Jesus spoke of no killing, no revenge in the Sermon on the Mount. Pope John Paul II condemned the invasion of Iraq as "illegal, immoral, and unjust." The ensuing conversation was tense, although disagreements were respectful.

Their warm, caring campus minister, Sister Ruth, had been excitedly bringing students from ECC for years. That time, the carnage of the Twin Towers led her to dismiss teachings about loving the enemy as "not relevant to this situation." Even though we were very fond of each other, she dismissively defended the invasion as "just." Forget the Pope this time, I guessed. Proposing nonviolence in a war situation can end up costing something, including disillusionment with the beliefs of dear friends.

Ethnic and Racial Diversity: A Challenge to a White Community

Attracting students to Agape from diverse ethnicities and economic backgrounds has always been a struggle. Undergrad students like me from lower-income families could not afford high-tuition colleges unless they received scholarships or financial aid. Students from urban colleges with larger mixed-age populations weren't drawn to a long drive into the deep woods with no street lights and miles away from the nearest store—too strange. Nevertheless, campus ministers committed to social justice faithfully brought students of mixed backgrounds and races.

On one occasion, a contingent of African-American college students, mostly women from St. John's University in Queens and St. Vincent's College in the Bronx, came to the retreat accompanied by their young campus ministers on fire with the message of peace. We learned later that the mostly female retreatants were wary of being in the woods, and the mother of one of the students sent her with a roll of toilet paper. They thought they would be in cabins without electricity. Brave hearts, all.

During one of our discussions about nonviolence, I mentioned the theological concept of voluntary poverty as a way that some Christians and we at Agape embrace to identify with the suffering poor in the world. I realized almost immediately by the body language and facial expressions of the students that I had lost or unnerved them.

Strongly disagreeing, an African-American female student from Wesleyan University took issue with the term and my depiction of it. In essence, she said:

Why would you want to be poor? I've spent my whole life being poor, wanting not to be poor, and now you [perhaps implying a white woman of comfortable means] want me to give up being involuntarily poor to be voluntarily poor. That's just crazy. I'm not gonna do it.

Straightforward and honest, that student's distress and disagreement registered with other African-American and Latino students. I became a quick learner of the consequences of presumptuous thinking from a position of white privilege.

Chastened by the exchange and what I learned from it, I never again used the term so glibly with a mixed-race group. Instead, I acknowledged my failure to realize that coming from a position of white privilege requires a studious effort to find language that does not offend sensibilities of those with whom I wanted to interact. Thereafter, Brayton and I used the term "simple living" when describing Agape to sisters and brothers in economically disadvantaged circumstances.

Before social media documented racially motivated police killings, the Black Lives Matter movement, and university rejection of slave-holding histories, we saw in ourselves the subtle stirrings of racism. In the eighties and nineties, we hadn't found the terminology. For that, we owe a debt of gratitude to the Black Lives Movement that thrust the vocabulary of white supremacy into the vernacular. No longer a term only for extremists with all of its controversial implications, we now felt the grip of the label "racist" on white people nationally.

We had a lot to learn about ingrained racism, hidden but identifiable in us. We conceived of Agape as a departure from mainstream consumer culture. Nevertheless, we had support to further our efforts from generous donors. We grew our own food and built green buildings of permaculture design, through a solid economic support base. A stark and necessary awakening had begun for us: many people of color do not have such contacts to begin with.

It wasn't necessary to denigrate our vision and call. We needed to put them in perspective as existing in a racist culture where a large percentage of the marginalized, most of them people of color, could not choose what we had chosen.

A case in point is that students who come to Agape from urban poverty in the inner city see Francis House, a huge barn-like structure with cathedral ceilings, six bedrooms, and three bathrooms, and comment, "You live in a mansion."

Alethia, an African-American woman from Brooklyn, asked, "Is this your summer home? What do you do here?"

The message comes through. Although many of them love tranquility, both Agape and Francis House are profoundly removed from their reality. We think of ourselves as attempting to live sustainably. Many students think of themselves as struggling to survive. The expense and benefits of solar energy and compost toilets are refined points in an elusive and unreal lifestyle to some undergrads who live in a world different from ours.

Our learning curve about racism had grown exponentially by the time we were invited in 2016 to teach at Wake Forest University in North Carolina. In a class entitled Christianity and Politics, most of the students were African Americans. Greg, one student with whom we had a rapport, was eager to share his perspectives on Agape. He listened attentively as I confided about my own sensitivities around language in talking about race.

After we began our PowerPoint presentation on Agape depicting our all-white community of individuals living simply on beautiful rural land, Greg raised his hand and asked, "Do you mind if I offer some gentle pushback?

"African Americans have no real concept of upward mobility," he asserted. "We are just trying to survive." The other African-American students and their white professor heard Greg pointedly ask, "How does your lifestyle in the country, miles away from urban poverty, speak to us?"

Greg was teaching us once again that, when we talk about downward mobility, people of color who have been discriminated against and robbed of the benefits of mainstream US culture don't identify. Christian communities like Agape and the Catholic Worker are created by people of white privilege who desire to adjust their mobility downward. The movements do not speak, to a great extent, to the experience of Black communities.

We gained many insights from Edgar Hayes, our sole African-American intern during our years as a community. He offered a disturbing view of his life to a large group of college students including a contingent of mostly African-American women undergrads.

He shared what happened frequently when, as a black man, he passed white women on the street. Often, they clutched their purses and moved quickly past him or even to the other side of the street. He engendered fear in people he didn't know, and the result demoralized him.

His comments elicited a discussion of white stereotypes of black men in society. Everything Edgar said resonated deeply because he was an African American who grew up poor in New York. We didn't frame the discussion. He did.

The Power of Nature and the Draw of Sustainability

Over the fifteen years of our college retreat weekends, students typically arrived in the evening to the beauty of Agape buildings, warmth in winter of the wood-burning stove, smell of freshly baked bread, and candles glowing in the darkened Francis House living room. The wood interior, stone hearth, and cathedral ceilings evoked spontaneous reactions like: "Wow, this is awesome."

Silence under the stars, prayer, and a moody night added an aura of mystery to being with people we were meeting for the first time. We watched the moon flit restlessly in and out of lightly stirring tree branches.

Students led the morning prayer after breakfast. We broke open the question, "Where do we see violence in our world?" A vegetarian lunch and dinner led to a discussion of vegetarian and vegan diets and how they relate to doing no harm, the Hindu concept of ahimsa, to animals as well as to humans.

During breaks, Francis House hummed with the sound of drumming, flutes, and percussion mixed with poetry. In the evening, we hosted a coffee-free coffee house when young people presented skits, often hilarious riffs on no-cell service at Agape or eating kale patties and tofu loaf.

We included a visit to Agape's hermitage for meditation. Journaling went on constantly with student writing shared later in the day delighting all of us. Evening bonfires displayed the mystique of the landscape and stunning starlight. Nothing can beat a bonfire for intimacy and a sense of wonder.

One BC student reported, "No cell phones or television, limited internet access, might be anxiety provoking. It was the opposite. I lived at Agape, more mindfully in the present."

Transition to Rural Immersions

Rural Immersions became popular educational forums following the growth of the ecological movement. Agape's unique setting provided students and staff an opportunity to spend from four to six days working the land, gardening, and preparing homegrown meals, sometimes with vegetables straight from our gardens. We cut, hauled, and split wood. Students felt a sense of purpose as they learned that Agape hosted hundreds of people throughout the year and that there is no back-up heat source.

Interactive discussions punctuated the day: How can we live without fossil fuel? Can we live more simply? How do I step away from the stressful, acquisitive American lifestyle? Can I find more meaning in my faith?

We introduced environmental components of our lifestyle: green-built Brigid House, a straw-bale construction; solar energy and hot water; composting toilet that saves forty percent of our drinkable water; and growing our organic vegetables, healthy and affordable. After her time at Agape with other students from Stonehill College, Celia Dolan wrote:

> I sense that we each discovered something important for ourselves during our time away. As for me, I realized that I arrived, broken, in ways that I didn't know I was, and I returned home, healed, in ways that I didn't know I needed.

Students reacted quite positively to the freedom, bonding, and outdoor nature of immersions. Peter from Brown University was struck by the "dignified work" and "Christ-centeredness with Jesus as the axis around which the entire operation revolves."

Greg, a student leader from the College of the Holy Cross in Worcester, commented in an article for Agape's *Servant Song Journal*:

> One of the most important takeaways . . . involved understanding the importance of listening...one of the essential cornerstones of community. The group covered an array of topics from ROTC to the pros and cons of affirmative action . . . We continued to share our opinions and grow in the new community we were fostering.

Internationals at Agape

International students have come to Agape over the years largely through World Wide Opportunities on Organic Farms (WWOOF). They represented a variety of European and Asian countries. Two delightful young women from Cavan, Ireland, spent a summer at Agape. Catriona Kennedy, one of them, observed:

> Through the tough times (eating kale and carrying logs down hills), we stayed smiling and laughing (not just when the cameras came out) and created some of our greatest memories.

Catriona and her friend Sharon also experienced their first public peace vigil at Westover Air Force Base. Dressed in black robes, they wore white masks to symbolize death emanating from cargo planes taking off from the base bringing weapons and supplies to American troops.

Under the watchful eye of Frances Crowe of Northampton, Massachusetts, then ninety-eight and a legendary peacemaker, they wondered if a photo taken that day might make it to *The Irish Times.* Frances held a sign reading: "Does Our Lifestyle Depend on War?"

The Creatively Maladjusteds

Over the years, we pulled together grad school students drawn to Agape with the hope that a self-perpetuating group might form as a core base to welcome others. Energy ran high among students who formed the first group. They called themselves the Creatively Maladjusteds after the famous quote of Martin Luther King Jr., who presented a model for living maladjustedly in a society that demands conformity.

The Agape Maladjusteds formed several groups in Boston over potluck discussions with friendships deepening as new ones began. They then related back to Agape as the base community. Sharing faith, morality, and social justice concerns in a post-faith, postmodern, and post-truth world, Emily Jendzejec, a BC grad, commented on her participation in the group:

> Spaces built with intention, founded on strong relationships, are where answers can arise, that are not to be discussed in just the peaceful woods of Agape, but to be taken back to wherever we live and put into actions.

After a year of grappling with issues of identity and purpose in the groups, one participant, voice elevated, with no little exasperation, burst out: "Sometimes I wonder why we can't just go for it?" It was a real cry of the heart. He touched upon something others may have wanted to express but didn't know how: "Why don't we take some risks, plunge into community life, do something?"

Many among the Maladjusteds wanted radical departures from their life routines but simultaneously admitted that some of them

Self-identified "creatively maladjusted" members of the younger generation meet at Agape.

might be risk averse. At least, they indicated, the Agape model was too radical. They were paying off loans after incurring numbing debt. Many felt they needed to experience careers before they could decide to give them up. This seemed imminently fair to me as I had a career well into my thirties.

Geoff Gusoff, one of the founding members of the group (which ended after three years when most members dispersed to different parts of the country) saw the reality of their predicament when he wrote:

How to avoid the endless talk, talk, talk that brings no action, but also the harried doing, doing, doing that fears real reflection (almost as much as it fears stillness)? . . . Thousands of questions crop up as soon as you take the term 'creatively maladjusted' seriously. ... I don't want to wake up when I am seventy-two and regret that I never actually went for it.

Portrait of a Creatively Maladjusted

Nathan Beall came to Agape via Yale Divinity School as an undergrad and is now an Episcopal priest. Nathan epitomized a young maladjusted who found a way to go for it.

After study, reflection and prayer, Nathan decided to noncooperate with the payment of war taxes by not earning enough income to be taxed. He worked out an arrangement with his college community, St. Mary's College in Maryland, to trade his salary for "a stack of meal tickets at the cafeteria so that I can eat with the students that I teach and serve."

Reporting that, as he made his decision, he often felt "isolated and frustrated," Nathan revealed that his dilemma underscores that, without intentional community support, the anxiety that accompanies such a dramatic departure from the adjusted in society can be excruciating. Nathan did receive some support from Agape, the National War Tax Resistance Coordinating Committee, and the Amistad Catholic Worker in New Haven.

In an account of his experiences, Nathan remarked about Agape's response to his new life as a tax resister:

> Someone else understood the conviction that we cannot profess love of neighbor while we fund bombs that murder children. Someone felt the agonizing tension between the Kingdom of God and the Kingdom of Caesar, between God and Mammon, between Jesus and the emperor.

Nathan observed that "young people in this country know that most of what the world offers them is worthless." He has decided that "there is a greater journey to take, a greater battle to fight." His advice to his peers: "Abandon the logic of this world, the logic of domination and violence, and turn again to the logic of love."

Ahmad al Hadidi, in plaid shirt, top, gathers with his audience from Assumption College, Worcester, after his presentation about racism. Williams Martinez, former Agape intern, raises a sign proclaiming "War Is Not the Answer" at a 2016 demonstration in Boston, bottom.

The muezzin or chanter from the Islamic Society of Western Massachusetts calls attendees to prayer at Francis Day, 2016, entitled "Listening to Muslim Voices in an Election Year." Presenters at the event, from left, below, include Bob Meagher, Nadia Alawa of Nu Day Syria, Mohammad Bajwa, MD, of the Islamic Society of Western Massachusetts, and Father Warren Savage.

Nathan found a home in the logic of Jesus when he decided to just go for it.

A Greater Battle to Fight

Millennial interns have sometimes been involved in the common work of pest control at Agape. One such occurrence involved Kyle, a BC grad school intern who alerted us that he had spotted a flying squirrel in Francis House. In a panicked voice, he called us on the community intercom to announce, "Flying squirrel manifesting. Flying squirrel manifesting."

The disoriented nocturnal creature had glided from the third floor into the living room, where my efforts along with those of four skittish interns to trap it resulted in the animal flitting from one corner of our sacred chapel to another. Our normal flying squirrel routine involved setting up Havahart traps, exercising nonviolent catch and release, saving us hundreds of dollars otherwise potentially spent on pest control while contaminating the environment.

The only trap available to me in the moment was my hands, heavily protected from possible bites by gloves used for the wood-burning stove. Except for one, the interns fled the chapel and clustered where they could still observe, just outside the door. My strategy included multiple catch boxes that the remaining intern and I moved from place to place as we followed squirrel flight patterns.

After we failed in several attempts to snag the skittish animal, I finally got him. An intern cheer went up. The chase was over. Jake, one of the interns, had recorded the movements of the dramatic capture in a notebook. Replete with sketches of a squirrel landing map, Jake's diagrams included accompanying medieval text. Jake titled the saga "The Battle of Squirrel Chapel."

A Burundian singer and Burundian dancers take part in a Francis Day observance entitled "Women and War," top. Edgar Hayes, leads a procession in memory of Tony Flaherty of Veterans for Peace on Francis Day, 2015.

Volunteer gardeners at Agape from Stonehill College, Easton, Massachusetts take their lead from Alicen Roberts, an Agape intern, right.

Green, the Color that Sustains All Life

Brayton

Teresa went to her mother and said, "Mom, I'm done with community life in Francis House. We need a new house."

We were ten years into community living where all interns and guests lived under one roof on two floors. We had very little to go on about how families actually live in community with non-family members.

Our daughter was making her thirteen-year-old nonnegotiable demand for more privacy. Her ultimatum encouraged us to acknowledge how fair and sensible it was for three of us to have our own separate living space. Family autonomy is essential in community with others. But if we long for too much privacy, we fall back into isolation and living sequestered as nuclear families.

We decided to yield to Teresa's assertion that we should build a residence for our family. But what to build? How to build it? We recognized that such a new residence had to be a sign of the environmental times we were entering. The year was 1997, the end of the second millennium, and we humans were waking up to a revelation of our grievously mistaken way of living life on the earth.

I observed the dawning of the new life-altering age in April, 1990, on the twentieth Earth Day. We could no longer explain away the raw facts of our environmental destruction. We had irretrievably altered our bio-systems. Through the greed of human domination of earth's natural resources, we have poisoned rivers, lakes, oceans, soil, animals, and air.

My first glimpse of such polluting came when I was living near the Charles River in Boston around the first Earth Day in 1970. That beautiful waterway that thousands sailed on every summer was considered a "dying river," dying from human pollution and sewage. Bostonians, full of the pride of hometown, sang out the top forty hit "Dirty Water" by the Standells:

Down by the banks of the River Charles . . .
Oh, I love that dirty water
Oh, Boston, you're my home.

Our ravaged, groaning earth was jarring us awake with life-or-death implications that the silly lyrics did not dare to mention.

The first Earth Day introduced me to the notion of living off the grid. That utopian call away from the mainstream was getting traction in the sixties and seventies with the condemnation of all fossil fuels. Back in the day, we were fairly light on specific action steps. There was plenty of youthful idealism about how we believed in possibilities for change. But most of us, especially the young people I knew, remained beholden to our economic privilege. Details of how to live a radical environmental alternative remained comfortably vague. We sounded so wise in our visions of the Age of Aquarius but often not the least bit self-sacrificing or pragmatic. Too many baby boomers had too much easy money and a zillion options for spending it.

Now we were getting chapter and verse from environmentalists about our lifestyle stuffing the atmosphere with CO_2, creating a greenhouse effect and catastrophically warming the earth's temperatures. The ruinous trend was melting polar ice caps and flooding our future. And what was a primary cause? Burning oil, gas, and coal, the big three of fossil fuels that drove the war against nature. We viewed living off the fossil-fuel-driven grid an urgent practical necessity for human survival.

A Straw House?

By the late 1980s, we finished Francis, a house made of stone and wood. In ten short years, green building exploded onto our scene. Sister El Maclellan of our mission council informed us that Sister Miriam Thérèse McGillis had recently built a hermitage of straw bales. Miriam is founder of Genesis Farm and a student of the "geologian" Catholic theologian of the earth, Father Thomas Berry.

El sent us over the design. Not having the knowledge and creativity of an innovative builder, I stuck it deep into our files under "too strange to imagine building."

By the mid-1990s, green building seemed everywhere, especially in New England and on the West coast. Our friends at Sirius Community, a nearby eco-village, had just completed a cob house made of mud, sand, loose straw, and lime. Cordwood houses were on the scene with cheap-as-they-come wood logs that insulated fantastically. Blown-in cellulose or pulverized newspaper became more mainstream insulation and nontoxic alternatives to the very likely carcinogenic fiberglass we had been using.

Straw-bale construction had gone from "out there" to a credible way to build. A friend told me of a two-story straw-bale house going up just west of downtown Northampton. Clem Watson from Vermont was the builder successfully perfecting and reclaiming the historic technique of building with thatch, straw, and grain.

Clem showed me his two-story, groundbreaking house, completed after a year of construction. His environmental selling points were:

- by virtue of its materials alone, the house insulates at R50, almost three times the R value of a house, such as our Francis House, super-insulated with fiberglass
- the materials to build the house, including straw, chicken wire, and stucco cement are half the cost of conventional house building materials
- straw constitutes a yearly renewable resource, so no need to buy lumber from corporations that are clear cutting North American forests for their own profit

Straw bale sounded like the best ecological design out there at a never-seen-before, simple-living budget.

For seven years, we were organic growers at Agape, and then we began straw-bale construction and entered the burgeoning world of eco-building. The word sustainable had become common parlance. Straw, a yearly renewable building material, emerged into a regenerative circle. Like the well-known recycling logo of arrows in a circle, we related everything we did to a circle in a motion that regenerates buildings into a healthy future for next generations. Straw-bale construction relied on organic straw material and involved almost no reliance on fossil fuel for production or construction. As we had with diet, we were learning that how you build, like how you eat, is either kind or toxic to body and earth. Having considered many ecologically imaginative building options, we decided on straw.

We needed a comprehensive plan to build a three-bedroom residence that would be sustainably green in all its functions. For novices like us, the concept was so newfangled that it required finding green-building specialists. We had Clem for straw-bale walls and timber framing. Bob, our architect at the ready but not experienced at building straw-bale design, suggested we find someone who could complete the building.

We built Francis House entirely within our community network, but the straw-bale house was another story, an ecological work of art and science, its artisans to be found in the world of cutting-edge innovators.

Permaculture Leads the Way

First on the site was David Stith, well known in circles versed in New England permaculture design. Permaculture teaches one to read the land and determine how best to position a house according to the four directions and topography. Our proposed house location seemed terrible to me, as it dramatically sloped up toward the south and not gently down, thus severely limiting the amount of light and heat from the sun.

David, a good educator, taught us that the fundamentals of permaculture design teach you to work with the natural world not bending nature to your will. Read the site, listen to the site and observe what it "says" you can do. Find solutions, not problems.

Having read our land, he confidently found the best site location with southern exposure.

The truth of permaculture speaks to a wider nonviolent application to life itself, echoing the *Tao te Ching's* spirit of nondomination—"yield, and you will overcome." The earth teaches humans a frugal restraint and pushes back against our drive to dominate her.

Digging a well came next, requiring the dowsing services of Don Roberts, chief of police in Hardwick. Dowsing is a spiritual gift that empowers one to feel water beneath as the dowser walks the land. Holding a stripped, y-shaped branch of a fruit tree with the stem pointing away from him, Don stepped across the proposed building site. When he walked over a groundwater vein or stream below the visible surface, the fruit branch he held gently bent downward toward a water vein, the point for digging a well.

Could I really believe what I saw?

"It's a spiritual gift," Don said. "I don't quite understand this myself, but it is reliable, and because it is a gift, there is never a charge." I wondered if I was learning environmental gifts and practices handed down from native traditions. Wherever it originated, we trusted our chief of police, as he was confident he found a water source. We dug down forty feet and hit the water vein.

Our next dilemma involved finding a courageous soul to climb onto the backhoe bucket, go down forty feet, and place hundreds of pounds of cement tile four feet in diameter to make our well. Fred Higgins was the man. Fred and his brother Tom, both born and raised in Scotland, had taught me how to build Francis House's stone hearth. As Fred climbed onto the bucket, he reminded us of his family history: "Because for generations my ancestors were coal miners in Scotland, it is second nature for us to go deep down into the earth." Down he went every day for a few days until the well was in.

The average cost of a professionally drilled, eight-hundred-foot-deep artesian well was five thousand dollars. Our do-it-yourself-by-hand forty footer cost us only a thousand dollars. Our frugal ways, however, were not always cheaper. Simple homesteading methods can be dangerous work for the average person like me and sometimes a costly risk to life and limb. At a minimum, frugality often results in a slower and more tedious process requiring patience and, for me at least, confusingly difficult, hard physical work. Well experts told us that a thirty-foot well would not yield enough water over time. We were taking a risk on the forty footer, I imagined.

We then approached the most demanding building stage— putting up straw-bale walls. We added Mark Korban, an old friend who helped build Francis House and himself a builder. He had just completed his own straw-bale house with the help of his wife, Reba, and their six kids. It was a reassuring boost to have a trusted friend on the worksite who actually knew some tricks on how to build such a strange and exotic abode.

Volunteers joined us and boosted the progress of our building. As with Francis House before it, we were dependent on the generosity and skill of those who could afford to donate their time. We were on a four-month time line to have the building weather tight before Christmas in order to protect exposed straw from ruinous freezing rain and snow. But first, we needed hardwood to finish framing.

The Beauty of Creature Machines

Up the driveway came two lumbering Belgian workhorses driven by the team driver, Don Phillips. We hired him to cut down and log seventy-five trees to build the frame of the straw-bale house.

Don Phillips drives his team of Belgian workhorses to the straw-bale house site.

As the horses came to a halt at the top of the driveway, Teresa and her friends from our extended community were instantly enchanted at the sight of these spectacular animals. These mythic, outsized horses were at Agape to haul hundreds of tons of oak trees from our woods. It was an intriguing glimpse of what a nineteenth-century homesteading life was like before oil-powered tractors. Don appeared to love the magnificent steeds more deeply than he could ever love a skidder, which is a tank-like gas guzzler that hauls the heavy tonnage of commercial logging.

Two months prior, we hired a skidder and driver to begin the process of bringing in trees for milling because we did not then know about Don's horse-logging service. When the skidder screamed its deafening way up the driveway, no one dared greet it and no children gathered around. It didn't possess the deep soul eyes of the Belgian horses. Also, the skidder smelled of burned fuel, not the sweet scent of a farm animal and pastures of hay. The skidder excretes greenhouse gas fumes while horses excrete fertilizer for the soil. Horses are self-giving. Modern machines are always a business deal.

I photographed Don's routine of leading his team into the deep woods, cutting trees down, and then hauling them in. I caught a moment of pure enchantment without his knowing it. He had just cut a seventy-five-foot-tall oak which, instead of falling to the ground, got wedged against another mighty oak—a precarious position for any large tree. It becomes more difficult to drop the tree in a clean and predictable direction.

Don's method for safely bringing the tree to the ground meant having the horses move out forty feet or so on command. The one movement was intended to slide the massive oak uneventfully down. As he stood behind them on his logging platform to drive his team, he wanted to move the horses out at a slight angle to his right.

He quietly signaled the horses' attention with his reigns and then called out "Hyaaah!" The horses lunged forward and then stopped short in a holding back pattern horses use when they sense some uncertainty. Don paused again.

Then he broke the silence with another commanding "Hyaaah!" Obedient to their driver, the Belgians jerked forward and again pulled up short. Silence . . . pause . . . a third "Hyaaah!" That time there was almost no movement to the right. Frustrated, I'm sure, Don sat quietly to assess his team's rejection of his three simple commands. He stepped off the platform and walked twenty feet in front of his reluctant team that normally functions as his right and left hands.

He turned toward them and paused. Then he signaled from his new vantage point, "Hyaaah!" Confidently, they moved out, first twenty, then thirty feet angling to the left, not the right as he had wanted. You could almost say the oak fell gracefully, without complication. Don then caught my eye and said, "Sometimes they know better than I do." He followed greater wisdom by relying on the intuition of two horses given the freedom to go where their horse instincts led them.

The experience was one of the most vivid five minutes of the entire building project. Two animal species worked together with mutual respect and need for what the other could provide. The animal of supposed superior brain capacity finally yielded to the native brilliance of two beasts of burden.

Log 'em In, Mill 'em, and Put 'em Up

The most generous gift of our good land, our hardwoods, helped us to build at half the commercial cost. After the Belgians did their job, Fran Bellamy from Belchertown took over with his portable mill. Fran was the only practicing Christian who was a part of our newly formed straw-bale-house construction crew. He was a gentle soul but very frank with me about what he thought was a true Agape tone on the worksite and what was not. We had our first serious worksite conflict.

"Clem doesn't treat people well. He doesn't really fit in the spirit of Agape," Fran complained. I respected Fran's opinion and felt he was making an uncomfortable but necessary point that, with his authoritarian style, the foreman of the job was

Bob Wegener auctioned straw bales to raise funds for our straw-bale dwelling, Brigid House.

undercutting the morale and camaraderie desired on the worksite. On the other hand, Clem was a superb carpenter, consistent with meeting deadlines, and a very hard worker but often a harder driver. Fran was right to say, "Good work is more than productivity." The challenge we faced was to establish a contemplative tone where everyone is accepted in spite of the fact that not all of us were there because of the draw of Agape.

We never worked our differences through productively. Negative feelings persisted until Fran finished the milling job in his remaining two weeks. The easy way out is usually the lesser way, and I regret I did not assist to improve worksite vibes.

Back on the job, Fran took the seventy-five trees of oak, maple, hickory, ash, and poplar and milled them down to posts, beams, oak boards for flooring, and trim for the fifteen windows in the house. Oak and maple have such a strong hardwood constitution that Fran had to spend only one month milling trees down to post-and-beam-construction size. Hardwood beams will check if not dried, but checking won't compromise the weight-bearing integrity of the beams. Because there was no need for drying time, all posts and beams were immediately available for building.

In two months, we had the interior of the house framed. But we only had another month to make it weather tight, and it was becoming clear we would lose our race against oncoming winter. Listening and yielding to nature provided another teachable moment among so many relearnings.

Straw-bale construction was my apprenticeship in learning eco-friendly ways under the tutelage of eco-believers and builders. My teachers had spiritual presence, a centeredness that comes from believing in something so palpably life-giving.

Volunteer Bob Ludwig works on the southwest corner of the straw-bale house.

We were not only learning marketable job skills but also life skills handed down from generations before us and adapted to our current age including

- learning to work with our hands
- understanding the harmonious integration of building and landscape
- discovering how to build a lower energy society by resisting the contemporary American temptation to construct buildings that are outsized energy hogs
- recognizing that how we use the earth's resources could uphold and protect the intrinsic worth of every living thing, logging trees selectively to improve the health of the forest while minimizing of their habitat for birds.

Finally, we are learning to make all landscaping and building decisions with an eye to their longevity thirty to fifty years out to insure a hale and hearty planet for the generations to follow.

Suzanne and I were in our early fifties, yet we felt like infants discovering how to walk lightly on the earth. By joining the vanguard of earth protectors, we woke up to how much we didn't know while realizing exactly what we had to change about ourselves from the inside out. Zen practitioners call it the "art of not knowing." We were immersed in an environmental science as we learned the language of the natural world. In that science, essential value is placed on biological health over ready access to toxic building materials, fossil fuels, and the "more" of speedy high tech progress.

Living Off the Sun

Clem and our building crew conceded the race against the frost and snow of December, wrapped the entire house in plastic, took the winter off, and looked toward spring and the final year and a half of building. Our earth told us to stop our building process wisely and definitively.

Wanting to eliminate burning oil and gas on the homestead, we chose a plan to evolve toward a hundred percent use of

Steve Kurkoski installs five off-grid solar panels on the roof of the straw-bale house.

renewables in building and maintaining all structures. The sun became our primary fuel.

First, we decided on a twelve-volt, off-grid battery system for electricity in the straw-bale house and a solar hot-water system powered by heat from the sun. We and our community network of people knew very little about solar energy. Yet, we considered living free of all fossil fuels even though we had never imagined what we dubbed air pollution in the 1950s could lead to catastrophic weather and threaten all life on earth.

A friend suggested we contact Steve Kurkoski as someone to install the direct-current, twelve-volt system. Steve is an electrician, and one of his many interests involved monitoring the yearly Massachusetts Tour de Sol Festival for battery-powered cars. A person whose passion is to develop and celebrate nonpetroleum cars had to be perfect for our job. He agreed to take on his first complete twelve-volt, six-battery-bank-system installation. We eventually absorbed volumes of material on all things electric, especially solar, from that knowledgeable man. I became Steve's student learning about electricity and photovoltaics.

Steve's first lesson was a reality check. "I hope you're not choosing photovoltaics because of the payback," he said. "Typically, solar is more expensive than conventional electricity with unknowns about how long the batteries will last and what long-term maintenance will cost."

Thankfully, I had no problem choosing solar energy on principle, not economics. It is interesting that he began our discussions with the expense of solar energy. Over the course of the year that he installed the system, he charged us ten thousand dollars complete, about half the going rate. Steve was the only paid subcontractor who actually donated several days to the good of the cause. Something told me there would be an eventual payback thanks to Steve's low-budget generosity.

After the site passed the solar test of adequate sun from ten in the morning until two in the afternoon, Steve proposed a half kilowatt system with six lead acid batteries. It was a modest-sized, affordable system for a residence with limited electricity use. That small act of noncooperation with the empires of fossil fuel was a kind of moral relief closely akin to not paying taxes for war.

Workers install a 4.5-kilowatt solar array on Francis House.

But I could not get out of my head a statement by Rex Tillerson, then CEO of Exxon Mobil: "Petroleum runs the world, and we are the best in the industry. We assume that will continue." Give up oil? Rex is correct. Just try to live one day without oil.

We owned a petroleum-fueled car, cut wood with gas-fueled chain saws, and on rare occasions flew in gas-fueled airplanes. Most everything we own and purchase needs oil to be produced from light bulbs to food, from pens to computers. Virtually all our possessions require oil-fueled transport. Sacrificing comfort and convenience? That is too steep a price for too many.

Americans tend to ridicule any talk of sacrifice as can't-do, so antithetical to our essential can-do attitude. To us, the privileged class, cutting back and doing without is an indication of impending failure. We continually learn from Jesus that to be faithful to the truth, we at the community have to discern new ways to back away from the advantages and death dealings of economic privilege.

Building with Straw Is Not Simple!

Steve and I spent the next month snaking electrical wire through eighteen-inch-thick straw bales. Experienced as he was, he had never wired a straw house. I thought to myself, Is this one of the first straw-bale houses in history to have modern electrical wiring? The first such houses were built in the late 1800s in the great plains of Nebraska. Those structures suited the timber-poor sand hills of the far Midwest, a land that yielded magnificent strands of meadow hay that constituted the first bale buildings. Hay was cheap, quick, and easier to build with than sod. Such houses were durable and comfortable in the extremes of a Nebraska winter and summer, especially with stucco cement plastering the outside surface.

Studying the history of the Midwest provided strong parallels to New England winters, but settlers in the 1800s didn't wire their straw houses for electricity. We were learning to do it from scratch with no previous method or blueprints.

As if to affirm that our building defied convention came the electrical inspector, Don. Solar-energy wiring in bales of straw confused him. He had never before inspected a house powered by solar electricity. Don had done some electrical work for us in the past, gave us great discounts, and enthusiastically supported of the mission of Agape.

"Look, Brayton," he offered with a bit of frustration. "I don't understand this building, and I know almost nothing about solar energy. I'll make you a deal. If you bring down the 120-volt grid wiring from Francis House, you can do anything you want with solar. I will inspect the house by the standards of conventional town codes for 120-volt electricity."

That was an offer we could not refuse! In addition, Steve saw the advantage of wiring the house both for 12-volt solar *and* 120-volt conventional. If, in the future, we wanted to increase the electrical capacity, then having 120-volt wiring would enable us to do so while continuing to run on solar.

Our ultimate goal was to power both the straw-bale and Francis Houses with solar energy within ten years. True believers, still light on skills, we sometimes felt as if it would take us another lifetime's experience to come up to speed with the wonder-working, deep science of the Ecozoic age. The surround sound of the new millennium and network of eco-believers gave us all we needed to strive on toward the unknowns of climate change one bale and one solar panel at a time.

Composting Unmentionables and Driving Vegetarian

Brayton

The Australian naturalist Bill Mollison coined the term permaculture in 1978 as a result of his growing up in a small village in the Tasmanian outback in a day when people made everything they needed and grew everything they ate. No one labored at what could be called a full-time job. Rather, everyone worked at multiple necessary but unpaid jobs. One of the principles to live by was, "Recycle all wastes." Now what could that mean? All wastes? Waste has value?

By the late 1990s, there was serious concern about landfills that were toxic and topping off. "Just throw it away" was the accepted practice I was reared on. As time passed, we were discovering that there is no "away" and that the garbage that goes out usually ends up in someone else's backyard or comes back around as some kind of poison in our own neighborhoods.

A new and revolutionary idea of zero waste was born and meant that the lifespan of our possessions was no longer from cradle to grave. From a new perspective, we need to consider the idea of recycling everything. Something is deemed waste when we are convinced it is useless

Are We Defecating in Our Drinking Water?

After the oil wars began in the Persian Gulf in the 1990s, we began hearing that the next war will be over clean water. Bruce at Sirius Community gave me *The Humanure Handbook* by Joseph Jenkins, who reads the riot act on water pollution and conservation as he builds a strong case for compost toilets. One estimate suggests that 40% of all drinkable water is annually flushed down American toilets into land, lakes, rivers, and oceans each day, a total of 5 billion gallons each day. Flushing a toilet is a flush-it-down-and-away, classic out-of-sight-out-of-mind practice. Some 3.6 trillion gallons of sewage yearly are pumped into our waterways, often polluting our groundwater. The chief culprit for water contamination? Faulty septic systems.

Bruce and his wife, Linda Reimer, founded Sirius Community in the late 1970s. They had several site-built compost toilets designed by Phil Claybourn, permaculture practitioner and Agape friend. It became gradually clear to Suzanne and me that green-built compost toilets must be included in our green-built straw-bale house. Phil called his design "The Moldering Toilet," meaning that the humanure broke down into rich humus without turning, much like tree leaves composting after they drop on the moist forest floor with little need for sunlight, exterior heat, or maintenance to transform the waste into compost.

When I called Phil initially, he was reluctant to take on the job. His site-built concept is a small toilet room that is always constructed as a separate structure conveniently adjacent to the house in order to vent odors more effectively. I wanted the room at Brigid House, the name we gave to our straw-bale edifice, to have the convenience of a toilet room right off the living area itself. I was excited to have Phil, the guy who created the brilliant moldering-toilet idea, help us build it. His design was considered state of the art by eco-village communities in the area and replicated at Massachusetts highway rest stops. He agreed to design the toilet for our specific site and get us started building the foundation. Then it was up to us to finish it.

Saving Our Precious Water

Our compost toilet was brilliantly simple to build and cost a mere five hundred dollars in materials. We have two chambers. It takes about four years to fill a chamber for a family of four when we switch chambers and continue. We give it one more year for the full chamber to complete the breakdown into composted fertilizer.

When we dug out the humanure five years later, it looked and smelled like sweet dark soil similar to well-aged cow manure. Miraculously, we then spread the best-there-is soil amendment around the base of our twenty fruit trees to encourage their growth in the most natural of ways. The process is simple, low maintenance, and feels like the most natural thing we could ever do.

The *Worcester Telegram and Gazette* newspaper did a front-page article on our compost toilet, "Compost Toilets—the Way to Go!" Our beautiful and ecologically brilliant space is at the same time the most controversial room on the homestead. Many, especially teenage friends and family, often refuse even to consider using the "weird and disgusting" room. Fifteen-year-old Sabrina said,

Autumn Rose Cutting happily digs humanure fertilizer out of the compost toilet chamber.

"I am going up to Francis House where there is a real toilet!" Our five-year-old granddaughter, Olivia, gazed into the deep dark chamber full of poop and said to Suzanne, "Will I fall in, Grandma?"

Rebecca, a nineteen-year-old from an inner-city Springfield parish, arrived with her youth group for a day at Agape to learn about sustainable living. A month earlier, we finished digging out one of the chambers and made a pile of aged-to-perfection humanure compost next to the garden. As the youth group walked past that infamous pile, I picked up a handful of that fresh, earth-smelling compost and proudly stated, "This will be fertilizing the fruit trees soon." With a look of terror, Rebecca let out a blood-curdling scream and ran a world-record fifty-yard dash to the safety of Francis House.

We give special thanks each day for the wild times and odoriferous, funny stories that only a compost toilet can bring!

Driving on Grease?

"You know a lot about solar energy," I said to Steve Kurkoski. "Can you build us an electric car that runs on solar?"

"It's not worth the time and money at this point," he said. "You can only run about fifty miles on a charge. But I have heard that people are running cars using vegetable oil."

Vermont family farmers, often cash poor and improvising how to hold on to limited profits, discovered that they could run their tractors using vegetable oil, even Fryolator grease used in restaurants. Soon mechanically savvy people fueled their diesel cars on grease. The discovery was tantamount to finding free fuel at minimal environmental impact. I could not get my head around the idea that we could eliminate the cost of gasoline, although I hadn't yet figured out how to acquire a diesel-powered car.

Running cars on vegetable oil was not a recent invention. It was the brain child of the visionary German inventor, Rudolph Diesel. In 1898, he patented the diesel engine to run on peanut

High school students filter Fryolator grease from a nearby Ninety-Nine restaurant for eventual use as auto power.

oil. That brilliant innovation relied on plants grown abundantly in petroleum-poor central Europe.

A historic discovery in 1901 in Beaumont, Texas, all but killed vegetable fuel. A newly drilled oil well gushed out what was thought to be unlimited oil. Two years later, off the assembly line came Henry Ford's Model T. And what was its fuel? Petroleum oil drilled from the most oil-rich wells in the known world, along the Gulf Coast, United States. Could the Model T fueled by petroleum-based gasoline constitute the single worst environmental mistake in all of history? It took us a hundred years to recognize the inconceivable devastation of petroleum's impact on all living things.

We purchased a four-year-old Volkswagen Jetta diesel with fifty thousand miles. Next, we had to convert the economy car to a grease car.

Millennials ... Save the Planet!

Online, I came across Justin Carven who founded greasecar. com. A mechanical engineering graduate from Hampshire College, where students conceive their own majors, he had invented a new and efficient fuel-line system that successfully fueled a diesel car using Fryolator grease. Many local restaurants made the grease easily available because their owners were eager to unload used grease that they otherwise had to pay to dispose of.

In rediscovering Rudolf Diesel's vision for our environmentally strapped times, Justin converted our Jetta from combustion engine to diesel power for fifteen hundred dollars. I calculated our savings on fuel would amount to approximately a thousand dollars yearly. In a short year and a half, I would have the new fuel-line investment paid off. In ten years, the savings would be ten thousand dollars, plus we were insuring against the inevitable rising cost of oil.

It was with great excitement and hope that I watched Justin and his under-thirty crew putting their minds together to help us save the world, if only modestly, from the horrors of our carbon-spewing autos. As he worked frequently on my grease car, he taught me something each time. For example, when you burn grease, it is an eighty-percent improvement in emission over oil. Given that twenty percent of all CO_2 emissions comes from cars and trucks, driving on grease is not a bad first move in noncooperation with oil. Our Jetta was only twenty percent shy of carbon neutral.

Next, I had to find a supply of grease. After a few months of buying biodiesel at the pump for three dollars a gallon, I discovered that Peter Wuelfing, our good friend and Agape supporter, was the dream contact. He managed a Ninety Nine Restaurant and Pub, one of a popular chain serving steak and potato fare. Restaurants must unload several gallons of Fryolator grease weekly at a cost to them in disposal fees. "Perfect," I told Peter. "I will take it off your hands for nothing." When they were ready to dispose of the grease, Peter had people on his staff filter it one extra time and put it in five-gallon containers.

I met with the Ninety Nine kitchen staff at the Springfield cable access television station, Focus Springfield, that filmed a piece about our new grease car. Peter's kitchen crew was enamored of what we were filming that day as they cheerfully filtered their very used, good-for-nothing canola oil. I could not tell my new friends at the Ninety Nine what I have been suggesting to my fast-food-eating friends. "All fast-food restaurants are great places to frequent—but please," I warned, "do not eat their artery-clogging food. Just run your car on their grease!"

Before we left, the head cook looked at me and said, "This is impossible, our Fryolator grease fueling your automobile and beating corporate oil almost totally. Why don't more people do it?"

That question was the most frequently asked, especially at grease-car demonstrations. My usual response is:

We Americans do not want the extra work. Locating a source of used vegetable oil seems like a strange job. Filtering it can feel tedious and time consuming. Finding a mechanic who is willing to repair grease cars has to seem nearly impossible. But principally, it is the precariousness of living outside the box that is just too much for most of us. Merely living securely inside the box necessitates a zillion hours at work and a life that is already laden with maxed- out demands and surprises. We can complain about climate change, but are we doing something about it?

I can relate to the preceding litany of excuses, because I distinctly remember my impatience with the filtering process when I first began driving a grease car. A voice in my head hounded me:

It takes me one-and-a-half hours to filter a twelve-gallon tank's worth of grease plus clean up. It would take me five minutes to fill my tank at the downtown Exxon Mobil. I don't care what gasoline costs—it is too much work.

Thankfully, a wiser voice counters: I do care what it costs both to pocketbook and to planet. I am reminded that, in our environmental age, to retrieve the planet back from inevitable climate-change Armageddon requires hard, creative work that is going to hurt and challenge our comfortable routines. The idols of convenience, efficiency, comfort, and pleasure serve as the drugs of choice for Americans living in our high-tech modern world— some expensive narcotics. And just how expensive?

A consensus of climate scientists agrees that CO_2-spewing petroleum is warming the planet, melting polar ice caps, so that rising seas will start flooding coastlines throughout the world sooner than we are ready for it. Some geologists determined that oil reserves in the US peaked in 1972. Just before the first Gulf War in 1991, gas at the pump was eighty-nine cents a gallon. Within a year at a dollar fifty a gallon, the price had come close to doubling.

Arriving just in time, fracking is our latest form of drilling. Fracking does ease the crisis of dwindling supply. Yet we must be forewarned, oil and gas from fracking are not cheap, either. Fracking releases potentially carcinogenic chemicals into the groundwater when water is pumped at high pressure. Many believe the shock from the explosions of fracturing underground rock is a reason for more frequent, high-Richter-scale earthquakes. Fracking is also an expensive mistake because it is a more difficult, costly, and time-consuming process than conventional drilling with petroleum quality inferior to Saudi oil.

Kai Wu, an economics PhD candidate at UMass Amherst, gave a talk at Agape. Kai shared damning scientific and economic facts about the disastrous impact of oil on the twentieth century. Kai informed us that "the worst-case scenario is not that we run low on oil and it becomes too expensive. The worst case is we find new ways of mining oil, increasing supply, burning it, and continuing to warm the planet."

Steve Kurkoski reminds me, "It's always good for renewable energy innovation to see oil prices go up."

Today 7.5 billion humans live on earth, most burning some sort of fossil fuel. In 1991, the US invaded Kuwait, then Iraq, in our first war over oil. One billion internal combustion engines worldwide release stored carbon. The hottest years in history began in the 1990s and continue.

The best hope yet is the growing number of people, especially young folks well educated on the subject and determined to stand up to climate deniers and those profiting from status quo energy economics. Slowing climate change by the way you live is arguably history's best idea whose time has come. So, we at Agape are throwing our lot in with eco-revolutionaries. But you could say our efforts amount to, yes, small potatoes.

Motoring a Potato Car?

Driving down the road in my grease car, I have the satisfaction of knowing the tail pipe smells like a vegetarian cookout, not poisonous fumes. Eric, one of our interns, was driving the grease car on the highway and came to a toll booth. As the toll operator counted Eric's money, he said, "I smell something. What is it?"

"French fries," Eric said.

"What?" the toll guy asked.

"Yup," Eric returned. "This car runs on restaurant Fryolator grease!"

My Aunt Rhoda called it "the potato car."

Winding my way around the neighboring towns near Agape, I can experience the non-rush-hour serenity of rural life. But that changed one morning as I saw a police car's lights flashing in my rearview mirror to pull me over.

The policeman walked up to my window, looked at me, and did not say "License and registration." Seeing the sign "This car fueled by vegetable oil" on my back window, he asked: "Does this car actually run on vegetable oil?"

"You bet," I assured him.

In sheer amazement that an automobile could actually run on used canola oil, he asked, "What is the catch here?" A ten-minute back and forth proceeded to be the best fun I've ever had with a cop who had just pulled me over for going ten miles per hour over the speed limit in a school zone.

When we finished, he gave me a big smile, wished me well, and did not ticket me. Instead, he issued only a friendly, "Watch the speed limit." Secretly many of us just love to beat the system, and besides, who but the profiteers really love the oil companies? Neither left nor right nor the cops in between.

Haiti—The Perfect Other

Brayton

On my drive home in January, 2010, after a five-day retreat at Saint Scholastica's Priory in nearby Petersham, I first heard the news report that Haiti had suffered a 7.0-magnitude earthquake. The epicenter was ten miles southwest of downtown Port-Au-Prince, Haiti's capital.

Before the disaster, I had planned to visit Steve and Nancy James, old friends who had spent twenty-five years as missionaries in Haiti. Their family of six children, all raised in Haiti, meant a lot to us, since they joined in shaping the early vision of Agape. The force and devastation of the earthquake compelled me to keep my February two-week commitment. I had previously traveled to Haiti eleven years before.

I landed in Cap Haitian on the northern coast. Steve, Nancy, and Herb, their long time missionary friend, met me at the airport amid a host of young Haitians, teenage and younger, begging from new arrivals for what they could get. The overwhelming scene reminded me of border crossings years before from Iran into Afghanistan and throughout India.

At home and around the world, I have always struggled to take desperate people seriously. That people beg from others in public signifies to me a world gone wrong, visible proof of grave economic disparities.

Agape raised a thousand dollars for me to bring along with two hundred granola bars to pass out to hungry Haitians and relief workers. Throughout my trip, not one of the mostly young Haitians refused my skimpiest of offerings, a sign of their near-starvation conditions. I surrendered my favorite hat to a very grateful fourteen-year-old boy when I had nothing else to give him. Odd that in such a suffering land, the mostly young males with broad smiles proved very good company.

The first night, I settled into the joys of Nancy's exquisite cuisine along with lively conversation and a good night's sleep. In the morning, Steve and I traveled to our first clinic on the outskirts of Limbe, the town where the Jameses live on the campus of a Baptist seminary. Since the earthquake, Steve combined his work assisting at local clinics with disseminating urgently needed pain killers and antibiotics to often overwhelmed and understaffed health professionals in full catastrophe mode.

I glimpsed a Haiti six weeks after an earthquake split open their earth, 250,000 had perished, and tens of thousands were seriously injured. An English woman doctor headed up the clinic with a young English couple in their early thirties. Brave souls. I could feel the toll their round-the-clock medical care had taken on the couple. They had recently admitted nine paraplegics airlifted from the rubble of Port-Au-Prince.

George, a paraplegic lying on his stomach, greeted me with the widest and most joyful smile I would see in all my time in Haiti. The remaining eight people, seemed decidedly more pensive and hurting. The staff members said all nine, like many of the million displaced and homeless people, would likely never return to Port. But George, like Haiti itself, displayed astonishing resilience as he directed an immediate warm smile to me as if he were the host and I the guest. Having broken my neck as a thirteen-year-old and so close to a paralyzing accident myself, I felt the immediate tragedy of paralysis. George's smile, nevertheless, as the nurses said, "lit up the entire room every day."

Heading to Port-Au-Prince

After a few days of delivering medicines locally, Steve, Herb, Jean-Jacques Mueller (our Haitian driver and guide), and I headed south to Port-Au-Prince to further assist the Baptist relief effort. The 150-mile trip took 6 hours, averaging 25 miles per hour on roads so moonscaped that, for much of the trip, we could go only 5 miles per hour. We passed towns devastated by the 2008 hurricane that killed 2,000 people and flooded four towns, thus driving tens of thousands from their homes. Mueller provided a constant commentary. "Erosion from rain and hurricanes," he said, "is soon going to cave in this major coastal road south to Port." Existing from catastrophe to catastrophe, the ever-vulnerable island of Haiti appears under permanent siege.

Ten miles outside Port, up over the hill on the left and a few miles in, we found mass graves. As we approached the unfathomable juncture and began to see earthquake-damaged structures, we noticed the smell of two hundred thousand bodies, more a waft than a stench. Steve said, "It's the smell of death."

Fabienne Jeanne, a Haitian ballet dancer, lost her leg in the 2010 earthquake.
Eventually fitted with a prosthetic limb, she slowly rebuilt her life.

Striking one of the most densely populated cities in the world with two million people inhabiting structures made of the cheapest cement largely without iron reinforcement, the earthquake had hit Port right between the eyes.

By the time we reached downtown, it looked as if the earthquake had pulverized one in every four buildings, a full half of them noticeably compromised or worse. Those left standing often had cracked at the foundation while many unknown so-called casualty statistics tragically remained underneath flattened buildings.

In Haiti, I gravitated to a saying going around: "Earthquakes don't kill people. Cheap buildings kill people." Entering downtown, we drove past the hotel where Mueller stayed on January 11, the day before the earthquake hit. He had wrestled with a decision to stay another day and then decided to return to the north. The following morning, his hotel pancaked in an instant, reduced to a massive tonnage of lethal concrete. Such impossible stories of the miraculous continuously pumped hope into us as we went along the torturous road.

Before the earthquake, four of nine million Haitians lived without electricity or running water. After the earthquake, add 300,000 newly orphaned and a million displaced. Forty days after the earthquake, people inched back into the city and, against the wishes of their government, quietly began rebuilding. Since only half the fault line had blown, the remainder could start shaking at any time.

As the smell intensified, we approached downtown and the seat of the government. Was it a metaphor of God striking down their corrupt politics that every major government building seemed in ruin? The presidential palace presented the most massively pulverized sight in this almost totally leveled city. Imagine a building once a quarter of a mile long literally cut in half. President René Préval expressed a common feeling as that forty-second earthquake began to shake Haitian lives into chaos:

"We thought it was the end of the world." When you see that city, you are deeply moved by the trauma Haitians have had to endure and continue to endure.

Jesus, Where Are You?

The Roman Catholic cathedral constituted the spiritual high point in the midst of the quake's devastation. While one can only imagine the massive force that destroyed the presidential palace, apparently even greater force threw Archbishop Joseph Serge Miot to his death from one of its balconies. Such complete ruin produced a steady stream of funerals, masses, and prayer vigils alongside the pulverized facade.

Steve and I had the rarest privilege of being in the presence of a young woman, hands and arms grasping the wrought-iron fence before the forty-foot high unharmed crucifix—another sign of the miraculous? Poised as if she herself were being crucified, she cried out her prayer: "Where are you Jesus? I love you, Jesus. Where is my precious one?" Steve and I said the rosary alongside the suffering woman who became an anguished, living Psalm with her primal cry of the grieved and those searching for missing family. How much of our world looked on, silently weeping the same prayer, "Why Haiti, Lord?"

For two nights, we slept in our Coleman tents on a cement slab in the makeshift Baptist headquarters that housed ten or so relief workers. The immediate task for the team involved distributing medicine, procuring additional tents to shelter people, and purchasing a truck to assist in the rebuilding of a local Baptist church and school ruined by the quake.

A veteran tsunami relief worker throughout Indonesia, India, and Sri Lanka, Scott Hunter served as the seasoned head of the Baptist effort. He signed on for three months, leaving his home in Albuquerque, New Mexico, and full-time truck driving job to provide sixteen-hour days of relief work. As a knowledgeable veteran of disaster relief, Scott felt the quake was the most devastating natural disaster he had seen or heard of. "Never before," he said, "has a city of two million been so completely leveled into total paralysis. Even countries in Asia damaged by tsunamis remained intact enough to offer significant and immediate relief to their own people."

Food and restaurants for vegetarians did not abound, so I settled for granola bars and fruit juice. "Living the inconveniences of the poor" rang a Dorothy Day adage in my ears. After experiencing the aftermath of the Haiti earthquake, I am tempted to vow never to complain again about the utterly manageable inconveniences in my own life. Haitians' inconveniences defied any imagination. The utmost suffering nevertheless produced few visible tears or long-suffering looks. To observe people in utter catastrophe without real resources renders my ordinary frustrations a luxury.

I indulged in one spaghetti and salad meal while in the city and paid for it for a month of untreated traveler's dysentery. The situation reminded me that I could have instant medical attention wherever I roamed, especially throughout the developed world, a painful reminder of economic injustice that we tried to alleviate but too often failed to accomplish.

Most relief workers operated on an emergency status for housing happy to have a tent to shield them from rain. Haiti's crisis of a million homeless made it necessary to build makeshift tents of the flimsiest sticks and any plastic tarp material relief workers could find. The terrible winds and downpour of the rainy season loomed only three weeks away. Possible hurricanes starting in July into August would follow. The UN reported 250,000 Haitians in unprotected extremity without adequate waterproof tents. Most of the residents left in Port conducted do-it-yourself relief work.

Earthquake Trauma

Before the quake, only fifteen psychiatrists served the entire nine million Haitians. More therapists certainly arrived after the quake. But in Haiti, there rarely seems to be enough of any necessity. People there offer a mesmerizing example of the indigent who never cease adjusting to the reality of not having enough of anything. One psychiatrist interviewed for the *New York Times* called Haitians "extraordinarily resilient."

A child pulled from the rubble cried, "Mother, don't let me die." A few precious days later, the child died. Incidents like that produced another saying going around Port: "You can be pulled from the rubble, but you are still in Haiti."

Another girl, Daphne, miraculously rescued from a collapsed house, cried, "Mama, I'm coming. Mama, I'm coming." Daphne ran, only to find her mother crushed to death and in the process of being loaded into a wheelbarrow for mass burial. Many trauma victims clearly just walked the streets barely making do with their trauma-wounded psyches. Haitians told me they turned to Jesus and their voodoo specialists in times of unmanageable trial.

Throughout the city, we saw rifles everywhere. A guard holding a rifle seemed to patrol every major store or institution, including one in front of an automotive showroom floor of a KIA dealership where I joined Steve as he bought a truck for the Baptist relief effort. Thousands of UN soldiers from all over the world carried rifles. Haitian police on patrol carried rifles. Ubiquitous US military personnel always sported their combat-ready firearms. More than an earthquake relief effort, it looked like a war zone.

As we traveled around the city, Steve, Mueller, and I reflected on the symbolism of those visible weapons. Does guarding everything with serious, visible weaponry tamp down fear of chaos? Many English-speaking Haitians continually complained to me that their country has no viable, day-to-day rule of law, and that fact engendered security fears especially with widespread looting after the quake. Guns like talismans in the hands of authorities would keep people in line while possibly holding at bay the potential chaos of theft and food shortage. Certainly we in the US have our own gun-loving talismans protecting our empire.

As nightfall began to darken the sky, I heard a jazz band playing a concert on top of rubble across from the cathedral. Earlier in the day, I saw Haitians in full tuxedos exit a long, black limousine to begin a New Orleans-style funeral procession. The joy, the bands playing, and normalcy, like the Phoenix rising, continuously promised hope amid the dusty cement ruins.

Walking at a brisk pace as night fell, a teenage Haitian girl startled me as she walked ferociously toward me. She looked intent on running me down only to stop short just two feet from a full collision. She stared straight into my eyes and playfully greeted, "Good morning!" then briskly pranced on.

"Only in Haiti," I marveled to myself.

The Other

For white North Americans, Haitians comprise the perfect other. Consider the 180-degree contrast. I am from the world's wealthiest country; they inhabit the hemisphere's poorest country. I spend more money getting to Haiti than the average $660 they make in a year. I am the theistic Christian; it is said of Haitians that they are 80 percent Catholic, 20 percent Protestant, and 100 percent voodoo. I do things with high tech, so-called labor-saving machines; Haitians often function like beasts of burden, many working at bone-crushing labor with bare hands. I could easily live to a ripe age of 80; they die at 47 on average due to high infant mortality.

Americans held and traded Africans; ancestors of Haitians mounted history's only successful African slave revolt in a French colony that became a nation. An earthquake brought everyday life in Haiti to a standstill; my nation presented itself as a savior. Our country has an aging demographic, while forty percent of people in their country are under 18. They function without viable rule of law; we have the highest incarceration rate in the world while successfully exercising world domination and spending one trillion on our military per year keeping world order. Their Christian worship often combines Roman Catholic traditions with robust African traditions; much of our Christian worship tends toward emotionless Caucasian reserve. We each stare curiously at the other. Do we each feel a certain sense of completeness in the perfect complement of other?

Driving out of Port-Au-Prince, we passed the infamous slum of Citi Soliel. Rain water had already built up in that tent city of thousands. The radio simultaneously reported round-the-clock negotiations on whether to rebuild Port with four smaller cities north of the fault line. As we looked back and remembered our stay in that lost city, I sensed Port-Au-Prince quite literally destroyed. I looked out the window and pondered. Were continual weather disasters in impoverished Haiti another stark indication of extreme climate events punishing first and hardest poor, coastal, and vulnerable nations? My new friend and driver Mueller nodded in agreement.

As I left that most memorable of all lands, I prayed that this tragedy will create an opening for emergence of a new Haiti, a Haiti that will truly capture the dignity of its long-suffering souls, the mysterious, intriguing, and faith-filled other. Please, I prayed, let that land become a living sign of the spiritual songs they sing from the depths of their reliance on Jesus, especially in the suffering chaos.

Beni swa l'éternel. Blessed be the Lord.

Judy and Dzhokhar

Suzanne

In the early eighties, we began an Agape witness against the death penalty at Boston's State House on days of US executions occurring with alarming frequency. The 2015 trial of Dzhokhar Tsarnaev, otherwise known as the Marathon Bomber, seemed to be the nightmarish culmination of years of Agape's witness against the death penalty with little sense that we as a country were moving any closer to abolition.

Our deep anguish around the issue of capital punishment intensified during the immediate aftermath of the horrific deaths and injuries caused by the brothers Tsarnaev in our beloved Boston during one of the most storied celebrations in the city, the Boston Marathon. The Tsarnaev brothers' homemade bombs resulted in the maiming and injuring of more than two hundred people and the deaths of three, including a young boy, Martin Richard, eight.

Given the severity of the so-called terrorist assault, the first since 9/11 on American soil, it was difficult to explore, even among friends, alternative narratives for the bombing, the brothers' motives, their radicalization and why. Empathy for the bombers was a nonstarter conversationally and morally.

Any suggestion that the carnage was the outcome of our complicity in destabilizing Iraq and Afghanistan drew an immediate "No comment" reserve from friends. The message was clear: Better not to talk about hunting down one nineteen-year-old, skinny, handsome, youngster of Russian-Muslim descent, whose face was projected across the world. Better to stick with "Boston Strong." People in Boston had to come together to remember the killed and maimed.

I understood the need to be respectful of the victims and their families, but did that mean forgoing our principled convictions as individuals and as a state whose citizens had voted against the death penalty? Holding the trial in Boston seemed to undercut the wishes of people in Massachusetts and even those of some victim family members who wanted to be spared the public spectacle.

After more than thirty years of working against the death penalty, many of us, including Pat Ferrone, peace activist, early Agape community core member, and the regional director of Pax Christi, Massachusetts, expected that an antideath-penalty coalition would emerge before the trial. Such a coalition never materialized. Dzhokhar's defense team petitioned for a change of venue from Boston, rightly citing that it would be unlikely that Tsarnaev could get a fair trial in Boston. Judge George A. O'Toole Jr. deemed otherwise.

The Need for Church Opposition

As people of nonviolence and members of peace communities, Brayton, Pat, and I thought we had to respond to the trial. Pat composed a plea to Cardinal Sean P. O'Malley of Boston to speak out against the death penalty for Tsarnaev.

We circulated a petition opposing the death penalty specifically regarding Dzhokhar. The petition went to hundreds of individuals and religious and peace organizations. We sent signed petitions to Cardinal O'Malley and eventually to news outlets as well as the defense and prosecution lawyers. Two years before, Cardinal O'Malley had rejected the death penalty for Dzhokhar Tsarnaev immediately after his arrest.

As I poured over newspaper articles and absorbed the mood in Boston, I became aware of Tsarnaev's lead attorney, Judy Clarke. My feminist-activist instincts were heightened by the modesty of Clarke's dress and the fact that she had taken on other heinous death-penalty cases while maintaining a passionate stance against execution. This was a woman to be reckoned with. How can anyone absorb all of this pain and public scrutiny while simultaneously dealing with the depressing narratives of the murdered and the murderers?

As I followed her sparring with the implacable Judge O'Toole during the Tsarnaev trial, I sensed the unfolding of a classic gender battle: a strong, tall, imposing woman of almost austere bearing vs. an intransigent ideologue, a pronouncedly pro-death-penalty judge who seemed to want a death-penalty conviction in Massachusetts at any cost.

A *New Yorker* article by Patrick Radden Keefe ("The Worst of the Worst," September 14, 2015) depicts Judy as a lawyer who is involved in a "labor of empathy," traveling as she did to the Caucasus to visit and interview Dzhokhar's family. Further, I learned that Clarke believes in "the essential goodness of each client," offering her clients "humility, generosity, and devotion." It sounded like the profile of a religious activist to me.

Vigilers oppose the death penalty at the trial of Dzhokhar Tsarnaev, eventually convicted in the 2013 Boston Marathon bombing. Vigilers include, from left, Catherine Flaherty, Scott Schaeffer-Duffy of Worcester's Saints Francis and Thérèse Catholic Worker, Pat Ferrone of Pax Christi, Massachusetts, Suzanne, and Brayton.

A legal drama took place between two women lawyers as Judy Clarke, the defense lawyer, squared off with Carmen M. Ortiz, US attorney for Massachusetts and the prosecutor. Ortiz pushed for the death penalty for Dzhokhar by presenting it as further protection for the injured. "We will continue to do all we can to protect and vindicate those injured and those who have passed away," Ortiz said.

Judy embodied the formidable. The first time I laid eyes on her as I stood in the vigil line outside of the Moakley Courthouse, I was struck by her serious demeanor with eyes to the ground and purposeful stride as she passed the few of us standing in the vigil line. As the trial began, Agape decided to hold a vigil in front of the courthouse once a week. The trial lasted four months, and we

Sisters of Saint Anne, Marlborough, Massachusetts, join Brayton in a weekly protest against the death penalty during the four-month trial of Dzhokhar Tsarnaev, convicted in the 2013 Boston Marathon bombing.

honored our plan, sometimes with others, including Sisters of Saint Anne from Marlborough, Massachusetts.

The Laborers Are Few

When I say "few of us," I mean few. Before the trial began, members of the Pax Christi/Agape alliance reached out to Massachusetts Committee Against the Death Penalty (MCADP), Amnesty International, the United States Conference of Catholic Bishops (USCCB), the office of Cardinal O'Malley, and the heads of all diocesan offices in Massachusetts. We urged them to make a definitive statement against the death penalty, to hold press conferences, or to join us at a public witness in front of the courthouse—all to no avail.

Initially, the lone daily courthouse protester, Joe Kebartas of Veterans for Peace, established himself as the only public face of opposition with his hand-made sign, "The death penalty is murder."

After Pat Ferrone personally delivered a plea from Agape and Pax Christi, Cardinal O'Malley and the Catholic bishops of Massachusetts Catholic bishops eventually released a terse antideath-penalty statement. Sadly and surprisingly, the statement included the words that Tsarnaev would be "neutralized" if sentenced to "life" in a maximum security prison. No mention of opposition to the torture that super max represents.

No creative middle ground seemed to emerge from any of Massachusetts faith leadership. Yes, let's hold prayer services for the victims, but let's also have open dialogue about the death penalty, we urged. It didn't happen.

The twenty-five of us who showed up to protest at the courthouse after Joe Kebartas paved the way made us acutely aware of the juggernaut of federal reach into liberal Massachusetts. The only consistent opposition to the federal trial included friends from Veterans for Peace, Just Faith, and Pax Christi as well as Quakers and Catholic Workers. Given our feeling of how tepid the support, I often wondered how Judy and the defense team must have felt with no significant vocal Massachusetts opposition to the death penalty from religious leaders, even though fifty-eight percent of Boston's citizens opposed the death penalty for Tsarnaev in April, 2015, according to the Boston University radio station, WBUR.

We invited members of MCADP to join Agape at the courthouse or to hold a press conference and assumed they would accept, but we received an email response stating that MCADP wanted to "emphasize our sympathy for the numerous victims of the bombing." Further, the group offered its view that "a presence on the opening day showing opposition to the death penalty will be seen as favoring the defendant and antivictim." MCADP promised that it was continuing to develop a "strategy" and that the group would keep us informed as to what the strategy might be. It never happened.

Given the wall of silence around opposition to the death penalty for Dzhokhar, I felt an even deeper sense of kinship with

Judy. What must she be feeling? I wondered. In a media room inside the courthouse reserved for those wanting to observe the public trial streamed live, I could see Judy's back as she leaned toward Dzhokhar to make a comment. In the process, she would occasionally touch his arm.

I felt the same maternal instincts toward the gaunt teen, whose face I couldn't see except in media clips. Of course, my empathy was counterbalanced by the anguish and horror I felt each time I saw one of the victims in a wheelchair or wearing a prosthesis and walking a slow limp by our vigil line. In addition to gruesome victim-impact statements, much reported in local media, we received steady commentary on Dzhokhar's downward gaze and what the media sometimes identified as his stony indifference. The media portrayed him as unfeeling, callous, beyond redemption—a detached zombie.

An Eye-for-an-Eye Drumbeat

During the drumbeat of death, Judy and the defense surprised everyone with the news that they had contacted Sister Helen Prejean, author of the best-selling book *Dead Man Walking,* to speak on Dzhokar's behalf. The book inspired the award-winning movie of the same name about Sister Helen's close relationship with a death row inmate in Louisiana, whose execution she witnessed.

Women of courage, I thought. Another shocker, which we hoped would turn the tide in favor of life in prison, was the revelation that Sister Helen had been visiting Dzhokhar for some months prior to the trial. She told the press that she found Dzhokhar repentant and remorseful.

Women were out in front in the case—Miriam Conrad, Judy, and Sister Helen pitted against Prosecutor Ortiz, a slick prosecutorial team, and the clearly biased male judge. Pro-death-penalty forces gained momentum daily in the face of the victims' unfathomable physical and psychic pain shared in testimony and observed as victims made their way to the courtroom.

The Verdict

Dzhokhar's death sentence was devastating—guilty on all thirty counts. Given Dzhokhar's age at the time of the bombing and other mitigating family circumstances presented at the trial, we had held out some hope for life. But the combined suffering of hundreds of victims obviously took its toll on the jury, death-qualified by virtue of being eligible for selection only if they identified themselves as able to vote in favor of the death penalty given the circumstances of the conviction. If a potential juror, acting in conscience, expressed moral grounds of opposition to execution, he or she would be disqualified from the beginning from serving on the jury.

We spent the day of defeat at the courthouse. When Judy passed by our silent vigil line, I sensed her as a woman of resolve and great strength. My impression heightened after reading Patrick Radden Keefe's September 14, 2015, *New Yorker* article, "The Worst of the Worst." He offers a portrait of Judy as a woman who "excelled at saving the lives of notorious killers." In addition to defending the "worst," Keefe maintains that Clarke "may be the best death-penalty lawyer in America."

Keefe calls Judy a soul searcher who "never lost a client to death row" and makes the point that other death row attorneys call her Saint Judy. For me, the article and others I read about her provided a spiritual if not religious context for Judy's life work.

A Plea for Mercy

Not unlike Jesus, Judy referred to those who committed the most heinous crimes as "the least of the least." About Dzhokhar, Judy said, "He is one of us." She has stated firmly and unequivocally that "people aren't born evil," and Keefe maintains that Judy learned "lessons in human behavior and human frailty" from her clients. Her attitude, he writes, is "There, but for the grace of God, . . . "

As Jesus called for "mercy, not sacrifice" (Matthew 6), so did Judy in her closing arguments at Dzhokhar's trial. According to press reports, she gestured and articulated like a preacher, reminding judge and jury:

> Mercy's never earned. It is bestowed. And the day allows you to choose justice and mercy. I ask you to make a decision of strength, a choice that demonstrates the resilience of community. We ask you to choose life.

Straight out of Shakespeare's *The Merchant of Venice* ("The quality of mercy is not strained . . . "), Matthew's Gospel ("Blessed are the merciful, for they will be shown mercy.") and Hebrew scripture at Micah 6:8 (" . . . act justly and . . . love mercy and . . . walk humbly with your God . . . "), Judy's almost biblical voice underscored the vulnerability and silence of Boston's Catholic community in the same complicity of silence shared by peace and justice communities nationally.

Outreach to colleges, universities, professors, and organizations that normally join in standing for peace and justice asking that they join us in some way or invite some of us to speak in classes went without response. Maybe religious communities in Massachusetts worked under the misguided belief that an antideath-penalty state like Massachusetts—which has had no death penalty since 1984—would not produce a jury that would descend to vengeance and retaliation when confronted with the federal government's ability to execute a convicted murderer.

A bright spot in the darkness was the work of the Catholic JustFaith Program at the Holy Cross Catholic Church in Springfield, Massachusetts, whose founder Bill Toller, also a Catholic deacon, asked Bishop Mitchell T. Rozanski of the Diocese of Springfield to intercede with the Boston hierarchy to take a public stand. Deacon Toller invited Brayton and me to speak several times on the issue at Holy Cross and to the JustFaith community, many of whom signed our antideath-penalty statement.

The Sentencing Drama

The day of Dzhokhar's sentencing, Judy passed those of us in the vigil line one last time She looked resigned and sad. It seemed that accumulated post-9/11 retribution and the resulting callousness and extremism were being made available to the nation vicariously through the trial and through the Tsarnaev brothers.

Absent from most news analysis was any critique of American invasions of Afghanistan and Iraq leading to the radicalization of some young Muslim men and women. That potential toward radicalization was reported by Milton Valencia and Patricia Wen in *The Boston Globe* after Tsarnaev's capture during the bloody attack on the boat where he hid, unarmed and already grievously injured. They wrote:

> As he hid in a dry-docked boat in a Watertown backyard, a wounded Dzhokhar Tsarnaev scrawled a message in pencil on the inside panels of the boat . . . interrupted by bullet holes and smeared with blood: "The US government is killing our innocent civilians. . . . I can't stand to see such evil go unpunished."

The prosecutors used the above words to demonstrate that Dzhokhar "articulated a clear motive for the Marathon bombings" while the defense lawyers attempted to show that "Tsarnaev was in a fragile state of mind when he wrote the message," thus suggesting that the sentiments of the note "were not genuine."

Representing Veterans for Peace in front of the courthouse, Tony Flaherty said they were opposed to America's wars and considered the Marathon bombing a predictable outcome of the US invasion of Iraq and bombing of Afghanistan.

Dzhokhar's "fragility," according to the *New Yorker*, elicited from Judy the opinion that Dzhokhar possessed a "well of compassion" that his friends say "runs a little deeper" than the average.

Her "labor of empathy" got a small boost from the plea of Bill and Denise Richard, whose son Martin was killed at eight years of age by the bombing. The Richards asked that the jury not impose the death penalty but rather life in prison. Their daughter Jane, seven, lost a leg in the bombing, and Denise, Jane and Martin's mother, an eye. Sentiments of the Richard family for life without parole underlined their exhaustion and grief, because they did not want to be dragged through a future trial or more hearings.

Before they began deliberations, Judy urged jurors not to act out of retaliation. "That's not who we are," she said and reminded the jury that they were "under no obligation to vote for death." That woman of empathy called the jury and the rest of us to our higher natures and to rise out of the abyss of media complicity in a tragic drama of revenge. The jurors, all death-penalty qualified, decided the opposite.

Outcome

None of the jury members were drawn to take a leap of empathy. When exposed to bombs on our own soil, we become paralyzed and fail to see the carnage we in the US—with our tax dollars—allowed to rain down on thousands of innocent civilians in Iraq and Afghanistan. After Tsarnaev heard the death sentence from O'Toole, according to Keefe, "Clarke reached out and placed her hand on (the defendant's) back."

Appeals have been filed while Dzhokhar sits on death row in federal supermax in Florence, Colorado. Among the grounds for appeal is the contention that Judge O'Toole failed to instruct the jury that, if they were not unanimous on death, the result could be life without parole. Another contention is, of course, that there was never a possibility of a fair trial in Boston.

Could Tsarnaev have been spared the death penalty if more voices had been raised nationally against his execution? Keefe says, "In this instance, Clarke had failed to paint a picture of her young client that was moving enough to save him." Further, Keefe suggests that Judy "never found the key" and that the "loss has been devastating" for her who, according to Keefe, shared with a friend, "You just have to figure out how to pick yourself up."

Keefe says the friend observed that for Judy, who is childless, "these clients are her children."

We may wait years for the outcome of a motion for retrial by Judy and her colleagues, who are no longer on the case. She revealed that Tsarnaev offered to resolve this case without a trial and had pled guilty and even written a letter of apology before the trial.

That information was sealed, according to Nancy Gertner, a senior lecturer on the law at Harvard Law School and retired federal judge in Massachusetts. She said, "There is no legal justification for the secrecy surrounding the proceedings" and that the "suppression of Tsarnaev's letter of apology on the grounds that it could be unsafe" is "absurd."

Perhaps the Richard family will eventually be moved to forgive their son's murderer or may even visit him and plead for him as they move through their ordeal and past future Marathon Mondays. As they observed in their statement to the press after asking the court for a life sentence in prison and not the death penalty, they embraced the "resiliency of the human spirit." They express readiness to "turn the page, end the anguish, and look for a better future," thus encouraging all of us to do the same.

Maybe, in such a future, the death of the Richards' son, Martin, and his parents' plea for clemency will become a symbol of the extraordinary power of mercy and bring with it the abolition of the death penalty in the United States.

A Pilgrimage to Standing Rock

Brayton

Suzanne informed me that our long-time activist friend Hattie Nestel called.

"She wants to send straw bales to Standing Rock for tepee insulation. Can you find her some?"

Hattie's request supported the Oceti Sakowin Camp at Standing Rock, North Dakota, established by the Lakota Indians to oppose the drilling of the Dakota Access Pipeline (DAPL) under the Missouri River.

When I returned the call, Hattie told me, "I found a local farm that sells straw bales. Tim Bullock is going to drive a truckload of them to Standing Rock, North Dakota. Are you interested in going and sharing the driving?"

"Yes," I blurted out spontaneously. "When is he leaving?"

"Tomorrow afternoon."

"I'm in," I told her.

I have known Tim through years of friendship with residents of the Buddhist New England Peace Pagoda in central Massachusetts. We got ready to go by noon the next day.

I started packing for the week, not forgetting riot gear—hard hats, ear and eye protection, and waterproof winter clothing that should hold up against police water hosing in arctic conditions. We knew that past police tactics against the Water Protectors got pretty violent.

Suzanne drove me to Greenfield to pick up the truck, a 27-foot closed rental truck, then on to the farm to load on the 238 bales of straw. Hattie, Tim, and I filled the entire bed with straw, leaving room only for our luggage. We all spent the night in the loving embrace of the Peace Pagoda before leaving for Standing Rock Reservation in Cannon Ball, North Dakota, at 7 AM. It would be a 30-hour, 1,800 mile ride—three days and two nights long. We drove it uneventfully and peacefully across two-thirds of the country in good company and the challenging conversations of like-minded souls. Nelia Sargent, longtime peace activist from Claremont, New Hampshire, joined us to make it a threesome in the front cab.

After our thirty-hour, hypnotic highway haul, we arrived at Pierre, the capital of South Dakota. Anticipation mounted in all three of us as we set our sights on the final three-hour leg toward reservation land. As I read the sign, "Entering Standing Rock Reservation," I felt a jolt of excitement as if I saw a pack of wolves in all their primitive wonder. We inhabited the snow-laden, frigid country of the Dakotas. We soon passed another sign that reads "Cannon Ball," and then, around the next bend, there it was: "Oceti Sakowin Camp," nestled in the flat, barren wilderness.

Oceti Sakowin is a Sioux name meaning Seven Council Fires. Like a Bedouin tribe in snow-covered badlands, the camp looked to me like the Promised Land. Imagine an area a mile-and-a-half square along a river bed with hundreds of tents, yurts, vans, and trucks housing roughly seven thousand people. We approached behind thirty cars and trucks lined up to get in. The sun was shining. The gatekeeper looked up at us and said, "Welcome home." Emotions began to well.

We informed the gatekeeper that Jimmy Betts, who works construction at Standing Rock, had requested bales of straw to insulate tents. We were directed to the construction site where carpenters were feverishly building two-by-four-foot walls to convert into housing sheds. I met up with Eric, a Vermonter heading up the entire building project with busy, maxed-out people around him constantly talking. Personable and funny, Eric greeted us and told me to offload the straw bales on the other side of the construction shed. He shared with me that he had arrived prepared to stay a week a month and a half before. Then he got into building and stayed six weeks.

"I can't leave now," he said. "I know too much. When life gets crazy here and egos get too large, the tribal elders tell us to humble ourselves."

We smiled at each other and admitted that our can-do white-guy blood makes humility difficult.

We began to unload the bales amid a tremendous buzz of excitement. The construction site was right in the middle of the camp, and hundreds of people were milling up and down Flagg Road, the main road through the camp lined by native flags representing 250 tribes supporting Standing Rock.

With volunteers, Tim and Nelia feverishly unloaded the truck while I recruited ten or so young people from different parts of the country to stack the bales. In the confusion of picture taking, I dropped my gloves somewhere. My fingers were immediately frozen. A local native guy saw my need and ushered me to the clothing tent. The woman in charge told me that more boxes than she could sort arrived at the post office daily, including all kinds of clothes.

Next, we needed a place to stay.

Soon after we arrive at Standing Rock, volunteers unload the truck.

The Great State of Michigan

Tim parked the truck across from the Michigan tent. Although we are not Michiganders and the tent seemed full, he negotiated some floor space in one of Michigan's two sleeping tents next to the food tent where thirty or so people routinely had dinner together.

Someone generously offered two spaces for Tim and Nelia as I decided to look for other lodging. Carly served dinner of venison soup and hamburger stew. She welcomed us outta-staters as if we were kin. Steve, a Vietnam combat veteran who had been at the camp since it began in August, kept everyone laughing and greeted us like old friends.

The encampment grew out of the response of native women to the crisis of young natives committing suicide. The young people dealt with their despair by traveling to Canada and resisting the Keystone pipeline there. They then discovered that the Dakota

Access Pipeline threatened their tribal lands in North Dakota. Through environmental activism, they healed from their despair and rediscovered their own tribal customs and spirituality. By August, 2016, their vibrant vision of resistance caught on. The camp grew from hundreds to thousands. The elders gave more than their full support to the movement of the young people. They insisted that the native young people lead.

I limited my dinner to a few apples and oranges, some bottled water, and saltines and left for the main gathering place to find lodging. That hallowed area is called the sacred fire of the Seven Councils. The original Sioux tribe was made of Seven Council Fires, each fire representing separate bonds based on kinship, dialect, and proximity to each other's fire. Sharing a common fire is a unifying ritual for the Sioux people. The prayer circle is the camp's constant heartbeat, with the fire always kept burning.

Oceti Sakowin, founded in the spring of 2016, was a ceremonial camp to maintain a prayerful intention for protecting the sacred Missouri River waters threatened by the Dakota Access Pipeline. When I arrived at the fire circle, a native elder informed all of us present:

This is the first time in 140 years that the council fires have been lit to symbolize our unity to protect these sacred waters.

As I walked toward the sacred embrace of the burning fire, I was immediately surrounded by college students who had that "just arrived at Standing Rock" look in their eyes. I sat by the fire. Matt from the Bay area immediately sat next to me and introduced himself. We started talking. Students from the University of California at Berkeley sat down to my right. I shared with them that our crew brought 238 straw bales from Massachusetts and that my wife and I live in a straw-bale house located on our community grounds. Although Berkeley students with a radical protest tradition, they seemed stunned, their eyes wide with wonder. "You actually live like that?" they exclaimed. The same scenario occurred over and over, and I was mystically transported back to Agape's own fire circle and its serenity when we are surrounded by college students during rural immersions we host at our community.

I decided to head back to the Michigan tent and negotiate a three-foot-by-six-foot piece of floor in one of the Michiganders' two twenty-by-sixty-foot military-issue, canvas tents that each sleep thirty. I lay back to sleep with my toes almost hitting one of two wood-burning stoves. I knew that, fully clothed as I was with winter coat and cap, I would be just warm enough on that cold, hard ground. We had to stoke the stoves every three hours. Just before dawn, I woke to freezing cold. The fire had gone out.

On the camp loudspeaker, I heard the announcement of morning prayer and made my way groggily in the dark to that most blessed of fire circles. One hundred of us prayed while standing in a circle. We did all prayer on our feet. Our tribal leader encouraged us. "Get up and pray every morning," he said, "and take the prayer through the day." We prayed together in a soothing, mesmerizing hour of chant, song, and drumming led exclusively by natives with intermittent testimony of tribal wisdom. The chant and testimony continued literally throughout the day until 9 PM.

As I traveled about the camp, I estimated a hundred fires burning inside the tents and in the many outside gathering areas. Trucks arrived in a steady stream delivering wood. Michigan folks hauled in fifty twenty-foot logs from home just for their use. That anthill of collective purpose had impressively good organization underneath. We were always just warm enough.

Looking at the Settler Colonialist Within

I met Tim and Nelia to attend the daily 9 AM orientation meeting. The staff informed two hundred of us present that our group was the largest orientation group Standing Rock had yet seen. Johnnie Aberon, event facilitator and spokesperson, gave the opening talk. A tall, thin Lakota man in his sixties with well-honed speaking skills, he covered how Standing Rock was born and shared, "The council fires are burning for the first time in 140 years."

After he finished, three young women took the mike—a Filipina-American, a Lakota Sioux from Standing Rock, and a white from San Francisco. The three women spent two hours advising us about on how to comport ourselves while living at the camp. As the women's talks unfolded, I felt their pain and the urgency of their message: five hundred years of oppression of Native Americans. And then I experienced the import and utter historic significance of white allies like me, of European descent, making a pilgrimage to Standing Rock since August 2016.

As the women spoke while fighting tears, I felt my own coming on. Approximately four thousand or so white allies learned the lesson: our settler colonialist behavior is ingrained. The women recited the code of conduct here: prefer to listen, not to speak; stand for prayer before and after all gatherings; refrain from all criticism, opinion, and gossip; accept and follow what the elders have established here as well thought out and trustworthy. Avoid behavior identified as settler-colonialist, that is, taking charge, taking over, looking to control, having everything figured out, or quickly fixing everything wrong. Whew! I could feel too many of those impulses brewing within me as I listened.

They also advised us to refrain from unnecessary picture-taking and to "be sure to ask everyone, especially natives, if you may take their picture." Then we heard the sacred prohibition: no picture-taking at any ceremony or prayer. I now feel awkward taking any photographs. Elders' advice: get used to feeling uncomfortable as you adjust to native ways, especially when noticing any takeover leadership inclinations inside you. But they also reminded us that when we inevitably tripped and fell, we were to practice getting up quickly.

Questions were taken in a specific order: from Native Americans first, then from people of color and, last, from white folks. Everything was geared to slowing down white-settler colonialist patterns of control, typically male patterns. Native peoples from all over the country spoke first in their mother tongues—often in chant—expressing gratitude. Emotions of appreciation and love moved through the crowd. The Filipina-American woman reminded us as we closed:

> Always ask permission to do something if you are not sure about the process here. Ask questions. Resist launching into gushy compliments of tribal peoples' dress or spirituality.

The more she tried to explain entitled behavior, the more tense her voice became.

"This is so hard," she finally confessed, "having to cover these topics that point to genocide and oppression of natives, blacks, people of color, and especially women." She fought back tears.

Food Served for the Ten Thousand

We filed out of that amazing tutorial on how to support Standing Rock and headed to lunch after having stood since 6:30 AM prayer. Although Standing Rock spokespersons instructed us to arrive at the site self-contained and asked people to bring tents, food, and clothing, still virtually every need was taken care of regardless—the organizers met all clothing, sleeping bags, and food needs.

Every meal was served on time. A few coffee and tea joints opened at 7 AM and served all day. Tent space was adequate with wood-burning stove heat for everyone who wanted it. Virtually all necessities for survival were mailed in or trucked in daily. I heard young people remark repeatedly, "I have never seen anything like this."

I had at least fifty conversations in four days at Standing Rock. I kept asking people, "Why did you come to Standing Rock?"

"I couldn't stay away," was the usual answer.

"And what exactly drew you?"

"Everything," people typically replied. Some elaborated, "My heart has been here since the summer, and I was finally able to come." Interesting that those were my exact responses.

We were moths to the sacred flame.

As night fell, I went back to the fire circle to listen to the chant and talks by the nations. A woman elder referred to the killing of the black snake, a metaphorical image of defeating the oil pipeline. She warned, "If we feed the beast, we will become the beast." The native idea of a black snake involves a long-held prophecy predicting the end of history due to human greed and arrogance creating a catastrophic imbalance in nature.

The elders at Standing Rock reminded the young organizers that renewal will come from the seventh generation, the millennials of all races. Those millennials will play an almost messianic role to aid in bringing order on behalf of all beings, according to the elders. I understood that Standing Rock youth leaders felt trepidation in the face of such a prophecy. I reflected on the black-snake image: Aren't the pipelines black because they are full of oil, and we who burn oil fashion those snakes? Haven't we, too, become the snake?

At six the next morning, it was five degrees and I was immediately awakened by the cold. I threw a few logs into the stove and headed for morning prayer. The elders spoke to us:

> This is a prayer camp and ceremonial camp to hold a prayerful intention for protecting the sacred waters. The land is sacred and powerful. Pray and act accordingly.

All spiritual needs were accommodated there, a breathtaking scene of prayer through action.

Women "Going Down to the River to Pray"

When the formal prayer ended at 7:30 AM, I was stunned to see Beatrice Menase Kwe Jackson, my bunk neighbor in the Michigan tent, take the microphone. She intoned rhapsodically: "Women are the water carriers. Water is life. *Mni wiconi.*"

"Water is life," the crowd called back.

She continued

> Water is the sacred element of life. Women are the protectors of this sacred element. Women will lead the procession down to the banks of the Sacred River we are protecting. The men will encircle the women as they walk, pray and chant.

Beatrice Menase Kwe Jackson and Brayton endure the cold at Standing Rock. She led the daily two-hour Standing Rock women's procession to the Cannonball River to proclaim "Mni Wiconi. Water is life."

Bea then led several hundred women one mile to what white settlers called the Cannonball River, a tributary of the Missouri, formerly and tellingly named Sacred Stone River by the Lakota. We men encircled and followed as a kind of cushion of respect and care. I finally laid my eyes on the river they protected with their lives.

That morning, we listened to the women as they chanted while walking in procession, "Water heals my body; water heals my soul; and when I go down, down to the water, water makes me whole." It was hard to keep the tears from flowing as we approached the Sacred Stone River.

Women arrived at the frozen water banks and offered tobacco. Men followed in their procession. I passed Bea, luminous with her shining smile. She looked directly at me as I passed her on the way to the water, and she said with the sweetest joy:

> I am so happy that my Creator has promised me that I can come back to my favorite sacred places after I die. I will come back to this Sacred River. It makes me so happy.

She cried out intermittently, *"Mni wiconi.* Water is life."

"Mni wiconi. Water is life," we called back.

"Water is life," others cried out in their own native and foreign tongues.

Tears flowed constantly in that camp. I wondered periodically: Why are people so readily weeping? Is it that we cannot adequately describe with words the natural and spiritual beauty we experience here? The place was emotionally overwhelming. Tears must be our purest eloquence.

Veterans by the Thousands Join the Camp

As I walked up the hill from the procession, I saw the camp drenched in veteran flags. For me most significantly were the flags of Veterans for Peace. Military men and women in uniform were everywhere. It was a powerful irony that, so frequently during my life, I have engaged in nonviolent protests against the very wars that those veterans fought. Now we were on the same side protecting the water protectors. The veterans' stated mission:

> To be human shields, to absorb the police violence directed against water protectors in the event of an eviction of the seven-thousand-person Oceti Sakowin encampment.

The Army Corps of Engineers owns the legal right to the land where we were encamped. Although an eviction order was rescinded, the veterans planned to march to the site of where the pipeline would begin to cross under the river in solidarity with the witness of Standing Rock. Veterans planned to meet with elders the next day in a special session. Some vets I spoke with said that they were at Standing Rock to protect defenseless native peoples who for five hundred years had been beaten down, driven off their land, and killed.

Many of the vets referred to police as militarized. Strange how the word militarized was used by water protectors and veterans alike to pejoratively depict the police. Can the word militarized ever be good?

It was eleven in the morning on a sunny Sunday, and I arrived at the interfaith service at the fire circle where some two hundred gathered. More people arrived as the ceremony began. As was always the case, Native Americans were at the center of the ritual with chanting and inspired talks. One of the first to speak addressed the crowd: "If there are any infiltrators in the crowd today, welcome! Turn on your devices now, and you will hear the truth."

Both wise and humorous, the challenge expressed how the Elders welcomed even the adversary.

Then, we heard prayers from practitioners of Islamic, Hindu, and Buddhist traditions interspersed with song and wisdom from native tribes throughout the West. Contributions finished with Unitarian-Universalist, Episcopal, nondenominational Christian, and Catholic speakers. All came to support and inspire the burgeoning crowd that eventually numbered several hundred.

Frank Fortier, a Jesuit priest, asked forgiveness from the indigenous peoples present for the treatment of Indians, especially by Jesuits and Christians. The tribal speakers tended to name whites and Christians as their primary oppressors. Father Fortier preached that Jesus was sent by God as a sign of the sacred. Jesus came to show humans living on earth how to treat all things as sacred gifts from a loving God.

As he delivered his homily, I felt outrage at the reality of how many self-professed Christians massacre the nonviolent Jesus and his fundamental message of honoring and protecting the sanctity of all life. Genocidal barbarity towards Native Americans by European Christians finds its origins in a papal bull issued by Pope Alexander VI in 1493 stating that any land not inhabited by Christians was available to be discovered, claimed, and exploited by Christian rulers. Further, it declared that Christianity was to be exalted and barbarous nations overthrown and brought to the faith. This proclamation was referred to as the Doctrine of Discovery and became the basis of European claims on the Americas and, thus, the foundation of US western expansion. For the next three hundred years, immigrants from European settler countries with the same intent felt morally entitled to drive native peoples from their land, kill them, and systematically destroy their culture from coast to bloody coast.

When Cornel West, stalwart African-American activist and writer, spoke at the service, he reminded us that "America's original sin was not slavery of Africans but the genocide of Native Americans. Slavery came second." West then evoked the legacy of nonviolent witness when he listed "Dorothy Day, Philip Berrigan, Martin Luther King Jr., and Gandhi: they are all present here at Standing Rock."

As Christian representatives invoked the name of Jesus, I felt the authority and prophetic power of Jesus in the steely, gutsy absolute of the fearless cry of indigenous peoples: "No to the pipeline."

Mercy: A Healing Salvation for Christians

Jesus was surely blessing those peoples and their water-protecting allies every day. Might that be the first time since 1492 that we can write a new chapter for Christians who are reconciled with and forgiven by indigenous people? Can we live together, honoring our sacred earth? Was Jesus blessing the leadership of tribal peoples who are, at last, leading white Christian people of European descent out of their own ecological self-destruction?

Then, Chief Arvol Looking Horse of the Lakota, Dakota, and Nakota nations himself rose to speak. With great nobility and grace, he stood before us with his six-foot-five-inch frame and broad shoulders. Chief Arvol himself is a standing rock.

He spoke of a dire vision that Crazy Horse had in the late 1800s. Chief Arvol portrayed Crazy Horse as the epitome of the fearless warrior who, according to legend, never cried. However, in his last years, Chief Arvol said, "Crazy Horse had a vision of the future depicting a devastating catastrophe that would soon decimate the people." After recounting the vision, Crazy Horse wept.

Chief Arvol Looking Horse continued:

> Today, I see an even greater catastrophe. Human beings have gone too far and have to be stopped. We must stop all of these pipelines. We must stop all of this fracking. All of it.

Of the native elders who spoke in the service, he offered words that call forth the most prophetic urgency:

If you are here at Standing Rock, you believe in the sacredness of all life. Water is life. *Mni wiconi.* Water is sacred. We will not move until the black snake is killed.

Drilling Halts

By the end of the three-hour interfaith service, we were poised for one final ritual. The thousands present were invited to encircle the camp in celebration and hope. Our section of the crowd headed for the Cannonball River.

A half hour into circling up, almost at the point of clasping our united hands, a young man drove up, leapt out of his car, and shouted: "The Army Corps of Engineers has denied DAPL a permit to continue drilling!!"

The mass of people erupted into shouts of joy and song, the timing symbolic and triumphant. We clasped hands. The permit was denied—a sweet burst of victory and necessary soul tonic.

Chief Arvol Looking Horse, nineteenth keeper of the white buffalo calf pipe on behalf of the Lakota Sioux Indians, speaks at the 2016 Agape observation of Francis Day.

Realistically, we knew DAPL was checked but not checkmated. Wendell Berry alerts us in his poem, "Watch Out," that corporations will "mercilessly sell the earth to buy fire." It will take more defeats of DAPL before true victory is won.

The circle made its way to the sacred fire where natives led us all in celebration. Voices in the camp erupted in joyous pandemonium. Even the bitter cold did not dampen our joy. We kept on chanting, cheering, and simulating animal calls, crying out into the frigid, barren beauty of the North Dakota wild.

For that week I so enjoyed not talking about the toxic election cycle, and then, a Trump supporter showed up at Oceti Sakowin— of all places! He rationalized Trump's racist attitudes towards Muslims while two California women patiently, firmly corrected him point by point. The tent was indeed wide at Standing Rock. Everyone was welcome, and the welcome was to a community of truth with love. An elder at the fire circle offered us an astonishing proclamation, "After five hundred years of oppression, all we have left is love."

"Standing Rock Is Everywhere"

As 2016 came to a close, many of us seasoned, nonviolent activists, agonized together: "Has the world ever looked worse?" Yet, parallel to our contemporary narratives of human horror was the truth of Standing Rock and the witness of the Sioux tribal people willing to die in the spirit of nonviolent love to uphold the sanctity of all life.

Will our native brothers and sisters lead us out of the darkness, a countersign to our self-inflicted ecological self-destruction and Trump's fear-driven politics?

These ennobled and humble ones liberate us with their grace and fearless confrontation of the corporate rape of Mother, the Earth. Their sign of ultimate hope was the camp called Oceti Sakowin.

Chief Looking Horse insisted, "We will be victorious through perseverance, prayer-filled and fearless nonviolent struggle. Standing Rock is everywhere!"

I began to feel the excitement and purpose of returning to Agape as a living demonstration that Standing Rock is, indeed, everywhere.

I ran into Stu, a Boston-area member of Veterans for Peace. His was the only familiar face besides those of my travel companions among the ten thousand. I noticed my phone mysteriously dead, and I borrowed Stu's to call Suzanne and fill her in on things.

The word was going around the camp that too many phones at Oceti Sakowin were mysteriously dead. Speculation was that the DAPL reconnaissance helicopters constantly flying overhead canceled the ability to charge cell phones. It was late. I was tired and decided not to consult with lawyers at the legal tent. I headed for the Michigan tent and a warm bed.

Morning broke in darkness, and I was up and out to morning prayer. As I walked back from the fire circle, I ran into Tighe, an activist friend who informed me that the vets were meeting with native elders at the casino ten miles down the road. There, Wesley Clark Jr., son of the legendary general, addressed a gathering of military veterans and Native Americans ten miles from the camp. With awe-filled cadence, Clark listed the cruel oppression and torture heaped on native culture by the US cavalry: "We drove you from your land; we took your children; we eliminated your God-given language; we killed you."

Dressed himself as a cavalryman, Clark finished his confession, wept, bowed his head, and begged forgiveness only to receive the merciful hand of the presiding chief. The hundreds of natives present shouted Ho in loving affirmation of Wesley's historically necessary, brave, and heart-wrenching contrition: another Standing Rock perfect moment.

How could Standing Rock possibly win against the inexorable forces of oil money? Native organizers were certain of one thing: they must stand firm to protect their water, their land, and their sacred burial grounds.

Naomi Klein interviewed a thirteen-year-old Lakota girl from Standing Rock and asked, "What has the Standing Rock campaign done for you?"

"It has given me back my future," the girl said.

Both Klein and the girl began to weep.

We nonnatives at the camp felt we were taking Standing Rock's brave witness and learning to fight nonviolently so we all have a future.

Those of us who believe in a healthy and sustainable future returned home with Lakota values of prayer, ceremony, and nonviolence while hoping to learn to protect humans from continual war and xenophobic hate engulfing our people.

Oceti Sakowin taught Americans that for our fossil-fuel-poisoned country to survive, we must by the grace of God defend the sacred—earth, air, water: all that lives.

Will Agape Enter the Next Axial Age?

Brayton

"Have you ever heard of Wayne Teasdale?" I asked Matt Riddle, a newly arrived intern in his late twenties. I pointed to a photograph in Francis House of Wayne with Bede Griffiths, a Benedictine monk who went to India as an experiment in Hindu-Christian community. In the photo, Bede celebrates a Hindu Eucharist, a sacramental unity of mysticisms—Hindu ritual prayer with bread and wine consecrated into Jesus's body and blood.

Wayne invited Bede to come to Massachusetts in the 1990s to meet members of Agape and other similar national communities. Bede was eager to hear about Agape's lay monastic vision of community dedicated to nonviolence. Wayne explained to us that Bede believed that the future of monasticism is not in the monastery. Rather, monasticism will endure in communities of lay people. He traveled to the US in his eighth decade to experience new forms of monastic life.

After that most unusual liturgy, Suzanne and I met alone with Bede, who shared with us something that we had never fully appreciated: "There is no better spiritual strength at the center of a community than a family." Soon after our meeting, we took a precious photo of five-year-old Teresa presenting Bede with an icon of Saint Francis.

Wayne and I, both in the class of 1970 at St. Anselm College, were intellectual friends who occasionally talked philosophy and unpacked jewels we learned in theology classes. We graduated, parted company, and twenty years went by. Enter Paul Gustafson, a recent Boston College graduate and volunteer at Agape who shared with me his plans for a trip to India. I insisted, "You must go to Shanti Vanam, a Hindu Christian community founded by Bede Griffiths."

In six months, Paul was back, moved by the experience in India. He mentioned that he had met a guy named Wayne

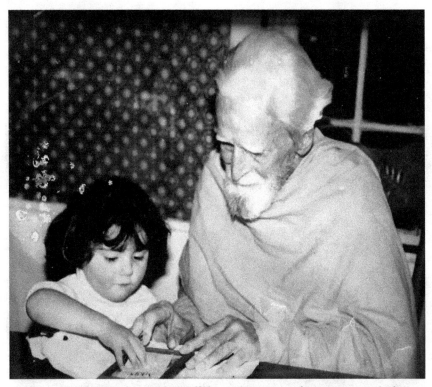

Teresa presents Father Bede Griffiths with an icon of Saint Francis before Hindu Eucharist at a New Hampshire monastery.

Teasdale at Shanti Vanam. Months later, Wayne traveled back to the US with Bede. Wayne wanted to meet with Agape folk and begin discussions with us and other religious communities about the future of monasticism, the essential role of laity, and the intersection of eastern religion with western Christianity.

The following year, Father Bede died, and my connection with Wayne fell off. A year or so later, I called him to get advice on contacts for a trip I planned to Rome and to see how he was doing. I shared how grateful I was for his recently published book, *The Mystic Heart*. It impressed me as the most comprehensive book on Christianity, religion, and mysticism from an interfaith perspective that I had ever read.

After he thanked me, Wayne's voice grew heavy as he said, "I have some serious cancer."

Wayne Teasdale, left, prepares Hindu Eucharist with Father Bede Griffiths.

I expressed my concern and promised prayers, and we hung up. A year later, another of my mystic-loving friends, Mike Boover, sadly informed me that Wayne had died.

Little did I know that Wayne's ideas of interspirituality and Bede's new monasticism were animating the currents of young spiritual seekers across the country. Our young intern Matt did, in fact, know all about Wayne and his spiritual father, Bede.

Matt was reading works by young writers who were paying homage to Wayne's notion of interspirituality as articulated in *The Mystic Heart.* Although Wayne had remained Catholic, he understood that spiritual-not-religious tendencies in the young were in fact "inter-spiritual emanations" and not a sign of the demise of religion. Here was an expression of a new religion of the next millennium. "The entire religious experience of history has been one single experience," Wayne wrote.

The young seekers he attracted were enthralled.

I was familiar with some of the new interfaith terminology that pointed to a reality composed of not one but of many expressions of ultimate truth. The term interreligious was used by Trappist Father Thomas Keating, who organized interfaith convocations in the 1980s. Those were historic meetings of representatives from all religious traditions to discover how to transcend differences that divide in order to experience a deeper sense in their oneness.

I had also encountered the concept of "religious pluralism" with the Dalai Lama, who implies that all religions are incomplete as isolated bodies and that each can learn from and be changed by the genius of the other traditions. Then there is, "interbeing," the essence of Thich Nhat Hanh's metaphysic that asserts that everything in existence consists of one interacting, interdependent life. We have no choice but to inter be, says Thay, as his followers call him.

Integration is the word whose time had come. We are living in times vibrating with integration: East with West, religious ideas with secular ideas, science with religion, humanity with earth. The convergence of these life forces pressures us to new levels of thought and inner experience. Such an "integral framework," Ken Wilbur writes, "is comprehensive and inclusive without adding any new content but unites East and West in a way that is revolutionary. The new human is integral."

First Axial Age

Karl Jaspers wrote of the first Axial Age in his *The Origin and Goal of History*. He refers to the six-hundred-year period from 800 to 200 BCE when today's spiritual patterns and forms of thinking were formed in the dramatic shift of consciousness including those generated by Lao Tzu and Confucius in China.

The Axial Age gave us Hebrew prophets followed by the Greeks, Socrates, Plato, and Aristotle. Siddhartha Gautama, the Buddha, added his spiritual genius, joining established Asian religions of Hinduism and Jainism. Before such historic movements of "inner revolutions," according to Jaspers, human cultures were primarily tribal. Humans, Jaspers explains, did not imagine ideas nor ways of being outside the boundaries of kinship. In the Axial Age, we began to reach out to unite ourselves with nature and up to the cosmos with our thinking evolving beyond the ken of the ethnic and religious birth communities that circumscribed us.

Individual revelation then began to shape our thinking and understanding of life, our belief in ultimate things and the nature of God, thus forming a new world apart from the limits of tribe. Informed by the Greeks centuries after the end of the first Axial Age, history began to see Jesus Christ as a culmination, followed by the birth of Mohammed and Islam, the last of the Abrahamic religions in the seventh century CE.

Does Traditional Religion Have a Future?

Since the onset of our college programs, we found that many youth born Catholic no longer considered themselves to be Catholic. They felt bound to no religion nor did they believe in God. Then, early in the new millennium, young Catholics who came to us began to talk about a new monasticism emerging out of Protestant denominations and people like Shane Claiborne, a young Evangelical Christian from Tennessee. Jonathan Wilson-Hartgrove and his wife, Leah, with their two children began Rutba House, a new monastic community in Durham, North Carolina. Jonathan traveled to war-torn Iraq and returned with an even stronger conviction of antiwar pacifism within the embrace of Christian-inspired new monasticism.

In a conversation I had with Leah, I shared my dilemma. "Why," I asked, "if you are not Catholic or celibate and live as a family with the poor as nonviolent activists embracing family life, do you call yourselves a new monastic?"

She answered:

We seek to reclaim the early wisdom of the desert fathers and mothers and to live inspired by these teachings. We want to be formed as they were, by a daily commitment to spiritual practice and the contemplative disciplines.

Assorted new monastics were discovering an experiential Christianity, not a faith heavily laden with obligatory doctrine. Instead, the movement draws from the simple, livable truth of early Christian nonviolent wisdom. Young seekers want the foundations of tradition but also demand the freedom to evolve ancient truths into something new.

Many of the disciples of new monasticism cite the Catholic scholar Raimon Panikkar, who writes, "Our task and our responsibility are to assimilate the wisdom of bygone traditions and, having made it our own, allow it to grow." Panikkar's father was Hindu and his mother was Spanish Catholic. He wrote of his spiritual evolution, "I left Europe as a Christian, found myself a Hindu, and return as a Buddhist without having ceased to be Catholic."

I have observed many of my generation born Christian resonate in an inter-spiritual way and drink from the wells of the Asian contemplative practices. We have been eager to learn yoga and practice Buddhist mindfulness and meditation while appropriating methods of Asian religion into Western cultures. Many of us seek out Chinese medicinal practices and absorb the wisdom of the sacred books of the East, the *Bhagavad Gita* and *Tao te Ching*. Ours is an integrated, spiritual world.

Enter Evolution

Throughout my life, I have observed from generation to generation people changed by the inexorable forces of evolution. The Gospel promises us as Christians that, with faith, we will evolve toward "the good," that is God.

I began to notice early in my life how different my generation was from my parents' and their Depression-Era, World-War II life journey. My choices and attractions were more varied and intercultural, complex, morally and philosophically based. I can see some of the same differences in how young people view religion, culture, and social acceptance today. They make far less a deal about skin color or sexual preference or even distinctions of gender, than we, their elders do, a sign of evolutionary progress.

It follows, then, that a new Axial Age will be more enlightened and more unified and make a higher stage of consciousness more accessible. We are all journeying through stages of moral development that I trust will lead us to greater potentials of universal, nonviolent Agape love.

"Everything that lives grows in complexity, unity, and interdependence," writes Teilhard de Chardin, a French Jesuit earth mystic. Spiritual experience extends out to include what was thought to be nonliving matter and an unobservable-but-felt infinity of cosmic forces.

I am learning a foundational tenet of young people who say they are spiritual not religious. Their primary desire for spiritual truth and commitment is linked to direct experience and not to presence in a church building on Sunday.

When our daughter Teresa turned sixteen, she began to resist going to mass. "I know plenty about the bible and Jesus," she told me. "I don't need to go to church to learn anything more." I had observed that, since her first days attending mass, she didn't relate well to the religious language or the priest's liturgical procedures behind the altar. Even the Eucharist did not grab her deeply, although at age eight, she was drawn to the ceremony of her first communion.

Another problem for Teresa was the ornate impersonal church building with only fifty or so rather unanimated parishioners every week, most of them older adults scattered around the church. Teresa had a proposal. "Instead of going to church, Dad, let's go into our chapel here and read the bible, and I'll tell you what it means."

We did just that, and she confidently taught a lesson on the meaning of the Gospel. When it came to the central importance of being a compassionate and loving person, no problem for Teresa. She simply wanted no more sermons or Church ritual.

Over the years at Agape, we have had fifty or so serious Catholic families in our extended network. Yet, by the time most of our children were in their late teens, it was rare that any of them would call themselves Catholic or attend mass on their own. Like Teresa, they found no real peer friendships at mass, no ritual that appealed to their age group. Traditional Christianity in North America was clearly dying back into forms we cannot yet see. Teilhard contributes insight into this dilemma. "We are surrounded by a fear that the world is floundering in atheism," he writes. "What it is suffering from is unsatisfied theism."

Further insight into generational differences came from my niece Joanna, who offered a counterpoint to established methods of social activism. "We are not going into the streets to protest injustice," she said. "We will go online and build a movement through the internet." Since the beginning of third millennium computers, internet and cell phones have defined our lives worldwide. Is the sea change of contemporary computer technology also an evolutionary stage, or does it distract us from developmental progress?

Digital technology instantly interconnects us on a massive scale. But does it keep us from real, face-to-face human connection or direct relationship with life on earth? Whatever becomes interreligious in our future, we fully anticipate spiritual seekers, especially the young, will maintain a primary reliance on hand-held technology.

We have lived through a most dramatic cultural shift in modern times as computers and cell phones have shaped daily life in the twenty-first century. One wonders, as the computer evolves, if we face a collision between the multitasking, fast pace of the digital world and the slower paced, monotasking world of spiritual practice and more mindful living?

Stay tuned.

Who Will Take Up the Mantle?

Regarding our future, an essential question looms: How do we at Agape set our sights on the next twenty years? Who among the younger generations will step up to lead communities like ours into the unknowns of future consciousness? Whatever brave and thoughtful souls may end up at Agape, they will be a breed of a different world from the one that shaped us, their elders

Matt Riddle shared with us around the breakfast table. "Don't look for the young people who are on their devices all day," he said. "Look for the young people on the margins." In the next years, we must begin to turn our sights from the intentional community margins of Agape to the creative borders of a new and evolving consciousness.

Petitioning for God's assistance, we have questions that loom. Will we attract readiness in the next generations or those eager for radical simplicity that divests from slavish reliance on fossil fuels and machines that require them? In such subcultures, perhaps we will find young people ready to evolve beyond war and myriad justifications for violence. Signs we see are not conclusive but suggest that the next Agape community will be inhabited by those who seek mystical union with Divine Love in ordinary, everyday life experience. They may not be found in church but in creative evolutions of Church, a renaissance in new religious forms.

As we move into the next twenty years of a world rebirthed into more interfaith and integrated ways, we will be absorbed into a second Axial Age. Communities like Agape that have always practiced rudimentary interspirituality find ourselves ready to offer our vision of what might come next. And yet, if we don't read spiritual evolution accurately and merge into it, I wonder if our Agape community will die out with other religions in a twenty-first-century, postmodern purge.

As a Christian, I continue to believe in grounding myself in one faith. The truth for me remains that Jesus Christ, even beyond the bounds of institutional Christianity, expresses the center and unity of the cosmic universe as no other being can. I trust the more enlightened age to come will maintain the spiritual design of the love, compassion, and mercy that Jesus lives and teaches. The unitive force of interspirituality that I can imagine drawing together adherents of the world's many faith traditions can be held together in nonviolent love. Such integration will be not only for the benefit of humans and our planet earth but for a loving embrace of the entire cosmos.

Life on the Margins: Looking Back and Looking Forward
an afterword

Brayton and Suzanne

Harmonizing forty years of perspectives as husband and wife into one story has been an arduous task leading to more than a few problematic moments between us, the authors. We agreed and disagreed, wrote and rewrote. Reviewing four decades in community as a family with our daughter Teresa, interns, and residents opened up memories painful, deep, and fulfilling.

We exchanged marriage vows that pledged a life in community. One of the sweetest outcomes of this sacramental union of being life partners is that we accomplished with others something that could feel so good. The demands have been emotionally steep, but they called forth deeper meaning and purpose than we could have ever imagined when we first pronounced them in 1980.

In this accounting of a community and its co-founders, we acknowledged missteps and regrets to each other and to our readers. We tried not to hide moments of despair and defeat nor to sound self-righteous and ideological. While writing, we shared our astonishment that the journey happened at all.

Sharing intimate revelations both biographical and spiritual meant realizing the personal cost connected to such vulnerability and transparency. In addition, the time to complete this book often took more from us psychically than we thought we could give. Then why bother? We pressed on, hoping in part that we were giving glory to God in the process.

The writer Thomas Merton has words worth recounting:

> If you write for God, you will reach many men and women and bring them joy. If you write for yourself, you can read what you yourself have written, and after ten minutes, you will be so disgusted that you will wish that you were dead.

Thus far, we trust that we have avoided a death wish.

Praise God, then, that this distilled version of the Agape story is finished. No more worry about too many self-referential accounts. We have attempted to write a chronological history although with many omissions of key moments and people because of the limited number of pages in a book. The resulting overview captured the narrower lens of two of its six co-founders.

As suggested in Paul's letters, we tried to rely on "Spirit and power" as we traveled the road of remembrance. Along the way, we received "persuasive words of wisdom" from many mentors and guides as we found ourselves called by collective summons to be among the "foolish of the world." (1 Cor. 2) After all, what could be more foolish in violent, post faith times than to dedicate one's life to the pursuit of peace and taking risks while relying on "wisdom from God"? (1 Cor. 1: 26-31)

The *Tao Te Ching* tells us that the wise person "yields" and does not "overwhelm, sows and does not worry about reaping." We learn from the *Tao* that sowers end up going to "where harm may happen" and risky endeavors flow from people who yield and "are not content with home." We gravitated towards sowing seeds of discontent, staking our future on the kind of friendships that derived from community bonds broadly shared.

Home came to mean sharing life with companions on the way who comprise a committed core. This cycle of departure and return to the community base is tangible proof of our souls' yearning for an authentic life, one dedicated to an ideal.

On our twenty-fifth anniversary in 1997, we took heart from words of the poet Denise Levertov. In her poem, "People Power at the Die In," Levertov seems to capture the essence of Agape, "the small, ephemeral harvest of our stirring."

"Small" and "stirring," the years break open into a promise—Yes. Agape's yes, Agape's promise, arises from our imagining and dreaming of joining together to create something so seemingly beyond our own capabilities.

In our modest attempt to paint a canvas of Yes, we focused on some of what has been made visible to us and much of what remains invisible as we yield—yield with a view to the future.

Acknowledgments
by Suzanne and Brayton Shanley

We gratefully acknowledge members of the Agape community advisory board, the mission council, representing the engine that keeps Agape running. Numbering between ten and fifteen people, the mission council meets five times a year, each time for a full day. The mission council has been the center of the community's decision-making process as members join us as teaching staff and in planning ongoing witness and participation in Agape's yearly events, primarily Francis Day every first Saturday in October. Mission council members staff the Francis Day celebration as they participate in a range of activities from greeting the more than two hundred people who usually attend to setting up and taking down the chairs lent by a local Roman Catholic parish.

Some council members who have been on board for more than twenty years and have achieved the status of elders or lifers include:

—Skip Schiel, steadfast confidante, photo-journalist, whose record of Agape events comprises a stunning tribute to his artistry and the community's collective memory since the beginning of our tenure in Hardwick and years before these Agape days; Skip wants us to tell you can reach him at skipschiel@gmail.com

—Bob Wegener, community comrade, architect, and friend, a visionary who has been with us from the beginning

—David Gill, SJ, mission council emeritus, who over the past two decades tirelessly, almost weekly, supported the community with his wisdom and wit

—Eleanor Maclellan, RSCJ, at our side on the council since the 1990s offering her indefatigable assistance with our Iraqi family and their needs

—Teresa Wheeler, has always been there for our entire stay in Hardwick beginning in 1990 with decades of minutes-taking for our meetings, a true Agape archivist

It does take a village to run a lay Catholic peace community. But some in this sacred village have given their all for countless years. We extend a deep bow of gratitude to all of you, our past and present council members, including the young people in our ranks.

We also extend our gratitude to

—Husband and wife Edgar Hayes and Ann Rader, co-founders of a sister community in Middletown, New York, who with their children, Micah and Josiah, have inspired us with their devotion to caring for the land and inner-city youth

—Samantha Leuschner, former Agape intern, social worker

—Bennett Comerford and Emily Jendzejec whose marriage in Agape's chapel is a sign of new beginnings, as is their daughter, Juniper, now two

—Alicen Roberts, who arrived at Agape at nineteen and is now a grad student at Yale Divinity School as she enriches us with her interfaith perspective and many trips to Jerusalem to study and grow

—Kate Carew, teacher and special friend to the Muslim community Nu-Day Syria

—James Robinson, candidate for the doctor of theology at Fordham University, whose thesis will include a chapter on Agape

—David Perkins, new addition to our ranks, with his family including wife, Katie, and two teenage daughters, Hannah and Grace, who make life easier with their smiles and Dave's IT expertise for Agape fliers

Thank you Dixon George, four-year permanent resident at Agape; Hazel Dardano, ever-ready for years on end with all kinds of assistance; Mary Bennett of Worcester, and our emeritus members, John Paul Marosy, Cornelia Sullivan, and Janet Poole.

And, of course, a special thanks to all of our readers and careful advisors, including Marcia Gagliardi, our publisher at Haley's who gave of herself generously to the completion of this book.

About the Authors

Suzanne Belote Shanley and Brayton Shanley

Suzanne Belote Shanley

Suzanne Belote Shanley completed her master of arts in English at the State University of New York at Buffalo and holds a master of philosophy in English from Simmons College, Boston. Suzanne teaches about ecumenical and interfaith nonviolence and facilitates a yearly New England-wide Francis Day—October 4—event at Agape. She has worked in prisons and co-facilitated a Death Row ministry as well as a yearly Good Friday nonviolent vigil in Boston. Suzanne offers classes on Eco-feminism and Women and War. She combines hospitality with a life of daily prayer, evangelical simplicity, and public witness. Editor of the Agape community journal, *Servant Song*, she is a published poet.

Brayton Shanley

Brayton Shanley earned his bachelor of arts from St. Anselm College, Goffstown, New Hampshire, and a master of arts in pastoral ministry from Boston College. Co-founder of Agape,

Brayton has been involved in the building and design of green structures on the homestead, including solar energy, a straw-bale house, and composting toilet as well as growing organic vegetables. Since 1982, he has taught courses and given lectures on nonviolence at colleges and other educational forums. He leads retreats and rural immersions on nonviolence and ecology at Agape. Brayton's first book, *The Many Sides of Peace: Christian Nonviolence, the Contemplative Life, and Sustainable Living*, was published in 2013 by Wipf and Stock.

Suzanne and Brayton received the Isaac Hecker Award for Social Justice from the Paulist Center, Boston, in 2015. In 2009, they received the Peace Abbey Courage of Conscience Award for educating youth and adults in sustainability, nonviolence, and peacemaking from the Peace Abbey, Sherborn, Massachusetts.

Colophon

Text for *Loving Life on the Margins: the Story of the Agape Community* was set in Utopia Standard. Utopia qualifies as a transitional serif typeface based on eighteenth- and early-nineteenth-century ideals of classical design. Adobe Systems release notes cite the fonts Baskerville and Walbaum as influences, and Sumner Stone, the renowned Adobe designer of fonts, has also compared it to Hermann Zapf's Melior and Aldo Novarese's Didone (ITC Fenice) as similar. Utopia Standard was one of the first typefaces in Adobe's Originals programme, designed to feature a large range of styles for professional use. Newspapers sometimes used Utopia Standard with its reasonably solid designs.

Versions of the typeface are released in the OpenType format and include features such as ligatures and small capitals. It is released in four optical variants for display, headline, regular, and caption text sizes, each in regular, semibold, and bold weights.

Titles for *Loving Life on the Margins: the Story of the Agape Community,* were set in Acumin Pro, a sans serif font created in 2016 by Adobe Systems.

CPSIA information can be obtained
at www.ICGtesting.com
Printed in the USA
FSHW010729080619